Men of Uncertainty

SUNY series in Japan in Transition

Jerry Eades and Takeo Funabiki, editors

Men of Uncertainty

The Social Organization
of Day Laborers in
Contemporary Japan

Tom Gill

State University of New York Press

Cover photo: Nakajima Satoshi

Published by
State University of New York Press, Albany

For information, address State University of New York Press,
90 State Street, Suite 700, Albany, NY 12207

Production by Kristin Milavec
Marketing by Michael Campochiaro

Library of Congress Cataloging-in-Publication Data

Gill, Tom, 1960–
    Men of uncertainty : the social organization of day laborers in contemporary Japan /
    Tom Gill.
        p.   cm. — (SUNY series in Japan in transition)
    Includes bibliographical references and index.
    ISBN 0-7914-4827-4 (alk. paper) — ISBN 0-7914-4828-2 (pbk. : alk. paper)
    1. Day laborers—Japan—Yokohama-shi. 2. Working class—Japan—Yokohama-shi.
    3. Yokohama-shi (Japan)—Social conditions. I. Title. II. Series.

    HD5854.2.J3 G55 2001
    305.5'62'09521364—dc21   00-039478

10   9   8   7   6   5   4   3   2   1

Contents

Contents

Illustrations

x   Illustrations

Tables

Acknowledgments

This book is a substantially modified version of a thesis I wrote for my doctorate in social anthropology at the London School of Economics and submitted in the fall of 1996. I would like to thank the Economic and Social Research Council for giving me the research grant (ESRC Award No. R00429234106) that made this project possible; and my supervisors, Professors Johnny Parry and Maurice Bloch, along with all the other staff and students at the LSE Department of Social Anthropology who argued with me and thereby helped me to develop the thesis. I enjoyed comparing notes with LSE anthropologist Gerald Mars. While I was conducting fieldwork I was given much useful guidance by Professor Sekimoto Teruo of the Institute for Oriental Research at Tokyo University.

In Kotobuki I was given a huge amount of help by Muroya Masa'aki, universally known as Kagoshima san, who has been working with the people of Kotobuki for some three decades. Takeuchi Masao, an official at the Kotobuki Labor Center, was also an invaluable source of information on the casual labor market, and Murata Yoshio of the Kotobuki Welfare Center is another Kotobuki veteran who gave me many insights into the district and its recent history. The members of Junichirō, the Kotobuki day laborers' union, were unfailingly helpful, and I would especially like to thank Yoshikawa san, Kondō san, and Yoneno san. On my travels to other yoseba I was also greatly assisted by Fukada Kazuo, Mizuno Ashira and Mizuno Mariko in Kamagasaki; by Ōtō Katsu in Chikkō; by Ōnishi Yutaka and his fellow unionists in Sasashima; and by "Gyaa" Suzuki, Nakamura Mitsuo, and other day-laborer activists in San'ya.

In the summer of 1997 I was appointed a research assistant at Kyoto Bunkyo University. This appointment gave me the time and facilities I needed to rewrite the thesis. I was also helped by the stimulating academic environment of Japan's biggest cultural anthropology department. In particular, Nakayama Noriko, Yasuda Hiromi, Kobayashi Yasumasa, Ōsugi Takashi and Ishikawa Shinsaku listened patiently to my problems and made constructive suggestions, while Harumi Befu's bracing criticism of my work was a necessary stimulant.

I owe a great debt of gratitude to my editor, Jerry Eades, for offering to include this book in his series on *Japan in Transition* and for reading the text several times and providing numerous invaluable suggestions. My thanks also go to Nancy Ellegate, Kristin Milavec, and the rest of the staff at SUNY Press, for their ever-professional support, to the copy editor Alan V. Hewat, and to the three anonymous readers who recommended the book for publication and suggested many improvements to the text.

This book has been greatly enhanced by the kindness of several very talented photographers who allowed me to use their work. I thank Nakajima Satoshi, Morita Ichiroh, Tokuda Masahiro, Umetani Hideji, and Kagoshima Masa'aki. Thanks also to Arimura Sen for allowing me to reproduce some of his "Kamayan" cartoons.

Some of the material in this book overlaps with other papers of mine—three in English (Gill 1999c, 2000b, 2000c), and three in Japanese (Gill 1999a, 1999b, 2000a). I would like to thank all the editors for allowing me to use reworked versions of the material.

I thank my parents, Rene and David Gill, and my friends Mark Jamieson, Tim Kalvis, and Ito Munemichi, for their encouragement and for helping to correct the text at various stages. Another friend, Steven Searle, kindly watched the Internet for me and supplied relevant news items. Him too, I thank.

I would especially and humbly like to thank my wife Kazuko, and my children Jake and Momoko, for putting up with me through the seven long years I have been working on this project. It has been quite an ordeal for the family and I truly appreciate their tolerance and understanding.

Above all, I would like to thank the day laborers of Kotobuki, San'ya, Kamagasaki, Sasashima, Chikkō, and Tobata for all the kindness and cooperation shown to a fat, suspicious-looking foreigner of obscure intent.

This book cost me my youth. I never dreamed that it would take me past the millenium to complete it. The longer the project has dragged on, the more I have envied my subjects, whose work is rewarded the same day, and not, like mine, at some point years down the line. That is not sentimentalism—it is the plain truth.

TOM GILL

Note on the Text

Japanese names have been given in the Japanese order, family name first.

I have attempted to adhere broadly to the Hepburn system of romanization in transliterating Japanese words, always aiming to convey the pronunciation of the word as clearly as possible.

Whenever a Japanese-language reference is cited, the translation is by myself unless otherwise stated.

Japanese words are generally italicized upon first reference only.

The yen-dollar and yen-pound rates varied constantly and violently during the process of researching and writing this thesis. The yen peaked at ¥80 to the dollar and later slumped to ¥140. Against the pound it peaked at ¥130 and then fell to ¥240. These fluctuations had virtually no impact on the standard of living of day laborers, and in the end I simply gave up trying to provide foreign currency equivalents. As a very rough rule of thumb, ¥1,000 was worth about six pounds or ten dollars for most of the period (1993–1995) in which I did most of my fieldwork.

Names accompanied by an asterisk have been changed to protect the informant's privacy. In most other cases I have used the first name only, and in a few cases, where I know that the individual would not object, I have used the full name.

There are many references in the text to the 600,000 words of fieldnotes I wrote during fieldwork. Anyone wishing to examine the fieldnotes can apply to myself or to my supervisors at the Social Anthropology Department of the London School of Economics, who also have a full set. Any reader with comments, criticisms, or inquiries is welcome to write to me via the publishers, or by e-mail at tpgill@yahoo.com in English or tomgill@yahoo.co.jp in Japanese.

Kotobuki: The Labor Welfare Center. The Labor Center and Labor Office are located underneath the extended roof on the right of the building. The crossroads in the foreground is the center of the early-morning street labor market. Note the fruit and vegetable stall on the corner. Photo by Umetani Hideji, 1994. Reprinted by permission.

1

Introduction

First Encounter

I WAS WORKING FOR KYODO NEWS, the Japanese wire service, in January 1986, when the murder of a day laborer union leader in Tokyo by a *yakuza* gangster briefly hit the headlines.[1] The story prompted me to visit San'ya, Tokyo's main day-laboring district, to write an article about the murder.

I had never heard of San'ya, yet it proved to be less than half an hour by underground from the Kyodo office in central Tokyo. When I did get there, it seemed at first like any other outlying district of Tokyo, albeit with buildings somewhat greyer and shabbier than average.

There were, however, several men lying asleep on the pavement, smelling of dried urine and alcohol. There were men who would accost me and talk with great animation, and others who would turn away as they saw me coming. Having arrived in the afternoon, I only saw men who had failed to get jobs for the day. Some slept in the street that night, others in cheap lodging houses, I in a nearby business hotel.

The next morning, everyone was up and looking for work by 5 A.M., and I realized that there were other kinds of day laborers besides the

1

battered old men that had first caught the eye: young ones, strong ones, skilled ones. The majority, however, looked over forty. They stood there in the pre-dawn dark, cigarettes and cups of tea in hand. Soon the labor recruiters showed up. They were a tough-looking lot; some were probably yakuza themselves. They went among the men, taking a few away to waiting trucks and vans after negotiations that were sometimes protracted and occasionally threatened to turn violent.

In a nearby park a small flea market was selling old boots, balaclavas, trousers, and bric-a-brac. There, another group of day laborers were gathering with some radical students, easily identifiable by their crash helmets, dark glasses, and bandannas. Some were armed with baseball bats. They set out with a large band of laborers on a demonstration, condemning the yakuza for the murder and the government for letting the yakuza get away with it.

Hundreds of riot police were deployed at strategic locations, apparently protecting the gangsters from the wrath of the day laborers. The laborers and students threw stones and bottles at the riot police, and a general shoving match ensued. But after a few minutes the demonstration continued on its way, leaving me to wonder how much of the violence was real and how much was symbolic. I later found that these early-morning confrontations happened almost daily, which surely affected the emotional involvement of the participants.

In 1986 I had lived in Japan for more than two years. Things that struck foreigners as strange now seemed readily explicable; I was on my way to becoming a "Japan hand." In San'ya, however, I felt suddenly disoriented. I resolved to research the phenomenon properly and have been trying to do so ever since.

Day Laborers in the Political Economy of Japan

The definition of a day laborer is, as they say, contested. According to the Ministry of Labor (MoL), there are some 42,000 day laborers in Japan (table 1), whereas another government department, the Labor Statistics Bureau of the Management and Coordination Agency (MCA), uses a different definition and says there are 1.26 million (table 3). This gross disparity will be discussed shortly.

"Day laborer" is the most common translation of the Japanese *hiyatoi rōdōsha*, which literally means "a worker employed by the day." Some Japanese workers and activists insist that *hiyatoi rōdōsha* should be translated "daily worker" because "laborer" corresponds more closely to the Japanese *rōmusha*, which sounds pejorative to them, implying unskilled, menial labor.[2] Others, by contrast, take pride in describing themselves as *hiyatoi rōmusha*—precisely because *rōmusha* has a more proletarian ring than *rōdōsha*.[3] I choose to use the term "day laborer" because it is familiar in the English language.

In fact, very few people satisfy the literal definition. Even the strictest day laborer will sometimes work on period contracts *(yūki keiyaku)* that last at least a few days and typically involve living near a construction site at a labor camp *(hanba)*. However, a substantial amount of the work done by my informants only lasts one day, with payment made in cash on that day. *Hiyatoi rōdōsha* is an occupational category recognized by most Japanese, and one with a long history that clearly differentiates it from other forms of employment (see chapter 2).

"Day laborer" does not only describe a particular working arrangement. It also carries a rich set of cultural associations: with poverty, struggle, loneliness, failure, vagabondage, and, like Hope at the bottom of Pandora's Box, freedom. From Yoshida Hideo's melancholy prewar reportage, *Hikasegi Aiwa* (lit.: "A Sad Tale of Earning by the Day," Yoshida 1930), through Mitsune Eiji's sentimental ballad of the 1950s, *Kamagasaki Ninjō* ("Kamagasaki Kindness"), to Okabayashi Nobuyasu's celebrated 1980s pop ballad *San'ya Burūsu* ("San'ya Blues"), day laborers have inspired writers and musicians to put the sadness of the disaffiliated worker before a mainstream audience. In a lighter vein, songs such as Soeda Satsuki's prewar *Sutoton-bushi* ("The Knockety-Knock Ballad") and the 1960s comic songs of Ueki Hitoshi, such as *Damatte Ore ni Tsuite Koi* ("Shut Up and Come with Me") have celebrated the happy-go-lucky aspect of the stereotyped day laborer. Miwa Akihiro's famous ballad, *Yoi Tomake no Uta*, pays tribute to the courage of a day-laboring mother. Thus a small but vivid branch of Japanese popular culture is dedicated to these people and their haunts.

Again, the Japanese language is peppered with terms to describe day laborers, from the stiffly bureaucratic *(hikasegi ninpu, nikkyū rōdōsha, hiyō kasegi,* etc.),[4] through the colloquial *(nikoyon, ankō, gonzō,* etc.) to the downright insulting *(tachinbō, pū-tarō)*.[5] To the Left they are *jiyū-rōdōsha* or *ryūdōteki-na kasō rōdōsha* (free workers, flexible lower-class workers), and a sizeable academic association[6] publishes frequent bulletins and an annual collection of papers on the political, social, and cultural significance of day laborers.

Strictly speaking, the main subject of this book is *yoseba* day laborers, traditional day laborers who look for work in urban labor markets called *yoseba* (Yamaoka 1984). Yoseba day laborers used to work in many industries, but nowadays they work mainly in two: construction and (to a lesser extent) longshoring. Like *hiyatoi rōdōsha*, the word *yoseba* is controversial. Day laborers are "free workers" in the strictly limited sense of not being legally bound to an employer. But the question of whether they are free in a broader sense is a fundamental one, embedded in the language associated with the occupation. The word *yoseba* derives from the causative form of the verb *yoru*, (to gather, meet, or assemble), and literally means "a place where (people) are made to gather." There is an alternative word, *yoriba*, which uses the ordinary form of the same verb and literally means "a place where (people) gather."

Many day laborers and activists are keenly aware of this distinction. Some prefer *yoriba* because it implies that they gather and seek work as free agents, not as passive objects of capitalism. Others prefer *yoseba*, because they think they *are* in fact victims of capitalism. Thus both terms are prone to accusations of political incorrectness. The question of free agency versus coercion was the strongest single theme running through my conversations with day laborers; I discuss it chiefly in chapter 8. In this book I use the term *yoseba* because it is the better known of the two.

The yoseba is typically a small area, embedded in the city, where men stand in the street very early in the morning and look for work opportunities. There are two basic ways of doing this: formally, through the casual labor exchanges set up in yoseba by national and local government agencies; or informally, through negotiation with street labor recruiters called *tehaishi* (lit.: "arrangers"), who usually have some connection with the yakuza.

The Ministry of Labor's day laborer population figure is derived by counting up people holding the MoL's white handbook *(shiro-techō)*, which is used to register at an exchange and to claim casual unemployment benefits (see pp. 52, 71–72). However, many day laborers do not carry the handbook: some have been stripped of it for making fraudulent claims, others work in areas lacking casual employment exchanges, yet others do not carry it because they are working informally, perhaps claiming social security at the same time. Hence the Ministry's figure is an obvious underestimate.

Even so, the Ministry of Labor statistics (tables 1 and 2 in the appendix) tell a dramatic story. The last three decades of the twentieth century have practically wiped out the formal market for day labor through the Ministry's labor exchanges. Three decades of steady decline have whittled down the population of handbook-carrying day laborers—by 84 percent in twenty-eight years, from 256,000 in 1970 to 42,000 in 1998. Person-days of registered labor have fallen faster still, from 4.3 million per month in 1970 to 51,000 per month in 1998 (table 1)—a decline of almost 99 percent, or an almost total disappearance, in twenty-eight years. The proportion of registered day laborers using their handbooks to get at least one day's work a month has also declined steadily, from 89 percent in 1970 to just 14 percent in 1998, indicating that a rapidly growing proportion of registered day laborers are effectively unemployed or relying on the informal, street-corner labor market.

Until 1994, day laborers needed to get stamps showing evidence of employment for an average of fourteen days a month in order to maintain eligibility for dole payments on days without work. In 1994 the Ministry of Labor responded to the long-running recession that started in 1990 by reducing the minimum to thirteen days a month, and raising the maximum daily dole payout from ¥6,200 to ¥7,500.

From 1970 to 1998 the number of days worked per month fell steadily, and in 1993 dole-claiming days exceeded working days for the first time (table 2). Whereas active registered day laborers got work through Ministry labor exchanges on six times more days than they claimed the dole in 1970, by 1998 they were claiming on more than twice as many days as they worked, signifying that the system was probably in its death throes.

That is not the same as saying that the whole institution of casual labor is in its death throes. Ministry of Labor figures include only jobs arranged through its own labor exchanges. Thus the apparent impossibility of active day laborers working eight days a month and claiming on eighteen (table 2; figures for 1996) can be explained by

1. workers on single-day contracts staying on for extra days at the work site and thereby acquiring more stamps without the work days showing up in Ministry statistics;
2. workers getting jobs via other labor exchanges, run by local government;
3. workers finding jobs through informal channels with employers who nonetheless subscribe to the unemployment program; and
4. unemployment stamp fraud.

The neat lists of numbers published by the Ministry conceal the true size and complexity of the casual labor phenomenon, and the fact that the ministry has less and less control over it.

The broad definition of day laborers used by the Management and Coordination Agency gives a very different picture. The MCA figure includes all workers on contracts of fewer than thirty days, or working without benefit of a contract (MCA 1995:72). Day laborers in the MCA definition show no sign of decline. The figure has hovered

around the 1.2 to 1.3 million mark for the last twenty-eight years—
the same period that has seen an 84 percent decline in day laborers
as defined by the Ministry of Labor. More than half the people
classified as day laborers by the MCA are women, many of them
working as piece workers at home (table 3). My study does not
cover these people: it is restricted to the almost exclusively male
population of the yoseba districts. It is significant, however, that a
government agency will admit to such a substantial population of
workers with zero security of employment. If one looks at other
categories of irregular workers—part-time, casual, temporary, self-
employed, etc.—we find that even official government statistics show
that some 15.5 million Japanese, or nearly one-quarter of the total
work force, are working with little or no job security (table 4).[7] In
other words, the yoseba day laborers are just the tip of a huge ice-
berg of insecure labor, which appears from government figures to
be declining, but much more slowly than the yoseba day laborer
population. The decline is largely being caused by the dwindling
population of rural smallholders which is a major element in the
MoL's "family workers" (kazoku jūgyōsha) category. "Casual employee" (rinji) is a large and increasing category, covering almost
five million people, although one doubts whether even this substantial figure fully reflects the vast number of corporate employees on
various forms of short-term contract.

Yoseba day laborers are hard to count. My own semi-informed guess
is that there could be up to 80,000 day laborers making regular or
occasional use of the yoseba, made up of the 42,000 or so registered
with the MoL plus a similar number of unregistered men.

Although a majority of broad-definition day laborers are women,
nearly all yoseba day laborers are men. In the Japanese countryside
all-woman road gangs are still a common enough sight, and women
do many kinds of demanding labor that tends to be reserved for men
in most advanced industrialized societies. There used to be many more
female construction workers,[8] and even in the modern yoseba a handful of women can be found who carry the white handbook, mostly
while doing office cleaning work. However, in cities the burgeoning
service sector has provided sufficient employment in restaurants, convenience stores, etc. to take women away from heavy manual labor,
and the yoseba are used overwhelmingly by men. These men are my
principal subjects; the role of casual female labor in the Japanese
economy is another vast topic, beyond the scope of the present study.

Yoseba day laborers are as clearly distinguished by residential patterns as by employment practices. Many of them live in cheap lodging

houses, called *doya* in Japanese (a street-slang inversion of *yado*, an inn). Areas with many doya are called *doya-gai* (lodging house towns). In three famous cases, the *yoseba* is also a *doya-gai*: Kamagasaki, in Osaka; San'ya, in Tokyo; and Kotobuki, in Yokohama, where I did most of my fieldwork. Day laborers sometimes refer to these three places as *Kama* (the first character of Kamagasaki); *Yama* (an alternate reading of the first character, "mountain," in San'ya); and *Hama* (the second character in Yokohama). Kama, Yama, Hama: the assonance expresses the sense of solidarity among these three great urban oases of nonmainstream culture.

In the mid-1990s there were reckoned to be roughly 21,000 day laborers in and around Kamagasaki, 9,000 at San'ya and 6,000 at Kotobuki, with another 3,000 using the yoseba at Sasashima in Nagoya and smaller numbers at various other yoseba.[9] In interviews with yoseba activists in September 1999, I was given the following estimates. Fukada Kazuo suggested that 21,000 was still a fair figure for Kamagasaki, made up of 14,000 based in Kamagasaki and another 7,000 coming in from outside to use it as a labor market. Nakamura Mitsuo suggested 2,500–3,000 for San'ya; Kagoshima Masa'aki suggested 2,500 for Kotobuki, where many former day laborers are now on welfare; and Ōnishi Yutaka suggested 2,500 for Sasashima.

Fieldwork

I spent twenty-two months based in Yokohama, from 15 May 1993 to 29 March 1995. I visited Kotobuki several times a week and also made field trips lasting several days each to San'ya, Kamagasaki, Sasashima, Chikkō (in Fukuoka), and Tobata (in Kitakyushu). I stayed in doya rooms in Kotobuki for several days on six different occasions.

In the yoseba, I made a point of getting up as early as possible in order to observe the daily job market. I attempted to get employed as a day laborer myself, but never succeeded. This was my greatest failure. My period in the field happened during one of the worst phases of the Heisei recession,[10] and work was very scarce even for day laborers far better qualified than myself. This, and deep suspicion on the part of the tehaishi about employing such an obviously foreign-looking worker, were the main reasons for this failure.[11]

However, I learned as much as I could about work from listening to hundreds of day laborers talking about it. I shared their lives in other ways, living in doya, drinking with them in the street, gambling in the numerous illegal gambling dens in Kotobuki, and generally mingling in as best I could.

I did not use a tape recorder, and only on one occasion did I take a camera with me to the field. Both these items tend to be viewed with suspicion by day laborers, many of whom have reasons for preferring to remain anonymous. I recorded material only on pocket memo pads, which I refrained from producing in front of an informant. I am convinced that any kind of simultaneous recording of conversations qualitatively affects the relationship between fieldworker and subject, usually to the detriment of the data obtained.

For similar reasons, I refrained from carrying out formal interviews, except on three occasions early in fieldwork; and I generally avoided asking questions except where they arose naturally out of the conversation. Nonetheless, I was able to build up quite a clear picture of several dozen day laborers whom I met on numerous occasions and most of whom I viewed as friends.

I attempted to make up for the lack of simultaneous recording by making notes in my memo pads as soon as possible after each conversation and incident, and by inputting data straight into my computer, usually the same day or the following day. This produced some 600,000 words of fieldnotes, which are the principal source of data for this book.

I also did my best to read the massive Japanese-language literature on day laborers. In one of these books (Kawahara 1987), the author tells how he went to Kotobuki in search of the truth about his younger brother, who joined the air force, quit after a couple of years, vanished completely, then showed up seven years later at the family home in Akita prefecture, ill and on the verge of death. He died three days later, leaving no evidence of where he'd been except for a few Yokohama place names, muttered in his delirium, which led Kawahara to Kotobuki. On his first visit he showed a photo of his brother to several men hanging around the Labor Center. One man said the brother had treated him to a meal a month before, another said he'd met him just the previous day. All said they knew him. In fact the photo was ten years old and the brother had already been dead six months. Time melts, identities blur and merge, people get confused and sometimes people lie . . . in Kotobuki.

It was not uncommon for people to contradict themselves in conversation with me. I would notice discrepancies between statements made several months apart; or a man might change his world view after another drink; or one man might accuse another of lying.

In this uncertain and disorienting environment, I used the following rules of thumb to evaluate statements: I gave greater credence to statements that did not have implications for the honor or social status of the informant, and to those by informants whom I knew relatively well; and where I was told two conflicting stories, I tended to give greater credence to the second version, told to me after I had got to know the informant better.

The fact remains that Kotobuki is the kind of place where one can make gross errors even after years of fieldwork. Thus I have the impression that contrary to conventional wisdom, there are relatively few ethnic Koreans or Burakumin (see glossary) among the day laborer population. However, people in both these groups are physically indistinguishable from other day laborers and, being subject to discrimination, have sound reasons for concealing their identity.

Outline of the Present Study

This book attempts to account for the persistence through time of day laborers and their gathering places in Japan, to understand the lives of contemporary day laborers, and to set them in the context of broader Japanese society.

The first step is to examine the history of day laboring, which accounts for much of the resonance now carried by the term (chapter 2). This is followed by a detailed ethnography of Kotobuki, the Yokohama yoseba that was my principal fieldwork site (chapter 3), describing the environment and the working and leisure lives of day laborers, plus the employment and welfare institutions that influence their lives.

At first glance Kotobuki looks much the same as the other yoseba around Japan. However, closer inspection reveals striking regional differences in the way casual labor is negotiated and perceived (chapter 4). The yoseba at Tokyo and Osaka have longer histories than Kotobuki, and the associations between the yoseba and other stigmatized zones, such as Burakumin districts, prostitution quarters and former execution grounds, are much clearer than in the young city of Yokohama. In northern Kyushu the yoseba have largely been supplanted by *rōdō-geshuku* (workers' boarding houses), which combine the functions of cheap accommodation and work introductions. All over Japan, freedom and security emerge as the issues involved in casual labor, but always in subtly varying ways.

In chapter 5 I consider the vital statistics of yoseba day laborers in Kotobuki, focusing on place of origin, previous employment, age, marital status and position in sibling birth order. My informants emerge as coming from largely rural, working-class backgrounds, and I have some suggestive evidence of a preponderance of eldest sons and youngest children in the yoseba population.

One set of associations with the day laborer category relates to homelessness. In chapter 6 I focus on the debate over literal homelessness ("rooflessness") versus detachment from traditional home life ("rootlessness"). For most day laborers, I argue, homelessness is seen as a risk to be avoided rather than as a defining aspect of their lives, although literal homelessness has been on the rise around the yoseba as day laboring contracts have dried up under the Heisei Recession. I also describe the ways in which homes and hometowns are replicated in the yoseba, for instance through festivals and the ad hoc institution of the bonfire.

In chapter 7 I look at the cultural identity of day laborers, attempting to show how their marginal position within Japanese society finds expression in contrasting, sometimes contradictory narratives of free agency and fate. Chapter 8 shifts from micro to macro perspective, analyzing the role of the yoseba within broader society, and contrasting the response of the authorities to that shown toward American skid rows.

Finally, in the epilogue I attempt to apply the findings of earlier chapters to the dangerous project of predicting the future of casual labor in Japan. I see it playing a growing role in the Japanese economy, but not in the traditional industries and not for very much longer in places such as the yoseba.

I conclude each chapter with a brief sketch of one of my day laborer informants. I have done this in the hope that elements in these men's stories will cast light on the themes of the book from a slightly different angle.

Sakae

Sakae was the first man I got to know in Kotobuki. Slim and trim, he was always respectably dressed and often carried a Walkman. He sometimes listened to an English conversation tape and he had a smattering of painfully memorized English idioms.

Sakae once told me that the trouble with life was that you had to carry on with it to the end. He wished it were like a film, where you could walk out in the middle if you weren't enjoying it. Indeed there were elements of fantasy in his self-presentation, and over time he contradicted himself several times. He was consistent on his age, though: forty-five in 1993.

In one early meeting he said he was the youngest of five children, and bitterly blamed his parents for making more kids than

(continues)

(continued)

they could feed in the hard years just after the war, living in a
rough district of Osaka. Later he had gone on to Nagoya Industrial University where he studied engineering. At a later meeting
he said he had just one sibling, an elder sister; that he was born
and bred in rural Gifu prefecture; and that his education didn't go
beyond high school.

The Gifu version of his family background continued thus. He
always went back to Gifu at Golden Week (a holiday period in
early May) to see his folks. They were very old, and his dad was
confined to a wheelchair, barely able to hear or speak. They were
looked after by his sister and her husband, who was a *mukō-yōshi*—
a man adopted to be a husband for one's daughter. Sakae described this as a deliberate policy by his parents to replace his
wandering self, their only son.

Sakae's account of his working life varied too: initially he told
me that he'd spent twenty years "digging holes" *(ana-hori),* but
later he said he had worked for Daikyo Oil until ten years ago, in
pressure turbine maintenance, until he got bored and quit. Since
then he'd been moving around the country doing a few months'
work here and there. He would disappear for long periods; after
one of these he said he had just completed a four-month stint
doing night maintenance at a factory in Kashima (Ibaraki prefecture). He said he had developed a seasonal pattern of work—for
instance, during the new year holidays he'd work as a night
watchman for one of the companies running pleasure boat rides
on Lake Hamanaka down in Shizuoka prefecture.

He consistently said that he had an apartment in Heiwajima,
Tokyo, and worked on relatively long contracts away from
Yokohama. He used to live in Kotobuki but had moved out
because there were too many people there who had lost the
will to work, and the defeatist spirit was catching. He came
back to Kotobuki to see old friends and sometimes to get employment. His infrequent appearances in Kotobuki seemed to
bear this out. On one occasion I saw Sakae talk to a tehaishi,
who he later said had fixed him up with a one-month job re-
pairing boilers in Osaka.

Sakae was keen on science and mathematics. He was a great
admirer of Werner von Braun, and tried to impress me with his
ability to solve trigonometric problems and to measure small irregular shapes using bits of paper divided into two-millimeter
folds. He had a project, of which he often spoke, to make an
improved embossing machine that would give him an income

(continues)

12

(continued)

and something to do in his old age. Several times he showed me embossed samples. At first these were rather crude impressions on small pieces of card, but over the months they gradually improved in definition and he became able to emboss images on flattened tin cans.

He had a pessimistic philosophy. The life of man was one of sorrows: the knowledge of pain, hunger, and poor circulation; poverty; the death of one's parents; parting from friends; suffering and sadness. He himself was born under an unlucky star. But everyone is subject to physical laws such as gravitational attraction: fat or thin, it would always take us nine seconds to hit the ground. This he found comforting. He also said there was balance in all things: if one person became happier, another became less happy, and vice-versa.

He believed that individual freedom was heavily constrained by material circumstances, and that men who wound up in Kotobuki did so because they had been "defeated by culture." Life was only as bad as one was culturally trained to believe: there were people in other countries much poorer than Kotobuki men, but they did not sense their poverty.

Sakae spoke at length about his friendship with a three-year-old boy called Tatsuo, whom he got to know in Kashima and to whom he became a sort of adoptive uncle. He credited Tatsuo with curing him of his addiction to *pachinko* (see glossary); he learned to spend his free time taking Tatsuo for treats rather than feeding money into a pachinko machine.

Ultimately his embossing project seemed to be a means of combatting fear of loneliness and mortality:

> When I die, I'll leave no family, no wife, no children, no friends, no property . . . nothing. I'll just fly away on my own. Over there. [Pointing beyond the high buildings again]. But there's one thing I want to do first. I want to get one of those big heavy stones—you know, a nice smooth, grey one—and I want to invent a better sort of embossing machine, and find some way of embossing my own face on it . . . not just a picture, the whole thing, in three dimensions. Then I'm going to go to some cliff, and throw the stone out to sea, so that even after millions of years, long after I'm dead, I'll still be there. That's my dream.[12]

2

General Historical Background

Overview

JAPANESE HISTORY OFFERS many examples of institutions for the control of workers that bordered on imprisonment and slavery. Slavery itself was nominally abolished in the Heian era (794–1185), but, "... there continued to be a body of semi-slaves such as serfs, bond servants, and indentured tenants" (Price 1972:16). During the Kamakura era (1185–1333) tradesmen called *hitoakibito* engaged in buying and selling servants, and in the Muromachi era (1338–1573) children were kidnapped, bought, and sold as servants (16).

Day laborers emerged from this culture of slavery and serfdom to pose a great challenge to their political and economic masters. Their history can be characterized as a long and continuous struggle between free workers attempting to express their autonomy, and employers and civil authorities that have sought to control them and at times incarcerate them. Sometimes these attempts to exert control have been made in the name of the workers' welfare, at other times they have been more obviously exploitative. But the struggle continues to this day.

Mushuku and *Hinin*

Short-term casual laborers appear to have played a significant role in the Japanese economy from about the middle of the seventeenth century (Leupp 1992:16). Toyotomi Hideyoshi, who ruled over most of Japan from 1582 to 1598, outlawed the employment of day laborers, which he saw as a threat to the stability of the feudal relationship between master and man, and to the all-important rice harvest. Thus, even four centuries ago, "day laborer" (the term *hiyatoi* was already in common use) signified far more than just a particular way of making a living. As Leupp puts it, "During the late sixteenth century day labor and abscondence had been nearly synonymous" (160).

Until the warlords—Oda Nobunaga, then Hideyoshi, then Tokugawa Ieyasu—went about unifying the nation from the mid-sixteenth century onward, Japan was a loose collection of mini-states, perpetually warring and intriguing against each other. Each state saw its vital interest as lying in keeping the peasantry firmly tied to the land so that the maximum possible rice tax could be extracted from them. All sorts of measures were taken to prevent peasants leaving the land, and after the Tokugawa shoguns unified the nation, regional strongmen *(daimyō)* further strengthened the rules. Leupp cites a 1612 edict from the province of Tosa (on Shikoku island) which is a case in point:

> It is a very serious crime to desert to another province. Those who assist in the getaway are equally guilty. Both ears and nose must be cut off. If, at a later time, the runaway is caught and brought back, he will be punished by death, and so will those who helped him. (7–8)

The main bureaucratic device used to prevent abscondence was the census register *(ninbetsu-chō)* kept by the local temple—a forerunner of the civic family register *(koseki)* used in Japan today. People travelling to other parts of Japan were obliged to carry a *tsūkō tegata*, a sealed statement from the temple certifying that the bearer was properly registered there and had been granted permission to travel. It was in fact a sort of passport. Anyone who travelled around without this document was defined as *mushuku*—literally, "without a home" (Mori 1988).

Strictly speaking, mushuku were homeless only in the legal sense of lacking a household of registered domicile. Literally homeless people were called *yadonashi*, written with the same characters as "mushuku" but in reverse order and with Japanese rather than Chinese readings (Takayanagi 1980:28–29). People could become mushuku by their own action, typically by leaving home without acquiring a tsūkō tegata, or they could be made mushuku against their will, being expelled for committing a crime. Dead, they would become unconnected spirits *(muen-botoke)*, and their names would be expunged from the *kakōchō*, the historical record kept by the temple. The term "muen-botoke" is still used today to describe people who die with no known relatives.

Another category that overlapped with mushuku and day laborers was *Hinin*, literally "non-people." The first written use of the term dates from the year 842, in the Heian era (Takayanagi 1980:12), and meant a person who had lost his rights of citizenship for some offense, typically failure to pay rice taxes. These people were struck off the village register and made to perform menial labor. By the seventeenth century several subdivisions had been defined. *Kakae-hinin* ("employed non-people") were registered, kept in workhouses *(koya)*, and set to work under workhouse bosses *(koya-gashira)*. *No-hinin* ("wild non-people"), by contrast, were unattached to any workhouse and were sometimes literally homeless. Many Tokugawa-era day laborers appear to have been drawn from their ranks. For the most part a blind eye was turned, but periodic roundups *(kari-komi)* expelled Hinin from the cities or put them into workhouses. The biggest of these roundups in Edo occurred in 1743 and 1837. Other ways of controlling Hinin included forcing them to wear close-cropped hair and identifying tattoos (Takayanagi 1980:214–215).

Hiyatoi : Burakumin :: Hinin : Eta?

Burakumin is a euphemistic term for an outcast group with an ancient history, now thought to number between 1.5 million (Sumida 1986:312) and 3 million (Yoshino and Murakoshi 1977:3). They have tended to live in ghetto-like settlements known informally as *buraku* (hamlets), some of which are designated "equality areas" *(dōwa chiku)* and are subject to government improvement programs. Burakumin still experience intense discrimination from mainstream Japanese, notably in marriage, employment, and education. The stigma against them is related to occupation, in particular to the meat and leather-tanning industries which were outcast monopolies until the outcast category was formally abolished under the "emancipation edict" of 1871 (Yoshino and Murakoshi, 1977:46). There is a massive Japanese-language literature on Burakumin (e.g., Kan 1986, 1988; Sumida 1986;

Takamoto 1993; etc.); English accounts include De Vos and Wagatsuma (1967), Yoshino and Murakoshi (1977), De Vos and Wetherall (1983), Kitaguchi (1998), and Davis (2000).

Mr. Fukada, a day laborer unionist in Kamagasaki, put it to me that day laborers are the cultural descendants of the Hinin, while the Burakumin are the biological descendants of the *Eta* (lit.: filth abundant), another despised group with ancient origins which became clearly defined during the Tokugawa era.[1] If true, this would imply an enduring pattern of what Murata calls the "multiple class stratification of discrimination" *(sabetsu no jūsōka)* (Murata 1988:19–24).

Fukada's claim that day laborers are modern Hinin is based on two main planks: They share the mobile, fluid lifestyle; and they are excluded from family life, though in the case of day laborers this is a cultural, rather than legal, exclusion. Being "non-people," Hinin could not legally marry, head households, and have descendants, says Fukada. Eta could marry, though only to fellow Eta.

The point about marriage is contentious. The Hinin status varied with time and place, and at least some of them were able to marry. However, the rest of Fukada's distinction between the Eta and Hinin is confirmed by Price:

> During the Ashikaga period (1336–1573) the Eta were the most fortunate of the pariah classes, that is, of the Eta-Hinin caste. They held special skills and economic monopolies, owned property, and had a stable community life; albeit this very stability assured their continuity as an outcast population. The Hinin trades usually required less skill, so that a person could move from one Hinin trade to another with relative ease. Also the Hinin were geographically more mobile. They could move in and out of Eta or Hinin villages or take up a respectable occupation in a commoner village and in time actually become a commoner. Written records from the Tokugawa period maintain that the Eta are outcasts permanently by inheritance whereas the Hinin are outcasts only by occupation and social status. (Price 1972:21)

During the Tokugawa period the main Buddhist sects maintained *Eta-dera* ("Eta temples"; "defiled temples") where Eta would be registered. Hinin were excluded from temple registration.

The historical relationship between Eta and Hinin was complex. In the early Tokugawa Era the terms were treated as synonyms, or even combined in a single word *(Eta-hinin;* Takayanagi 1981:116). Some modern scholars casually conflate them (e.g., Komatsu 1987:S37), while others argue that Eta became subsumed within the class of Hinin (e.g.,

Yoshino and Murakoshi, 1977:33), and yet others argue that the categories were clearly distinct from each other, at least until well into the Tokugawa Era (e.g., Price 1972:21). Sumida has it that the Hinin category disappeared at the end of the Tokugawa Era (1866), while the Eta continue to exist—renamed Burakumin—to this day (Sumida 1986:310). It seems that no two accounts of these two groups concur.

Takayanagi, a historian who has written a book-length account of the Hinin, says that the two classes were mixed together until the seventeenth century, but were deliberately separated by the shōguns (1981:116), as an extension of the divide-and-rule policy under which they divided the rest of society into a four-class hierarchy. Takayanagi identifies the key differences between the two classes thus:

1. *Eta* was an inherited status, whereas the status of *Hinin* was generally imposed as a punishment, usually for absconding from one's village; participating in a failed double suicide; petty theft by people under the age of fifteen; or running illegal gambling games. (Takayanagi 1981:17–26)
2. Eta were officially recognized as being superior to Hinin. For example, in eighteenth century Edo the *Hinin-gashira* (head of the Hinin) in Asakusa, Kuruma Zenshichi, was officially subordinate to the *Eta-gashira* (head of the Eta), Danzaemon, and was obliged to supply him with one thousand man-days of Hinin labor each month.[2] (116)
3. There was considerable friction between the two groups, developing into a protracted feud which broke out in 1720, smoldered on for the next 150 years and erupted in a major uprising of Hinin against Eta in 1838, "because the contempt of the Eta had become too much for the Hinin to bear." This ended with the execution of the Hinin leader (121). The feud was still in full swing as the Tokugawa era came to an end and the classes were abolished. (125–130)

Although there is nothing between Burakumin and day laborers remotely resembling the Tokugawa-era feud between the Eta and Hinin, it is fair to say that there is very little sense of solidarity between them. Sumida Toshio, himself a Burakumin and a famous campaigner for Burakumin liberation says (1986:313) that the Burakumin in Osaka contemptuously refer to day laborers as *tachinbō*. Sumida divides the day laborers into two groups. The former are in fairly regular employment, may have families, and contemptuously refer to the Burakumin as *eta*. The latter are "drifters and down-and-outs" and, he says, do not discriminate against the Burakumin.

In Sumida's division of the yoseba population one hears an echo of the old distinction between "controlled" and "wild" Hinin (*Kakae-hinin, No-hinin*). Sumida himself concedes that day laborers show some resemblance to Hinin (Sumida 1986:313). This brief sketch of a very complex historical question suggests that the stereotyped model of Japanese society, of mainstream and margin, insider and outsider, may require modification. There does seem to be evidence of a fairly consistent pattern of dualistic discrimination here.

The Preindustrial Proletariat

Tokugawa Ieyasu came to power in 1600 after crushing his opponents at the Battle of Sekigahara, and took the title of *shōgun* in 1603.[3] This was the start of the Tokugawa shogunate, a 265-year period (1603–1868) also known as the Edo era after the city of Edo, present-day Tokyo. The shogunate was born during a period of frantic urban construction: twenty-five cities were founded between 1580 and 1610 (Leupp 1992:11–12). As the era wore on, the policy of the shogunal government was marked by an increasingly irreconcilable contradiction between the shoguns' desires to maintain a large, settled agrarian population that could be relied on to turn in the rice harvest every year, and develop a large, flexible urban labor force that would help in the rapid construction of cities and castles. In the rural districts, exploitation provoked large numbers of peasant rebellions—2,700 big enough to be recorded during the Tokugawa era (8)—while in the cities, periodic crackdowns to send absconders back to the country alternated with periods of turning a blind eye because their labor was so obviously needed.

Migrant labor became prevalent, and a preindustrial urban proletariat developed, which was useful to the shōguns in supporting the Tokugawa economy—especially in mining, construction and transportation—but was also big enough and rebellious enough to pose a potential threat to shogunal control. The urban equivalent of the peasant rebellions were frequent violent street riots called *uchi-kowashi* (lit.: "smashings"), often directed at rice shops or pawnbrokers and demanding cheaper rice or the free return of pawned items (Kodansha 1989:174).

One reason why day laborers were such a potent threat to law and order was their strength in numbers. In the castle town of Okayama, for instance, 28 percent of the registered households belonged to day laborers by the mid-seventeenth century; corresponding figures of 17 percent for Okazaki in 1801 and 39 percent for Yamaguchi in 1844 have also survived (Leupp 1992:4). Even the poorer samurai did day labor on the side for extra income (126).[4] Moreover, the cities were huge: in 1700 the population of Edo was roughly one million, making it one of the world's biggest cities. Osaka had a population of four hundred thousand, and some 15 percent of Japanese people were living in cities. Only Britain and Holland had higher rates of urbanization (11–12).

The Tokugawa shogunate's attempts to control and repress the day laborer population were hampered by the frequent labor shortages that afflicted the big cities. Smith (1959:110, 124–125) contrasts this situation with the labor surpluses that were common in western European cities during this period, and Leupp suggests that this difference in the supply and demand of labor enabled Tokugawa day laborers to enjoy considerably better working conditions than their European counterparts (Leupp 1992:146–147). Even so, economic fluctuations and poor rice harvests occasionally reduced large numbers of day laborers to vagrant status and made them into a greater threat to law and order. At such times the blind eye policy toward rural-urban migration would be discarded.

License, Welfare, Control

Early attempts at licensing systems for day laborers in Edo entailed the appointment of day laborer chiefs who had the job of issuing licenses. The earliest surviving edict dates from 1653:

> As it was formerly commanded, people working as day-laborers must receive a license *(fuda)* from the day-laborers' chiefs *(hiyatoi-gashira)*. Anyone employing persons without such a license will be fined. This is a criminal offense.[5]

These *fuda* were wooden tags to be worn on the person, and were similar to licenses already issued to beggars (Leupp 1992:161). The Edo authorities also attempted to set maximum wage levels for day laborers, expressed in terms of the number of laborers to be supplied by an *oyakata*—small-time boss, leader of a work gang—for a fixed amount of gold. Provided he did not exceed that maximum, the oyakata could skim off as much of the wage as he could get away with, much like a modern-day street labor recruiter.

In 1665 the shogunate moved to strengthen the licensing system by setting up a day laborer registry, the *Hiyatoi-za*. The authorities frequently tried to tighten their control of day laborers, by adding new professions to those covered by the registry, by cracking down on day laborers who avoided paying the license fee by sharing one license between several men, by obliging the registry chiefs to collect lists of day laborers from their landlords, and by holding the chiefs responsible for the behavior of registered men (Leupp 1992:162–163).

The Registry finally collapsed in 1797. Yoshida suggests two reasons for this: (1) The post of registry chief had become a financial liability and was therefore very hard to fill; and (2) the whole system was based on a faulty premise: that "day laborer" could be defined as an occupational status *(mibun)* comparable to that of a samurai or artisan, when in fact it was a mere "condition" *(jōtai)* that people easily drifted into and out of.[6] That ambiguity survives today.

Probably a third reason for the collapse of the Registry was a shift in the shogunate's approach to the control of day laborers. During the Kansei reform (1787–1793), the concept of regulation was giving way to a dual approach of carrot and stick. During this period the Edo authorities collected 22,000 *ryō* from house-owning townsmen, and another 10,000 from the shōgunal treasury, to fund the establishment of a poor relief office called the Machikaisho. "Up to 410,000 needy townspeople were receiving assistance, in the form of rice and money, by the Tenpo period (1830–1844)" (Leupp 1992:159).

The *Ninsoku Yoseba* of 1790

The period of the Kansei reform also saw the birth of another famous Edo establishment: the *ninsoku yoseba*, or "navvy gathering place." According to which scholar you listen to, this was either a highly progressive institution, designed to make solid citizens with useful skills out of vagrants, or a forced labor camp for innocent victims. Takikawa (1994) is typical of the former position, Matsuzawa (1988a, b) of the latter.[7] Several day laborers told me that this was the origin of the word "yoseba" as used today.

The most direct inspiration for the ninsoku yoseba was the *hinin goya*, or workhouse for outcasts, popularized by the authorities of Kanazawa, who opened their first workhouse in 1670. A more immediate forerunner was launched on Sado island in 1778 (Leupp 1992:166–169). There is evidence that the categories of laborer *(ninsoku)* and outcast *(Hinin)* were confused, especially by the officials on Sado (Leupp 1992:170).

In 1790, spurred to action by the Tenmei uprising of 1787, the Edo *bakufu* (shogunal government) decided to take action against the growing number of unregulated laborers and vagrants on the streets of Edo. Hasegawa Heizō, an Arson and Theft Inspector, proposed a brand-new yoseba for Edo.[8] It was built (in just two months, by Hinin laborers brought over from the prison at Asakusa) on an island of reclaimed land in the Sumida River. It was close to the estuary, between two existing islands, Tsukudajima and Ishikawajima (Takikawa 1994:117). A deep moat was excavated between the yoseba and the two neighboring islands. The new island became known as Vagrant Island (Mushuku-jima) by the people of Edo (116).

The inmates were not necessarily guilty of any crime. At first it was simply a place for vagrants, including "sons disinherited because of their dissipation and merchants whose morals have deteriorated" (Leupp 1992:171). After 1820 the authorities started to put petty criminals in the yoseba as well (171). The site area was 12,000 square yards, and though it was designed for 120 to 130 inmates, it was always overcrowded, housing up to six hundred by the Tenpo period (1830–1844; 171).

Inmates were put to work making charcoal briquettes, recycling old paper, dredging rivers and milling rice (Hayashi 1988). Two centuries later, paper recycling and river dredging are still representative underclass occupations.[9] Work parties were sent out from the yoseba to other parts of Edo, and their members became known as water-drop navvies (*mizu-tama ninsoku*) from the distinctive pattern of water drops on their light-brown uniforms (Takikawa 1994:117). By the mid-nineteenth century, "[O]il squeezing became the largest enterprise, bringing the workhouse eight hundred gold ryō in profits every year" (Leupp 1992:171). Inmates were paid wages and forced to save one-third of their income (171).

Three years was the usual term at the yoseba. Three times a month the yoseba inmates were subjected to moral lectures from scholars of Shingaku—a Confucian-Shinto-Buddhist amalgam with a stress on the dignity of hard work (Leupp 1992:173–174). Those who tried to escape from the yoseba faced draconian punishments, including the death penalty for escaping; tattooing and flogging for evading work within the yoseba; three hundred days in manacles for conspiring to escape even if the attempt was abandoned; and flogging or island exile for gambling (172–173).

The rules attempt to distinguish between yoseba laborers and Hinin, stating that anyone discovered to have concealed their Hinin identity will be handed over to the Hinin headman. But interestingly, in the same year the yoseba was set up, the authorities also tightened their control over the Hinin:

If the Hinin broke the rules by stealing, using coercion, or *leaving their assigned areas,* they were subject to fixed penalties. The first time they left they were just scolded and told to stay. The second time they were tattooed on the upper arm, the third time around the left wrist, and the fourth time they were killed. These penalties were strengthened in 1790; the first time they were tattooed on the upper left arm, the second on the left wrist, and the third time they were killed. (Price 1972:27; italics added for emphasis)

Leupp says the yoseba movement lasted about eighty years, from the 1780s to the 1860s (1992:174). After Edo, yoseba were established at Nagasaki (1814), in Osaka (c. 1840), and in Nagaoka (1851 or 1852). However, Fukawa describes one set up at Kobe in 1871, after the Meiji Restoration (1994:90–91). It only lasted three years. At the very end of the Tokugawa shogunate, most of the inmates of the Edo yoseba were relocated to Usubetsu, on Hokkaido, and put to work fishing (Leupp 1992:174). The site of the yoseba became a straightforward prison, which was later relocated to Sugamo in 1896 and then to Fuchu, where the main Tokyo prison remains today (Takikawa 1994:173–174). Among modern day laborers who know their history, the ninsoku yoseba is remembered with special loathing: in one year alone, more than one thousand inmates died (Leupp 1992:173). Today the word "yoseba" is still used to mean "prison" in yakuza slang (Matsushige 1988:207).

But as the shōguns' grip on power weakened in the mid-nineteenth century, Edo and the other great cities were hit by wave upon wave of street protests. The blind fury of the uchi-kowashi gave way to more overtly political protests called *yonaoshi,* or world rectification movements. Walthall (1986) says that day laborers, vagrants, and drifters played a major role in these urban uprisings, and in the end they contributed to the collapse of the shogunate.

The Industrial Revolution

Labor arrangements bordering on imprisonment persisted into the Meiji era (1868–1912). The shift from feudalism to capitalism happened very quickly, and capitalists viewed their relations with employees in terms of lord and retainer (Crump 1983:158). The role of the oyakata expanded, and he became a kind of employer-landlord, who would sign up laborers on exploitative long-term contracts and house them in primitive on-site dormitories called *hanba* or *naya* (Matsuzawa 1988b:152).

Employers were supported by a series of governments that made virtually any kind of attempt by workers to improve their situation illegal, most notoriously through the Public Peace Police Law *(Chian Keisatsu-hō)* enacted in 1900, Clause 17 of which forbade workers "to stop work or refuse offers of employment for the purpose of bringing about a strike" (Crump 1983:20–22).

While organized labor struggled in this hostile environment, individual resistance appears to have been widespread, often expressed in systematic disloyalty to employers. Many workers put a positive value on mobility, and felt something like contempt for those who stayed in the same job for long. Here is an anonymous machinist writing in 1898:

> A worker is someone who enters society with his skills and who travels far and wide with them. Who could possibly credit with a spirit of advancement those workers who cling to a single place and put up with all sorts of abuse? . . . Past and present, whatever the occupation, a worker is someone who travels broadly, enters factories here and there, accumulates greater skills and, overcoming adversity, finally becomes a worker deserving of the name.[10]

Gordon describes how frustrated managers in turn-of-the-century industry tried various tactics to prevent "spontaneous job-switching," including seniority-based pay systems (forerunners of the stereotypical modern Japanese corporate pay system), withholding of wages that would be lost if the worker left without notice, and mutual pacts with other employers not to take on workers who had run away from each other's factories. Gordon argues that these control systems largely failed, the reason being that workers did not change jobs simply to look for better terms, but because, as the machinist's comment just quoted suggests, mobility was valued in its own right. Figures for the Ishikawajima Shipyard and the Shibaura Engineering Works, two of Tokyo's biggest manufacturing centers, show that in 1902 more than 80 percent of the workers had been there for five years or less, with about half the workers apparently moving back and forth between the two companies (Gordon 1985:33–36). This picture contrasts sharply with the *immobility* observed among nineteenth-century East London casual laborers (Jones 1971:81–84).

Why this high degree of mobility in Japan? Littler (1982:148–150) points out that the Japanese industrial revolution (c.1880–1915), unlike its British predecessor, took place at a time of economic expansion, so that the economy was more often troubled by labor shortages than by unemployment. It is striking that Smith and Leupp say much the same about the Tokugawa era (see p. 19), and this long-running tendency toward labor shortage—perhaps related to the labor-intensive nature of rice cultivation?—may be one of the factors differentiating Japan from other countries in the transition from feudalism to capitalism.

While the labor aristocracy embraced job mobility, those further down the labor hierarchy had it thrust upon them, picking up casual work wherever they could find it. Their desperate lives were vividly recorded by two astute observers of the Meiji underclass: Yokoyama Gennosuke and Matsubara Iwagorō. Some of the worst-off lived in *kichin yado*, cheap flophouses that were the forerunners of the doya. Yokoyama counted 135 of these around Tokyo in 1898 (1985 [1899]:62–63). The disgusting conditions in one kichin yado are described by Matsubara (1988 [1888]). The patrons included peddlers, mendicant monks, and traveling actors along with day laborers *(hiyatoi; tachinbō)*. Five or six residents would share a single room, demarcating territory by laying out their possessions. Most of the men were travelling, some of them with wives and children in tow. The kichin yado charged three *sen* per night (Matsubara, 1988 [1888]:21–23), only one sen less than the rent quoted by Matsubara for the cheapest kind of family accommodation (158; 100 sen = 1 yen).

One technique often used to maintain some kind of stability in the work force was to employ indirectly, via an oyakata. He would be paid a lump sum, out of which he would pay his apprentices (who often lived in his house or in a dormitory owned by him) an amount agreed between them without reference to the end employer. Matsubara says that the oyakata of late-nineteenth-century Tokyo are:

> the section commanders *(shō-taichō)* of this society, and are called foreman *(tōryō; also implies pillar of society)* or room-boss *(heya-gashira)*; they have a certain amount of authority, and are influential men about the neighborhood as becomes one who has some 40 or 50 men under his command. (Matsubara 1988:156)

There is something of the modern tehaishi or *ninpu-dashi* owner (see glossary) about these oyakata, and in both cases the exact status of the individual varies greatly—from wholly independent operator to employed company operative via all points between. In Matsubara's day the principal end employer was the public sector—often the civil engineering department of the prefectural government *(fuchō no doboku-ka)*. Sometimes the bureaucrats would go directly to the oyakata with their labor requirements; sometimes they would go via a private company, which in turn sometimes used a higher-level middle man called an *ukeoishi* (contractor) to pass on requests to oyakata (Matsubara 1988:156). So in some cases the employment chain went bureaucrat—private company—middle man—foreman—worker. As I will shortly show, very similar chains may be found in the modern construction industry.

Yokoyama offers further interesting parallels to modern conditions. He divides day laborers *(hikasegi ninsoku)* into six categories: repairers of roads and bridges; general navvies *(dokata)*; those employed in factories; those working for carpenters, plasterers and stone masons; those engaged in road haulage *(shariki)*; and the tachinbō—men who would wait, typically at the bottom of a hill, and help the shariki get his cart up the hill by pushing from behind while he pulled from the front. For this service they would get a very small payment (Yokoyama 1988 [1888]:33). The other kinds of day laborers often sustained a household, but "the tachinbō has no house" *(tachinbō ni wa ka'oku nashi)*. The tachinbō of Tokyo would sleep in kichin yado in Asakusa and elsewhere during the cold months, and on benches in Ueno Park, Kudan, or Asakusa Park when it was warm enough (39–40). Yokoyama remarks that bad diet has broken the spirit of these men, yet still they will remark that they "wouldn't do something so stupid as to get a steady job" *(Oraa, jōyatoi no yō na baka-na koto wa shinē)*; a comment that may still be heard in the yoseba today (40).

If the tachinbō seem to correspond to some of the more marginal modern day laborers, several of Yokoyama's other late-nineteenth-century types show the shrewd, tactical approach of the more successful day laborers known to me. The road and bridge repairers routinely had their wages skimmed by recruiters (a practice known today as *pin-hane*), with a forty sen day wage paid by the local authority being reduced to thirty-two or thirty-three sen by the time the ukeoishi and oyakata had taken their cuts. Women workers got just twenty sen (Yokoyama 1988 [1888]:33–34). Workers responded to this exploitation by having a relationship with their boss (oyakata) that Yokoyama describes as "extremely weak." The majority of them worked on different jobs in different places every day, and they would not hesitate to work for a different oyakata if he was offering one or two sen a day extra. They had "no sincerity or compassion towards the boss." In dramatic contrast, some allowed themselves to get into debt to an oyakata by accepting advances on their wages, and were forced to work for as little as twenty-five or twenty-six sen a day (34). These free and unfree day laborers have their counterparts in the yoseba and ninpu-dashi workers of today (see pp. 104–108).

There are also numerous Meiji era accounts of employers struggling to physically restrain their workers from escaping. Women were being rapidly drafted into the labor force and were especially prone to prison-like conditions, generally justified on the grounds that the employer was acting *in loco parentis*, and had to defend the women's sexual virtue (Crump 1983:17). This often had tragic results, as when thirty-one young spinning girls were burned to death in the sealed dormitory of a spinning company in 1899 (Katayama 1918:57).

Men were also subjected to forms of forced labor. On coal mines and construction sites, bond laborers were kept locked up in prison-like quarters known as *tako-beya*.[11] "Our miners live in congested barracks like rows of sheds, which are built by the mining company," runs an account from 1918 by the early Socialist leader, Katayama Sen (Katayama 1918:79).

But as Katayama points out, the physical closeness in which miners lived their lives, and their ability to talk in secret while working underground, also gave them a special solidarity and made it easier for them to organize (Katayama 1918:79–80). Throughout the period there were uprisings by miners, peaking in 1907 when there were major, violent insurrections at the Ashio copper mine in Tochigi (February),[12] at the Horonai coal mine in Hokkaido (April), at the Besshi copper mine in Shikoku (June), and at the Ikuno silver mine near Osaka (July). Each one was put down by military intervention (Crump 1983:163–164).

In this economy of coercion, day laborers had an important role to play for the capitalists and political authorities, as what Marx called "a disposable industrial reserve army, . . . for the changing needs of the self-expansion of capital, a mass of human material always ready for exploitation."[13] For this reason, some Marxist theoreticians have tended to label day laborers as class traitors, part of what Marx called "the 'dangerous class,' the social scum, that passively rotting mass thrown off by the lowest layers of old society . . . [whose] conditions of life . . . prepare it . . . for the part of a bribed tool of reactionary intrigue" (Marx and Engels 1977 [1888]:92).[14]

Matsuzawa dates the birth of the modern-style yoseba to the end of the nineteenth century:

> Between 1885 and 1890, yoseba were established for the first time
> in back streets and flophouse quarters to keep up with the grow-
> ing hanba demands for day labor power. (Matsuzawa 1988b:153)

The hanba were strictly controlled work camps. Recruiting agents would come to the slum districts of big cities in search of labor for the mines and factories. The alternative to a lengthy spell in a hanba would be casual work "as navvies, carters, ricksha men, scavengers and buskers" (Matsuzawa 1988b:153). Here we see the origins of the choice facing the modern day laborer, between period contracts (often at work camps still known as hanba) and one-day contracts.

In 1879 the Ryūkyū islands (now Okinawa prefecture) were annexed, and during the Meiji era the Ainu were steadily dispossessed of their land in Hokkaido. Displaced people from both areas came into the yoseba as day laborers.

There were some efforts to organize day laborers. In 1882 a short-lived union for rickshaw drivers was set up (Matsuzawa 1988b:153), and in 1900 a Japanese Day Laborers' Union was launched. At one point Katayama was among its officers.[15]

The Interwar Years

As Japan built up her economic and military muscle on her way to becoming a major colonial power, coercive labor practices flourished. Convict labor (kangoku rōdō) was widely used, especially in the development of Hokkaido, and non-convicts worked in conditions that were little better at the tako-beya. These workers were trapped by brokers (shūsenya) who lent them money and then forced them to sign up for six-month contracts to pay off the debt (Furukawa in Takada 1977:220). Takada (1974, 1977) has a vivid firsthand account of life in the tako-beya on railway and other construction projects in Hokkaido, 1930–1944. Wanted posters were put up for escaped workers, and "you couldn't even go for a crap or a piss without permission" (Takada 1974:33). The tako-beya system persisted until it was dissolved under the allied occupation in 1946 (Matsuzawa 1988b:157).[16]

Similar to tako-beya were *naya*, literally "barns." These were all-male establishments, and the men lived in tiny rooms. Discipline was maintained by the *naya-gashira*, or barn boss, and was notoriously harsh. Allen found naya still standing during his recent fieldwork in the Chikuho region of Kyushu, and describes a system of "virtual incarceration of miners in company housing" (Allen 1994:5).

The day-laboring population grew rapidly in this period, and was officially estimated at some 24 percent of the working population by 1931 (Kusama 1932:293).[17] Nakagawa finds that day laborers formed a large and growing part of the urban underclass in the period just after World War I (1985:119–126). Many factory workers escaped from the underclass, leaving casual building workers and porters behind in *nagaya,* long wooden terraces where whole families would live in rooms three to six tatami mats in area (116). Kusama Yasoh, a government expert on casual labor and homelessness, visited a nagaya at Minowa, very close to the present-day yoseba at San'ya. Amid Rabelaisian squalor, he found seventy-five households totalling some three hundred people in one building. About fourteen or fifteen of the households belonged to factory workers, most of the others to "miscellaneous laborers or day laborers" (Kusama 1936:115–116).

The global depression of the early 1930s hit day laborers hard, with 11.5 percent officially unemployed by 1932 (Kusama 1932:293).[18] There were 31,106 officially unemployed day laborers in Tokyo on 29 February 1932. Kusama describes a number of ineffectual measures that were taken to deal with the problem, one of which, instituted in 1928, was a forerunner of the present bureaucratic employment system for day laborers.

This was a registration system "aimed at safeguarding bonafide unemployed Tokyo citizens against the unfair competition of workers flowing in from places outside the city" (Kusama 1932:294). Rather like the Tokugawa era distinction between Kakae-hinin and No-hinin, the system recognized "good workers" (permanent Tokyo citizens) and "bad workers" (typically peasants who would come to Tokyo in the winter months when there was no work in the country). The division was replicated within the population of registered workers, who were further divided into "specified or regular workers" and "non-specified or irregular workers" (295).

> To the former category belong those who have won the confidence of their employers and have secured regular employment, while those belonging to the latter category are employed only temporarily in miscellaneous work and without any fixed location. To them fall such jobs as road making one day and, perhaps, street cleaning the next."[19] (Kusama 1932:295)

The Municipal Labor Exchange would pay wages, later recovering them from employers.

During 1931 the Exchange was supplying work for some 6,000 men a day out of some 18,000 registered day laborers. Some 2,000 of these men were "specified workers" and got work every day, while the other 16,000 were divided into four groups of 4,000, getting work roughly once every four days on a rotation system, usually at the minimum day wage of ¥1.35. Even worse off than these were the unregistered day laborers, who "have only a very remote chance of securing employment" (Kusama 1932:296). The rotation *(rinban)* system is still in use today in Ministry of Labor casual labor exchanges, as is the concept of the specified worker, whom an employer has requested by name.

During the Depression, some day laborers were forced onto the streets. A national census found that 1,799 people were sleeping outdoors in Tokyo on 1 October 1930, of whom 60 percent were categorized as day laborers (Kusama 1932:297). Kusama further estimates that the number of rag pickers in Tokyo rose from about seven hundred in 1921 to five thousand in 1932. The daily earnings of three hundred rag pickers interviewed by Kusama's staff averaged "the incredibly small sum of 13.7 sen per man" (298).

The interwar years saw a rapid influx of foreign workers, especially Koreans. In 1923 there were 62,000 Koreans working as "irregular laborers" in Japan, out of an ethnic Korean working population of 79,000; by 1931 there were 525,000 irregular laborers in a Korean working population of 630,000 (Matsuzawa 1988b:154). Koreans played a notable part in the day laborer movement, first through the General Alliance of Korean Laborers in Japan *(Chōsen Rōsō)*, founded in 1925 and swelling to a membership of 24,000 over the next five years; and then within *Zenkyō*, the "National Conference of Trade Unions of Japan," launched in 1928 by the Japan Communist Party. Despite its imposing name, Zenkyō was a small affair (16,000 members in 1932), with many day laborers and about 50 percent Koreans in its membership (Matsuzawa 1988b:155–156).

According to Fukada Kazuo, there were two prewar day laborer unions: *Zenkyō Doken* (the construction workers' section of Zenkyō) and the Kanto Union of Free Workers *(Kantō Jiyū Rōdō Kumiai)*. The former was militant, often organizing demonstrations at labor exchanges; the latter was more charitable in approach, organizing food handouts for unemployed laborers, etc. Both unions, he says, grew out of the struggle of Korean laborers, who were the principal victims of the vicious prewar forced labor camps (personal communication, 5 August 1994).

In the run-up to the Pacific War, unions were banned and day laborers were herded by the government into groups called *Rōmu Hōkoku Kai* (Patriotic Labor Society) and *Rōmu Kyōkai* (Labor Association), and put to work by force (Matsuzawa 1988b:156). As Japanese men were put into military service, yet more Koreans and other people from Japan's new colonies were press-ganged to Japan to replace them in the work force. By 1945 there were some 2.4 million Koreans living and working in Japan; the postwar repatriation still left 544,903 behind, a number that has edged upward since then (De Vos and Wetherall 1983:9–10).[20]

The Postwar *Yoseba*

There was no role for a free labor market like the yoseba in the war-time command economy. But they soon reappeared after the war, when there was a massive demand for flexible labor to rebuild Japan's shattered infrastructure, matched by a massive supply of workers who had lost their livelihoods during the war.

During the allied occupation of Japan (1945–1951), two important items of legislation attempted to bring a degree of order to the casual labor market. One was article 44 of the Employment Security Law *(Shokugyō Antei-hō)*, which states in part that: "It is an offense to op-erate a worker supply business, or to use workers supplied by a per-son operating such a worker supply business." This outlawed private-sector employment agencies, in an attempt to prevent the ex-ploitation of casual workers by intermediaries such as the workers' boarding houses of western Japan (see pp. 104–108). These businesses remained illegal until the passing of the Labor Dispatch Business Law *(Jinzai Hakengyō-hō)* by the government of Yasuhiro Nakasone in 1985.

The second important measure was the establishment of the unem-ployment countermeasures *(shitsugyō taisaku* or *shittai* for short) in 1950. From this time on, day laborers fall into two bureaucratic categories: ordinary ones, and those employed under the countermeasures. The latter were called *shittai rōdōsha*, a term translated by Caldarola as P.E.S.O. workers, from the Public Employment Security Offices, which administered the program (1968:513). The program was intended as a temporary measure to cope with the postwar employment crisis, but it took on a life of its own and was only finally terminated in March 1996. In 1950 there were 283,000 P.E.S.O. workers (including 70,000 women). The program peaked in 1960, with 350,000 workers (includ-ing 142,000 women),[21] before the government stopped adding new people to the program, allowing it to go into a long, slow decline until by 1995 P.E.S.O. workers accounted for just 2,635 of the 48,517 regis-tered day laborers in Japan.[22] P.E.S.O. workers formed 13 percent of the doya-gai dwellers surveyed by Caldarola in the mid–1960s (513)— but I never knowingly met one during my own fieldwork. Only one prefecture had significant numbers in 1994–1995: Fukuoka.[23] The steady decline in numbers of day laborers shown in Ministry of Labor statis-tics (table 1) must be seen in the context of the gradual winding down of what was a major program for several decades.

After the war a more extensive system of public casual labor ex-changes was set up to regulate the labor market and keep it out of the hands of gangsters—a mission that has never enjoyed more than limited

Photo 2.1 Day Laborer with White Handbook. The white handbook is needed to claim the day laborer dole. Photo taken in a two-mat doya room in Kamagasaki, by Nakajima Satoshi. Originally published in Nakajima Satoshi: *Tanshin Seikatsusha* (People Who Live on Their Own). Osaka: Kaifu-sha, 1990.

success (see chapters 3 and 4). The white handbook system (see pp. 4, 52, 71–72) was launched, in a half-hearted attempt to bring a measure of security, and in 1965 the Dock Workers Law created a separate system for longshoremen, with a blue handbook. This latter system was abolished in 1988.[24]

The high-growth economy of the 1950s and 1960s brought strong demand for casual labor. Yoseba in particular cities went through regional booms with events such as the Tokyo Olympics in 1964 and the Osaka Expo of 1970. These booms would push up casual wages, but would also attract more people to the day-laboring life, until wages fell back again. A very pure form of free-market economics prevails in the yoseba, and it has meant that there have always been men struggling to survive on the edges of the day laborer population, in good times and bad.

In 1974 the first oil shock hit the yoseba, creating major problems of unemployment and homelessness and spurring on the nascent yoseba protest movement. Thirty years of campaigning for better welfare provision for day laborers have had varying degrees of success. The day laborer union movement is alive and kicking, though plagued by political factionalism (cf. Funamoto 1985), and since 1982 some of the yoseba unions have managed to unite in *Hiyatoi Zenkyō*, the National Federation of Day Labor Unions. Since 1987 the Federation has published its own monthly newspaper, *Hiyatoi Zenkyō News*.

Postwar day laborers have maintained the rebellious, street-fighting tradition of their forebears, but there has been a marked tendency for the men to riot in relatively good times rather than during recessions. In Kamagasaki there were twenty riots from 1965 to 1973—high-growth years—and then none for the next seventeen years of the oil shock and after until 1990. In San'ya there were thirteen riots from 1959 to 1968 and then none until 1984, and in Kotobuki the last riot I know of was on 25 May 1975 (Kawase 1985:349). Ministry of Labor figures for officially registered day laborers have shown a steady decline for the last thirty years (table 1), and the population has been aging rapidly, to the point where the average yoseba day laborer is now in his mid–fifties (cf. tables 5, 8, 10).

The range of industries using casual labor from the yoseba has greatly narrowed in the postwar years. Transportation and manufacturing, both major employers before the war, have virtually ceased to use the yoseba. The docks, another traditional mainstay employer, still use casual labor but in much smaller quantities now that containerization has come to pass. The one industry that can still be relied upon to recruit day laborers in substantial numbers is the construction industry.

The Modern Construction Industry

Of all major industries, construction is among the least amenable to automation and mass production. It remains a high-risk business, at the mercy of the elements, and prone to massive fluctuations in demand with the changing economic climate. It is a big-unit industry, where companies can see their business thrive or fail on the outcome of a single big-ticket tender. Although building techniques have developed, there will always be a need for skilled and unskilled help on the building site. These factors make the construction industry a natural user of casual labor (Applebaum 1981), and it is here that Marx's concept of the "disposable industrial reserve army" can be seen most vividly illustrated.

The big Japanese construction companies, such as Kajima Construction and Shimizu Construction, are classic instances of the "core and peripheral workforce" commonly associated with Japanese management methods (Chalmers 1989). They maintain the smallest possible permanent, salaried work force, and supplement it when necessary by using subcontractors (*shita-uke*, lit.: "under-takers") and sub-subcontractors (*mago-uke*, lit.: "grandson takers"). Day laborers are never employed directly by the likes of Kajima and Shimizu; rather, they are employed by a small company at the very bottom of the line of subcontractors.

This system, sometimes compared to a pyramid, or the tentacles of an octopus, is highly favorable to the company at the top, a general contractor or *zenekon* in its Japanese abbreviation. They win large contracts, do the more profitable work themselves, and subcontract most of the hard labor to smaller companies, which feel indebted to the general contractor for giving them the work and are usually too small to dispute terms. When contracts are in short supply, a subcontractor may be dropped, or given less work so that it has to cut off a sub-subcontractor. The general contractor can usually evade legal responsibility when industrial accidents occur, though it may discreetly pay off the subcontractor that suffers the legal consequences. The general contractors' unions connive: the insecurity and low pay of nonunionized workers at subcontractors contribute to their own security and high pay, and there is no sense of solidarity (cf. Mouer and Sugimoto, 1986:353–354).

The structure of the Japanese construction industry closely resembles that of the criminal underworld. In major yakuza syndicates a boss (*oyabun*) rules over the pyramidal hierarchy of a central gang (*kumi*), which in turn dominates descending chains of lesser gangs. Even today many construction companies have the word *kumi* (often softened to *gumi*) in their names, and the two institutions have common historic origins (see, e.g., Itō 1987:58, who says that in the Taisho era, 1912–1926, the two were virtually indistinguishable). Even today, many smaller subcontractors are directly or indirectly controlled by yakuza.[25] Likewise, the yakuza oyabun is a close cousin of the oyakata[26] who manages day laborers. Both terms literally mean "father figure"—and this overt paternalism is a prevalent control system in contemporary Japan.

In my field trips I have come across exploitative lodging/employment institutions reminiscent of the hitoakibito and similar institutions of the Tokugawa era—the ninpu-dashi. The signs are that this kind of institution is making gains at the expense of the yoseba in the casual labor market. As recently as 1995 Japan was criticized in the United Nations for her practice of hiring out imprisoned convicts to work for private contractors. These are reminders that the historic struggle between coercion and free labor is not yet over.

Tadao

Tadao was slight, thin, with a deeply lined face, grey-white hair and few teeth. He smiled a lot and spoke with a lisp. He once told me the following in a conversation at the Apollo cafe:

I was born in Yaizu, Shizuoka prefecture, on March 6, 1939. It's a port city and there were always plenty of girls waiting for the sailors to put in. My father worked on cargo ships. He made captain. They were small ships of about 250 tons, and mostly carried coking coal. He'd sail to Kobe or Tokyo, and be away for a week or so each time. There'd be five or six crew on board, eight at the very most. The fact that he was a captain gave him a certain amount of status in town.

I was the third of ten children. The first two were both girls, so I was the oldest son. Normally I'd be the one to inherit the family house, but now my younger brother, the second son, is there. I never got on with my dad. He was very strict and always drunk on *shōchū*. Mind you, he worked very hard: supported a wife and ten children. He did carpentry and house building as well as sailing. He's long dead now. I pray for him every day.

But I hardly talked with him at all. If I had any problems, I'd discuss them with my mother. She'd always listen. She died three years ago, aged eighty.

I was born just before the war. We were always hungry. We ate potatoes, corn, and pumpkins. My mother grew them in the garden. When I was five or six, U.S. battleships bombarded Yaizu. We had to turn all the lights out, and dig holes to hide in. I was very scared. The B-29s came roaring over too.

At last the war ended, and I went to primary school. The teacher was very tough: he often used to push me around. I didn't study much, and I got into fights. I had some good friends at school, but we all went different ways after leaving. I don't seem to be very good at making friends. I try, but other people don't respond. Here in

(continues)

(continued)

Kotobuki, I have drinking friends but they're only friends as long as we're drinking. There's no one to look after me when I'm in trouble.

I went to junior high school in Yaizu, and then to the Maritime School in Takahama, Aichi prefecture. I was there for one year, and got my seaman's license. I graduated at sixteen or seventeen and immediately got a job with a shipping company in Osaka called Iino Kaiun. They operate cargo ships around Japan, carrying coking coal between Kobe, Kawasaki, etc. This was the best period of my life. I enjoyed life at sea, and we would always get drunk when we reached port. Sailors usually drink a lot. I think it's because when you're at sea, you never know what's going to happen. You might sink at any time! So when you get into port, you spend all your money on drink.

I was with Iino for four or five years. Then I had a traffic accident. A taxi ran into me while I was crossing the road and broke my thighbone. It was partly my fault: I was drunk, and not crossing the road at the right place. Still, I got ¥2.5 million compensation. There was no litigation—we settled the matter out of court. I was in hospital for nine months, and unable to move freely for a couple of years. When I finally recovered, I think I could have gone back to Iino, but I decided not to. There was just too much drinking.

For a year I did no work. I lived on the compensation. I had an apartment in Mikawashima, near Minami Senju [i.e., near San'ya]. It was a very tough year. My thigh kept hurting. Eventually I got some work as a *tobi*, [spiderman, see glossary]. But I have low blood pressure, and I get dizzy in high places. I fell off several times, and was saved by the safety harness each time. This was about 1960–1965.

I had to quit being a tobi. After that I got various jobs around Tokyo and Osaka, mostly at nightclubs. I was a barman at various times; I also spent several months as a *yobikomi* [barker; see glossary]. I never stayed more than a few months in any job; I just couldn't settle down. I never got on with the management at these places, though I got on well enough with the girls. The relationship between cabaret girls and their yobikomi is a special one.

(continues)

(continued)

In 1961 I married a cabaret girl, two years younger than myself. It wasn't arranged, of course—we married for love. We had one child, a daughter. We had six or seven years of successful married life. We both worked at the Hollywood cabaret in Shinjuku. I was a bartender and she was a waitress.

What finally broke up the marriage was my gambling. I spent *all* my money on gambling. I used to go to the off-course gambling center in Asakusa. . . . "[27]

At this point Tadao abruptly got up and left, apparently overcome by shame. But in other conversations he told me that later on he'd worked in a bar at the U.S. naval base at Yokosuka. While there, he got into a fight with an American serviceman, knifed him, and got six years. He converted to Christianity while in prison.

By the time I met him, he was falling to pieces. He was usually drunk, and once I saw him with a head wound which he said he'd got from falling down the stairs under the influence of drugs. Twice during our acquaintance (August 1993–April 1994) he spent time in a mental hospital.

For some time he worked nights at a Coca-Cola bottling factory, 10 P.M. to 8 A.M. for ¥10,000 a night. But within a few months he was on welfare. He stayed in at least three doya while I knew him, and I also found him sleeping on the street once. He would get very aggressive when drunk, especially when trying to defend me from imagined aggressors. On one occasion he slipped me a note in a crowded bar that said, in English, "I love you."

Tadao disappeared from 6 January 1994 to 4 April 1994, when I found him standing gaunt but upright on the street corner. He said he had been back in the mental hospital, but was OK now. He looked a year older but scrubbed and clean.

I was in a hurry. I suggested we should have a drink when next we met, but though I was frequently in Kotobuki for another year, that meeting never happened.

3

Ethnography of Kotobuki

Location

MY MAIN FIELDWORK SITE was Kotobuki, the day-laboring district of Yokohama (map 3.1). It is a yoseba and also a doya-gai, with just under a hundred lodging houses (as of early 1999) in an area roughly three hundred meters square. In the Japanese literature this district is often referred to as Kotobuki-chō, "chō" being an urban sub-division similar to the American "precinct." In fact, the Kotobuki district covers only part of Kotobuki-chō, and also covers parts of the neighboring precincts of Ōgi-chō and Matsukage-chō. It is located in Naka ward, the traditional center of Yokohama, within a ten-minute walk of the fashionable Motomachi boutique street, Chinatown with its famous Chinese restaurants and bijou ethnic craft shops, the Yokohama Bay Stars' baseball stadium, the ward office, and City Hall (see map 3.2). In short, this rough center of underclass life is slap in the middle of the most desirable real estate in the city of Yokohama. The location is a historical quirk, replete with meaning for the future of Kotobuki.

Kotobuki's main natural boundary is the Nakamura River, which runs northeast through Naka ward on its way to Yokohama Bay. For

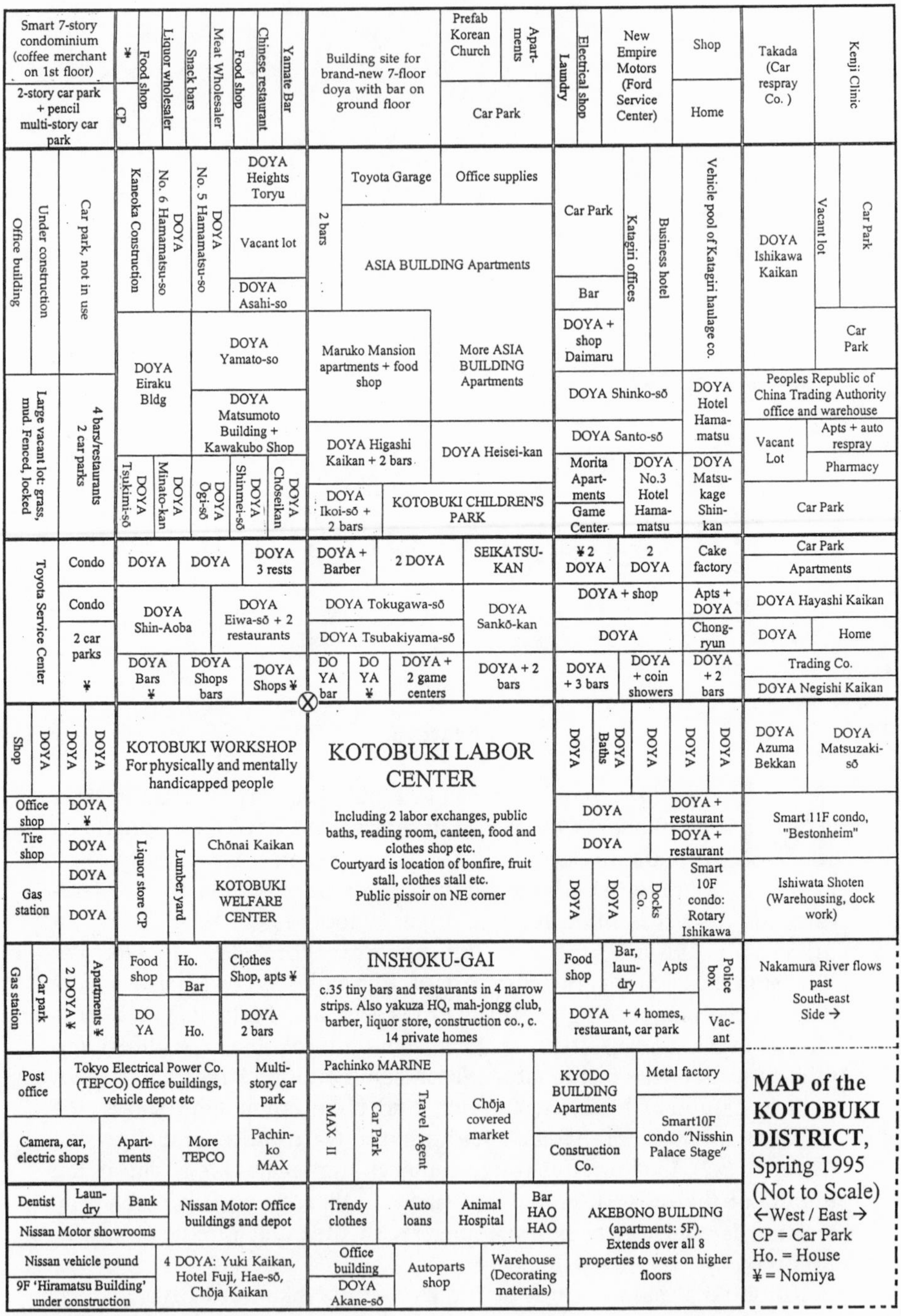

Smart 7-story condominium (coffee merchant on 1st floor)
2-story car park + pencil multi-story car park
CP
¥
Food shop
Liquor wholesaler
Snack bars
Meat Wholesaler
Food shop
Chinese restaurant
Yamate Bar
Building site for brand-new 7-floor doya with bar on ground floor
Prefab Korean Church
Apart-ments
Car Park
Laundry
Electrical shop
New Empire Motors (Ford Service Center)
Shop
Home
Takada (Car respray Co.)
Kenji Clinic
Office building
Under construction
Car park, not in use
Kaneoka Construction
DOYA No. 6 Hamamatsu-so
DOYA No. 5 Hamamatsu-so
DOYA Heights Toryu
Vacant lot
DOYA Asahi-so
2 bars
Toyota Garage
Office supplies
ASIA BUILDING Apartments
Car Park
Bar
Katagiri offices
Business hotel
Vehicle pool of Katagiri haulage co.
DOYA Ishikawa Kaikan
Vacant lot
Car Park
Car Park
DOYA Eiraku Bldg
DOYA Yamato-so
DOYA Matsumoto Building + Kawakubo Shop
Maruko Mansion apartments + food shop
More ASIA BUILDING Apartments
DOYA + shop Daimaru
DOYA Shinko-sō
DOYA Hotel Hama-matsu
Peoples Republic of China Trading Authority office and warehouse
Large vacant lot: grass, mud. Fenced, locked
4 bars/restaurants 2 car parks
DOYA Tsukimi-sō
DOYA Minato-kan
DOYA Ōgi-sō
DOYA Shinmei-sō
DOYA Chōseikan
DOYA Higashi Kaikan + 2 bars
DOYA Heisei-kan
DOYA Ikoi-sō + 2 bars
KOTOBUKI CHILDREN'S PARK
DOYA Santo-sō
Morita Apart-ments
Game Center
DOYA No.3 Hotel Hama-matsu
DOYA Matsu-kage Shin-kan
Vacant Lot
Apts + auto respray
Pharmacy
Car Park
Toyota Service Center
Condo
Condo
2 car parks ¥
DOYA
DOYA
DOYA 3 rests
DOYA Shin-Aoba
DOYA Eiwa-sō + 2 restaurants
DOYA Bars ¥
DOYA Shops bars
DOYA Shops ¥
DOYA + Barber
2 DOYA
SEIKATSU-KAN
DOYA Tokugawa-sō
DOYA Tsubakiyama-sō
DOYA Sankō-kan
DO YA bar
DO YA ¥
DOYA + 2 game centers
DOYA + 2 bars
¥2 DOYA
2 DOYA
Cake factory
DOYA + shop
Apts + DOYA
DOYA
Chong-ryun
DOYA + 3 bars
DOYA + coin showers
DOYA + 2 bars
Car Park
Apartments
DOYA Hayashi Kaikan
DOYA
Home
Trading Co.
DOYA Negishi Kaikan
Shop
DOYA
DOYA
DOYA
Office shop
DOYA ¥
Tire shop
DOYA
DOYA
Gas station
DOYA
KOTOBUKI WORKSHOP For physically and mentally handicapped people
Liquor store CP
Lumber yard
Chōnai Kaikan
KOTOBUKI WELFARE CENTER
KOTOBUKI LABOR CENTER
Including 2 labor exchanges, public baths, reading room, canteen, food and clothes shop etc.
Courtyard is location of bonfire, fruit stall, clothes stall etc.
Public pissoir on NE corner
DOYA
DOYA Baths
DOYA
DOYA
DOYA
DOYA
DOYA + restaurant
DOYA
DOYA + restaurant
DOYA
DOYA
Docks Co.
Smart 10F condo: Rotary Ishikawa
DOYA Azuma Bekkan
DOYA Matsuzaki-sō
Smart 11F condo, "Bestonheim"
Ishiwata Shoten (Warehousing, dock work)
Gas station
Car park
2 DOYA ¥
Apartments ¥
Food shop
Ho.
Bar
Clothes Shop, apts ¥
DO YA
Ho.
DOYA 2 bars
INSHOKU-GAI
c.35 tiny bars and restaurants in 4 narrow strips. Also yakuza HQ, mah-jongg club, barber, liquor store, construction co., c. 14 private homes
Food shop
Bar, laun-dry
Apts
Police box
DOYA + 4 homes, restaurant, car park
Vac-ant
Nakamura River flows past South-east Side →
Post office
Tokyo Electrical Power Co. (TEPCO) Office buildings, vehicle depot etc
Multi-story car park
Camera, car, electric shops
Apart-ments
More TEPCO
Pachin-ko MAX
Pachinko MARINE
MAX II
Car Park
Travel Agent
Chōja covered market
KYODO BUILDING Apartments
Construction Co.
Metal factory
Smart10F condo "Nisshin Palace Stage"
MAP of the KOTOBUKI DISTRICT, Spring 1995 (Not to Scale)
←West / East →
CP = Car Park
Ho. = House
¥ = Nomiya
Dentist
Laun-dry
Bank
Nissan Motor showrooms
Nissan Motor: Office buildings and depot
Nissan vehicle pound
9F 'Hiramatsu Building' under construction
4 DOYA: Yuki Kaikan, Hotel Fuji, Hae-sō, Chōja Kaikan
Trendy clothes
Auto loans
Animal Hospital
Bar HAO HAO
Office building
DOYA Akane-sō
Autoparts shop
Warehouse (Decorating materials)
AKEBONO BUILDING (apartments: 5F). Extends over all 8 properties to west on higher floors

Map 3.1 Map of the Kotobuki District
⊗ = Central Crossroads. Names of doya included only where space permits.

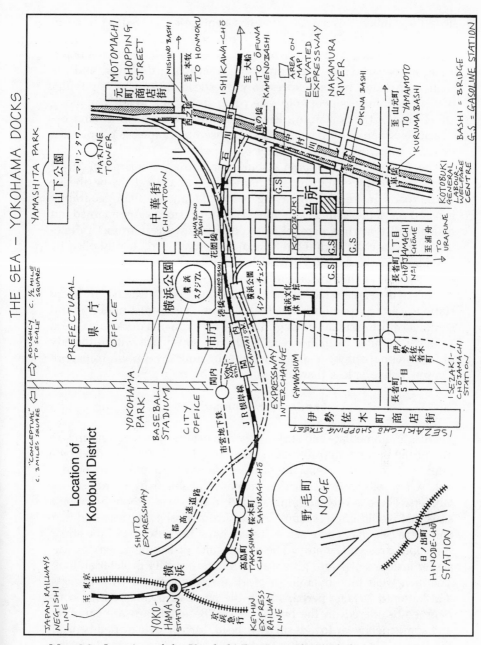

Map 3.2 Location of the Kotobuki District within Yokohama

its last few miles, this narrow river has a concrete elevated expressway (the Kanagawa No. 3 Kariba line) running directly above it. The river is rather polluted and has fishing boats and pleasure craft moored along its banks. There are many bridges crossing the river, and the shelter provided by the expressway overhead makes these popular places for homeless people to take cover from rain. Roads run along either side of the Nakamura River, and the narrow strip of land between river bank and pavement is also used by homeless people as a place to construct shacks (chapter 6).

The river forms Kotobuki's southeast border. Chōjamachi Street forms the southwest border and Shin-Yokohama street the northeast. These roads are rarities in having names; Japanese urban geography is based on points rather than lines. The fourth side is an unnamed but major road that runs parallel to the Nakamura River from Urafune-chō to the baseball stadium at Kannai. This road is frequently plied by ambulances taking sick or wounded day laborers to the emergency casualty unit at the hospital in Urafune-chō.

The two nearest stations are Kannai and Ishikawa-chō, adjacent stations on the Japan Railways Negishi line; the nearest underground station is at Isezaki-Chōjamachi. The main Yokohama docks are fifteen to thirty minutes' walk away and virtually any place within the city of Yokohama can be reached within an hour by public transport. Central Tokyo is less than an hour away by train.

Landscape/Atmosphere

There is an immediate and striking change in atmosphere as one crosses any of the borders into Kotobuki. The boundary is often marked by a litter of abandoned cars, some of them smashed up and some burned out. A few of these vehicles are actually inhabited by homeless day laborers. There is rubbish lying around in the street—though not on a scale that would impress slum dwellers from most countries—and here and there one may come across a man lying unconscious in the street.

People dress differently. The smart suits of businessmen and designer fashions of youth give way to a determinedly proletarian look. The men wear blue overalls or work trousers covered with pockets, and battered jackets, perhaps with the name of a construction company embroidered on the breast pocket. Baseball caps are common, and some men wear towels on their head, turban style or tied beneath the jaw. A few still wear the traditional baggy pantaloons (*shichibu-zubon*) and canvas boots (*tabi*) of the Japanese working man.

People walk differently. In the rest of Yokohama they walk quickly, in a straight line, on the sidewalk, eyes fixed ahead of them. Here they walk slowly, meandering around the road, looking about them or surveying the ground for cigarette butts, paying no attention to cars that hoot at them. They urinate in the street, sometimes even when standing right next to the public pissoir located in the middle of Kotobuki. The smell of stale urine hangs in the air.

Altogether, people behave differently. They sit on the pavement, drinking and talking. Many will happily talk to a stranger, and it is easy for a strange-looking foreigner like myself to get into conversation with a man I have never met. In this respect, it is the most sociable place in Yokohama.

The area is dominated by the Kotobuki-chō General Labor Welfare Building (*Kotobuki-chō Sōgō Rōdō Fukushi Kaikan*), generally known simply as "the Center" (*sentaa*). This is a grim, grey ten-story fortress of a building opened in October 1974, containing two casual labor exchanges, a large canteen, a shop stocking working clothes and daily necessaries, a public bath, the Kotobuki Clinic, a reading room, lockers, and even a bank (it has just this one branch and is run by the social services). The higher floors of the center are given over to municipal apartments, some of them used by the city authorities to house single-parent families. The building has a large central courtyard; this and the outdoor stairways of the labyrinthine construction are natural meeting places for men and pigeons alike.

The streets of Kotobuki form a fairly regular square grid, with the Center filling one block. South of the Center is the eating-and-drinking quarter (*inshoku-gai*), a very narrow alley lined with tiny bars and restaurants. Despite its raffish appearance, I never noticed an obvious instance of prostitution here or in any other part of Kotobuki; the mama-sans who run the bars are generally of mature years and brook no nonsense.

On all other sides, the streets are broader and lined with buildings, typically five or six stories high. These are the doya (lodging houses). A few small wooden ones still survive, but most are concrete structures built within the last thirty years. Many have pretty names such as *Tsukimi-sō* (Moon-view Mansion) or *Shirayuki-sō* (White Snow Mansion); other names are geographical references, often to resort towns near Yokohama—the *Atami-sō* and *Hamamatsu-sō*, for instance. Though all signboards are in Japanese, the doya are nearly all owned by ethnic Koreans, and on closer inspection a few of them prove to be patronized by Korean migrant laborers. On the ground floor there may be a bar or restaurant, with the menu as likely to be written in Korean as in Japanese.

Another landmark is the *Seikatsu-kan* (lit.: "Livelihood Hall"), a shabby four-story building run by the local authorities,[1] with an office where city welfare officials offer consultations on labor and welfare matters, plus a TV room and meeting space, free showers, cooking facilities, and washing machines, and a children's day care center that was founded in 1983. A small alternative school for school refusers that was there during my fieldwork period has since been closed. The tiny Kotobuki Children's Park, used mostly by adults, is right opposite the Seikatsu-kan. Nearby is the Kotobuki Welfare Center (*Kotobuki Fukushi Sentaa*), an even shabbier two-story building containing a nursery, an office for welfare consultations, and a self-help group for alcoholics. Next door is the Precinct Association Hall (*Chōnai-kaikan*), a rickety two-story building that houses the Kotobuki Day Laborers' Union (*Junichirō*).

Just behind that is a much smarter, three-story building called the Yokohama Workshop. It contains three facilities: the Hope Revival Center (*Kibō Kōsei Sentaa*, founded 1983) for physically handicapped people from all over Yokohama and outlying towns; the Light Center (*Hikari Sentaa*, founded 1983), a workshop for blind and partially-sighted people; and Bird (*Baado*, founded 1997), a small workshop for physically and mentally handicapped people living in Kotobuki itself. All three workshops attempt to train users in crafts that will give them satisfaction and some income. Products include ceramics, cake, and wooden toys.

Also in central Kotobuki is the Kiraku House (*Kiraku na Ie*, 1997), a social center for elderly people. Just outside the district is the Matsukage Temporary Shelter, which houses seventy homeless people at normal times, doubling up to 140 during the year-end holiday period (see chapter 6). On the edge of Kotobuki is the Sanwa Building, an office block housing three more support operations: on the second floor is the Alc Day Care Center (*Aruku Dē Kea Sentaa*, founded 1993), for alcoholics trying to kick the bottle. On the third floor is the *Roba no Ie*, literally the "Donkey House." This embarrassingly named institution, founded in 1989, is a workshop for people with learning impediments, run by Christians. On the seventh floor is the Kalabaw Association (*Karabao no Kai*, founded 1987), a volunteer group supporting foreign workers in Kotobuki and elsewhere.

Another workshop, the Shalom House (*Sharomu no Ie;* founded 1989), is located in a nearby apartment building. Despite the name, it too is run by Christians. Yet another, this one run by the social services, is the Kotobuki Welfare Workshop (*Kotobuki Fukushi Sagyōsho;* 1983), located on the first floor of an office building just behind the police station. The latter is a modest affair, usually with just four officers

attached to it. It does, however, have a fairly large fenced-in com-
pound where the patrol cars are parked, with plenty of room for extra
police vehicles in case of disturbances.

Then there are two churches, an imposing red-brick Baptist one and
a much more modest one run by a Korean evangelical group; and the
Yokohama branch of Chongryun, the representative organization of
Japan-resident Koreans who support Pyongyang rather than Seoul.

These landmarks tell us a number of things about Kotobuki.
Firstly, the population is not exclusively male. There are some
women; there are a few children. The children of Kotobuki used to
enjoy a formidable reputation. The book *Barefoot Primitives* (*Hadashi
no Genshijintachi;* Nomoto 1974) paints a vivid picture of the gangs
of urchins that used to roam the district. Murata Yoshio, who has
been running the Kotobuki Welfare Center for more than twenty
years, recalls that when he first arrived in Kotobuki, in 1968, he was
amazed to see small children jumping up and down on the roofs of
cars. In the early 1970s there were 1,200 children living in Kotobuki,
attached to 550 households (Murata 1992:11–12). My own informants
tell me that it used not to be uncommon for whole families to live
in doya rooms; and there was even a children's baseball team, the
Kotobuki Bears, which played its first game on 7 July 1973 (Kawase
1985:347).

Nowadays the Bears are a distant memory. There are far fewer
children in Kotobuki; a few live in the municipal apartments and a
few more come in from outside to take advantage of the alternative
child-care and educational provision in Kotobuki. Figures from the
Welfare Center for late 1994 show sixty-two Japanese children in the
Kotobuki district: twenty-two preschoolers, twenty-three of elementary-
school age, five of middle-school age, and twelve aged up to seventeen. Nearly all of them were living in the municipal apartments. In
addition the figures show twenty-five foreign children, mostly living
in doya. Nearly all day laborers live alone, and the families living in
doya rooms are nearly all foreign. Still, the history of Kotobuki children raises the question of how far the isolation of modern day laborers is culturally ingrained and how far it is a product of changing
economic circumstances.

Secondly, the steadily growing concentration of welfare facilities in
the area testifies to the tendency of the Yokohama authorities to put
all their problems in one basket. People with any kind of disability are
likely to be sent to Kotobuki, there to mingle with the long-term unemployed and chronic alcoholics. It is common to see blind people
and wheelchair users making their way home from the Kotobuki

Workshop, and it is a tribute to the tolerance of the day laborers that the staff of the workshop reported almost no cases of bullying or abuse directed at users of the facility.[2] Meanwhile, the difficulties encountered in locating facilities for people with disabilities anywhere else in the city demonstrate the *lack* of tolerance in mainstream society.

Thirdly, the presence of the two churches—and the absence of Shinto shrines and Buddhist temples—tells us that this is a special zone in terms of religion, too. Officially Christians make up only 0.7 percent of the Japanese population,[3] yet Christianity plays a far larger role in the day-to-day affairs of Kotobuki than either of the two major faiths. During fieldwork I met a Baptist missionary, the Reverend Satō, who conducted Salvation Army–style hymn-and-prayer meetings in Kotobuki. He had hopes of turning the place into a Christian stronghold in the heart of Yokohama.

Fourthly, we see that as well as being an island of outsiders in a sea of conformity, Kotobuki is also, in a sense, a Korean island in a Japanese sea. The historical reasons for this I will shortly discuss.

One more feature of the Kotobuki landscape deserves mention. There are two buildings, designed as private residences, that house the offices of yakuza gangs (cf. Herbert 2000). They are much newer and cleaner than most buildings in Kotobuki, made of shiny grey laminated prefab units and studded with air-conditioning vents. Gangsters, immediately recognizable by their loud clothes, permed curly hair, and dark glasses, come and go. Expensive cars, usually white Mercedes-Benzes, are moored outside like private ships.

Police figures say there were fourteen gangs with offices in Kotobuki as of spring 1994. Some were operating out of doya rooms, or from more respectable apartments across the Nakamura river. Ten of the gangs, and all the ones active in Kotobuki, were affiliated to the *Sōai-kai*, a minor yakuza syndicate with bases in Kanagawa and Chiba prefectures. The boss is an ethnic Korean, but most of the rank-and-file members are thought to be Japanese. The other four gangs were affiliated to the Yamaguchi-gumi, Japan's biggest syndicate. Their operations were at the docks; Kotobuki merely provided a convenient base, at a time when citizens' movements against the yakuza were making it difficult to maintain premises elsewhere.[4] Nowadays the traditional labor rackets are less important as a source of yakuza income than gambling. Dotted around Kotobuki are some twenty illegal bookmakers, operated by the yakuza and heavily patronized by day laborers and, to a lesser degree, by slumming salarymen and taxi drivers.

Population

Kotobuki is subject to regular population surveys, with respect to age, gender, ethnicity, household composition, number of welfare recipients, handicapped people, etc., by the Kotobuki Welfare Center and several other agencies (see tables 5 to 12).

These figures clearly show that the traditional doya-gai population of single Japanese day laborers is steadily aging and leaving the work force, without being replaced. They are either ending up on welfare, which now covers well over half the population, or are drifting down into the poverty class, sometimes via an intermediate period as occasionally working day laborers. Meanwhile, much of the really tough work, demanding youthful energy and muscle, is being done by foreigners—mostly illegal Korean migrants. The foreign population peaked in 1994 at around 1,100; it fell sharply in 1995 as many went home because of the lack of jobs caused by the continuing recession, or tried their luck elsewhere, for instance at earthquake-ravaged Kobe. By the end of 1998 there were fewer than four hundred foreigners left in Kotobuki. Roughly 70 percent were Korean, 20 percent Filipino, and 10 percent Thai. My impression was that most foreign workers were in their twenties or thirties, whereas the average age of Japanese day laborers in Kotobuki was estimated by Junichirō at around fifty-four or fifty-five.[5]

The distinction between functioning day laborers (gen'eki, lit.: on active duty) and those who are no longer up to it is keenly felt in Kotobuki. Among the latter are the yankara (see glossary), who sit drinking round the bonfire under the outdoor steps of the Labor Center in the colder months, sometimes getting black in the face from the soot. Various degrees of sympathy and contempt are felt by the gen'eki for the yankara, and the lack of solidarity between the two groups is a major source of concern for the union.

Komai remarks that Kotobuki is the only doya-gai with a significant concentration of foreign workers resident (1995:112). He suggests three reasons for the general absence of foreign workers from yoseba: They are easy targets for immigration officials (nearly all the foreign workers being illegal); many doya landlords bar foreigners; and building improvements in San'ya and Kamagasaki have pushed up room costs. In contrast, he argues, Kotobuki's landlords have renovated and raised rents more slowly, but more important, as ethnic Koreans they are more sympathetic to Koreans and foreign workers in general.

Komai's points are generally valid. However, recent shifts in the ethnic balance of the population suggest a further factor. Ventura (1992) describes a thriving underground population of Filipinos, large enough to be subdivided into gangs based on provincial background in the Philippines. Though he offers no estimate of the size of the Filipino population, it must have been far larger than when I arrived in Kotobuki just a couple of years after Ventura left. By then the Filipinos had largely been supplanted by South Koreans. Komai dates the start of the increase in the South Korean population to 1988 (1995:112), and it is no coincidence that this was the year that Roh Tae Woo, then president of South Korea, lifted the republic's previously very strict travel restrictions. Once it became possible for ordinary South Koreans to acquire passports, they started to target Japan as a destination for well-paid migrant labor. In Kotobuki they easily established a presence, helped by the fact that the doya owners were ethnic Koreans who spoke the Korean language and had a natural sympathy for their fellow countrymen. They had the added merit of looking more Japanese than Filipinos do (an advantage to employers who want their illegal foreign workers to look as inconspicuous as possible), and these two factors seem to have given them a decisive edge.

A large proportion of the Koreans in Kotobuki, doya owners and migrant laborers alike, are originally from Cheju island, off the south coast of the Republic of Korea.[6] Within Korean society, Cheju people are subject to discrimination and have a strong sense of solidarity. This helps to account for their preponderance among the Korean population in Japan: for them, unlike most other Koreans, life in Japan has tended to mean *less* discrimination than in the home country. Cheju fishermen have maintained links with Japan for several centuries (Delores Martinez, personal communication), and a ferry service opened between Cheju and Osaka back in 1922.

The Great Cheju Massacre of April 1948 killed perhaps 60–70,000 people, or about a quarter of the island's population (the figures are hotly disputed). The islanders were basically being punished for boycotting the south-only presidential election of May 1948, which confirmed the division of the Korean peninsula (Kim 1994). This event was a powerful incentive to Cheju Koreans left in Japan after the war to stay there, and for those who had returned home to re-migrate to Japan. In Yokohama, Cheju people stuck together and concentrated their capital in Kotobuki. The genocide inflicted on the people of Cheju by the South Korean government gave them a natural sympathy with North Korea, which helps to explain why the local headquarters of Chongryun are situated in Kotobuki. So even in international terms, Kotobuki may be seen as a zone of tolerance for people who suffer discrimination elsewhere.

To sum up: Being in Kotobuki has different meanings for Japanese and foreign workers. For many (though not all) of the Japanese, it signifies failure. They are at the bottom of the pile, and estranged from their families. For the Korean and Filipino workers, by contrast, the risky venture of illegal migrant labor is a heroic challenge to better the lives of themselves and their families. As Ventura (1992) observes, migrants rarely come from the poorest class in their own country.[7]

Most of the Koreans and Filipinos I met had families to which they were still attached. Occasionally, the families would be living with them; alternatively, they would come over to visit during holiday periods. Moreover, the migrants were generally younger and fitter than the Japanese, so much so that some labor recruiters would employ only foreigners.

History

Compared with the doya-gai of Tokyo and Osaka, Kotobuki has a very short history. Until the 1860s, the area of Yokohama that includes Kotobuki was under the sea.[8] During the Meiji era (1866–1912), land reclamation works turned the area first into marshland and then into inhabitable dry land. The reclaimed land was divided into seven precincts (chō): Yoshihama, Matsukage, Kotobuki, Ōgi, Furō, Okina, and Bandai. Collectively they used to be known as *Umechi Nanakamachi*— the Seven Reclaimed Towns.

The earliest reference to Kotobuki in the city histories dates from 1877, when the people of Kotobuki-chō and Matsukage-chō demanded of the city authorities that water be supplied to their part of town. But the water supply was still a problem in 1886, when emergency water supplies were taken to Kotobuki-chō and Matsukage-chō to cope with the cholera epidemic of that year. Kotobuki seems to have been a poor part of town even then, and 1903 saw the start of its career as a focus for Christian good works, when the Yokohama Corps of the Salvation Army was established at Kotobuki 1-chōme, under the command of Colonel Henry Broad of Britain.[9]

The district gradually developed into a fairly prosperous area of small-scale silk manufacturers and merchants over the first half of the twentieth century, only to be burned to cinders during the American fire-bombing campaign of World War II.

Kotobuki's association with day labor did not begin until well after the war. In prewar Yokohama, day laborers had been scattered around the city, with the main concentrations being in Nakamura-chō (across the Nakamura River from Kotobuki) and Noge-chō. After the war, a day-laboring district rapidly grew up at Sakuragi-chō, a couple of miles west of Kotobuki and directly fronting the bay. The allied occupation forces were making heavy use of the port of Yokohama to import essential supplies (for several years school meals for the whole of Japan were imported via Yokohama, for example), and Sakuragi-chō became a major regional communications center.

There was an immediate and substantial demand for casual dock labor. Moreover, unlike Japanese enterprises, which discriminated against Koreans and other minorities in their employment policies, the occupation forces would employ anyone who they thought could do a job. Accordingly, the sociological cocktail we find in Kotobuki today began to come together: people from despised minorities such as Okinawans, Ainu, and especially ethnic Koreans; men with criminal records or "difficult" personalities who would struggle to find employment elsewhere; and men from poverty-stricken rural families attempting to support the people back home through urban migrant labor.

Soon a busy doya-gai grew up around Sakuragi-chō. Doya were rapidly thrown up, often by ethnic Koreans catering mainly to their fellow countrymen. They could not accommodate all the day laborers, and the overflow were put up in three permanently moored ships that became known as "floating hotels." But the district developed a reputation for drunken lawlessness, possibly exaggerated, which led to mounting protests from the well-organized local shopkeepers. An outbreak of typhoid intensified calls for the doya-gai to be broken up.

The allied occupation ended in 1952, but large areas of land around Japan were not immediately released from requisition. Twenty-eight percent of all requisitioned land was in Kanagawa prefecture (of which Yokohama is the prefectural capital), and even today the U.S. military maintains major bases in the prefecture. The Kotobuki district itself was home to a transportation regiment. In 1950 Kotobuki-chō, Ōgi-chō and Matsukage-chō were each listed as having a population of zero in official Japanese statistics—U.S. servicemen evidently did not count. In 1955 the three precincts were listed as having a combined population of thirteen (table 11). Derequestioning was not completed until 1956.

At this point the city fathers saw a golden opportunity to quell the protests of the Sakuragi-chō shopkeepers. With a few bold strokes of the bureaucratic pen, the doya-gai was shifted lock, stock, and barrel from Sakuragi-chō to Kotobuki. The doya were demolished and the floating hotels destroyed (the last one in 1959), their largely Korean owners being compensated with money and land on which to build doya at Kotobuki. To this day, nearly all the doya in Kotobuki are owned by Koreans—a unique feature among Japan's doya-gai. The first doya, appropriately named the *Kotobuki-sō,* opened there in October 1956; the casual labor exchange was shut down at Sakuragi-chō and reopened at Kotobuki in April 1959; and in 1961, despite local protests, the blood bank was also moved to Kotobuki.[10]

Within five years (1956–1961), sixty-three doya had been built (Saitō 1994:131). They were filled immediately: the high-growth economy had spawned a large population of day laborers (131). By 1960 the three precincts in the Kotobuki district had a combined population of 2,131, rising to 7,968 by 1965, falling back to 5,648 by 1970, and settling at around five or six thousand to the present day (table 11).

Kotobuki was a tough district in the 1960s. There were several riots, including one on 30–31 October 1967, when "several hundred" men besieged the Kotobuki police box from 9 P.M. until 4 A.M. the following morning (Nakada 1983:218–219). In October 1960 the Isezaki-chō police reported finding seventeen children who had never been to school and six long-term nonattenders in Kotobuki-chō (Matsunobu 1989).

Precincts in Japanese cities usually have their own local representative associations, called *chōnai-kai* (precinct associations) or *jichi-kai* (self-governing associations). In 1945 a joint association for the seven precincts on reclaimed land *(Rengō Chōnai-kai)* was set up. However, this body tended to be dominated by shopkeepers and landlords living in the non-day-laboring districts, and in April 1969 a group of Kotobuki residents set up their own independent body, the Kotobuki District Self-governing Association *(Kotobuki Chiku Jichi-kai).* This idealistic attempt to bring together day laborers and non-day laborers from the area eventually foundered; the differences in interest were too great (Murata Yoshio, personal communication). Today the day laborers are represented mainly by the union, and the doya and shop owners have their own organizations. There are two associations of doya owners, divided on political lines between sympathizers of North and South Korea. The chōnai-kai is practically defunct, though it still exists on paper to collect government grants and to administer the *Chōnai Kaikan,* the building which it owns.

In 1974 the first oil shock plunged Japan into recession. Bereft of employment and with no money saved, many of the day laborers of Kotobuki were plunged into poverty. In the winter of 1974–1975 activists supporting the day laborers held the first Winter Survival Campaign *(Ettō),* supplying emergency accommodation and food for homeless men during the new year period when government welfare offices were closed. This became an annual Kotobuki event, the twenty-fifth being held in the winter of 1998–1999.

Junichirō, the Kotobuki day laborer union, was founded on 18 May 1975, amid mounting anger at the authorities' failure to provide assistance for day laborers during the recession. A week later there was a riot provoked by the contemptuous attitude shown by police toward the body of a dead day laborer. The riot police went in and fourteen were arrested. On 25 November 1975, sixty workers from Kotobuki held a sit-in at the prefectural hall, demanding funds for the winter survival period and jobs (Matsunobu 1989). In 1978, the union and other sympathetic bodies launched the annual Kotobuki summer festival, held in mid-August every year, the twenty-second being celebrated in 1999.

The family aspect of Kotobuki life had virtually disappeared by the end of the 1970s. The very low population/household ratios for 1980 onward (table 11) show that the prevalence of single men was well established by 1980. Employment picked up during the construction boom of the mid–1980s bubble economy, but toward the end of the decade the bubble burst and casual employment went into a decline from which, as I write, it has never recovered.

On 23 April 1983, nine middle-school boys from Yokohama were arrested for assaulting at least sixteen homeless day laborers in areas near Kotobuki, killing three (see pp. 177–178). This appalling incident prompted the formation of the Thursday Patrol *(Mokuyō Patorōru)*, which has been patrolling the areas used by homeless people ever since—every Thursday in winter and one or two Thursdays a month in the warmer seasons. Every winter a few men die of cold, starvation, or injuries around Kotobuki, but the patrols, plus some improvements in welfare provision, have helped to reduce these numbers.

Employment

Formal Institutions

There are two casual labor exchanges in Kotobuki. The Kotobuki Labor Center Free Employment Introduction Office *(Kotobuki Rōdō Sentaa Muryō Shokugyō Shōkaijo)*, located at ground level in the Center building, is operated by an external organization of the Yokohama city and Kanagawa prefectural governments called the Kanagawa Prefecture Labor Welfare Association *(Kanagawa-ken Rōdō Fukushi Kyōkai)*. Directly above it in the same building is the Yokohama Port Labor Branch of the Yokohama Public Employment Stability Office *(Yokohama Kōkyō Shokugyō Anteijo, Yokohama Minato Rōdō Shutchōjo)*, officially nicknamed the "Hallo Work Yokohama Port" *(Harō Waaku Yokohama-kō)*, which is administered by the Ministry of Labor. Here I refer to these two insti-

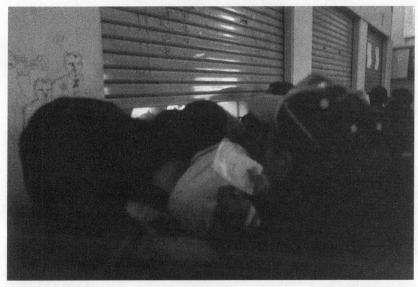

Photo 3.1   The Rush for a Job As the Shutters Go Up. Kotobuki Labor Center, 6:15 A.M. Men struggle to get their employment cards through the window as the shutters start to rise. The graffiti on the left are by Nishikawa Kimitsu. Photo by Umetani Hideji, 1994. Reprinted by permission.

tutions as the Labor Center and the Labor Office respectively, for simplicity.

This split between local and national government in administering casual labor is also found in San'ya and Kamagasaki. The bipartite system appears to reflect dissatisfaction among city governments regarding the bureaucratic mindset of the Ministry of Labor. Nomura Yoshiaki, a veteran official at the Labor Center who was there when it opened in 1974, told me that many Kotobuki men were unable to supply the fixed address required by the Ministry of Labor to become a formally registered day laborer, and consequently were driven into the arms of the illegal street-corner recruiters. The Center was designed as a place where men could get employment in a regulated market but without having to negotiate painful bureaucratic procedures.[11]

The two institutions look similar. Job-seeking workers do not enter either office: instead, they wait for metal shutters in front of the office to rise, revealing job advertisements displayed on a line of rectangular back-lit panels with reference numbers at the top, above booths where officials allocate jobs from behind reinforced glass windows. The job details are telephoned or faxed by employers the night before or early in the morning. Once a job is arranged, the official will give the day laborer a contract, often with a little map showing how to get to the work site. The worker usually has to make his own way to the work site, which may be as far as a two-hour train journey away.

Thus far the two exchanges are much the same. However, there are important differences between the two.

The Labor Center opens Monday to Friday at 6:15 A.M., and at 4 P.M. on Friday for weekend work. Jobs are allocated on a first-come, first-served basis. My fieldwork was conducted at a time when jobs were very scarce, and I witnessed many a desperate scramble for work. Men would gather outside the shutters an hour or more before they went up, crouching in the dark on scraps of cardboard like the devout at prayer, or sprinters awaiting the starter's gun. In a sense, they were both: they prayed for work, and sprinted to get it. A job for the day could make the difference between hunger and a full stomach, sleeping on the cold street or in a warmish room.

The moment the shutters started to rise, there would be a great rush forward—but only as far as a *second* set of shutters, which would rise half an hour later. The advantage of all the waiting was only to secure a more favorable position in the almighty scrum when the inner shutters rose. Men would memorize the numbers corresponding to each panel and shout out the numbers when the shutters had risen just high enough to show which panels were lit up, but not high enough to reveal the nature of the job, the location, the conditions or the rate of pay. They would thrust their identity cards[12] under the shutters, knowing that they would get a job if one of the officials took it out of their hands. As one day laborer put it to me, "the long arm wins" *(nagai ude ga katsu)*.

Officials justified this procedure on the grounds that it was simple, and functioned as a crude form of natural selection. Stronger, fitter men had a better chance of getting jobs, and those were the kind of men employers wanted.[13]

The Labor Office opens half an hour later than the Center, at 6:45 A.M. The system is very different. Workers must acquire a Ministry of Labor white handbook, bearing their name, address, photograph, and registration number. Jobs are allocated according to a strict rotation *(rinban)*: each morning, in principle, the first man allowed to choose a job from those on display is the one with the number after the last number that got a job the previous day. In practice there are some rather complex modifications to the system to deal with situations where one or two jobs are "refused" by a large number of men because they require skills or qualifications, such as the ability to drive a truck, that most of the men do not possess.

In short, we have a free-market free-for-all downstairs, and a brand of fair-shares socialism, half an hour later, upstairs. The difference in system is reflected in the atmosphere outside each exchange. The desperate struggle for jobs at the Labor Center is often over in less than a minute, whereas at the Labor Office men do not start to gather until well after the shutters have gone up, and the air is of apathy rather than desperation. Once the jobs have been allocated, typically to just a handful of men, a far larger number will deposit their handbooks to claim the dole. The dole system will be discussed later.

This bipartite system sometimes presents a day laborer with a difficult choice: whether to go for a tough, badly-paid job at the Labor Center, when his number is near enough to the top of the pile to stand a fairly good chance of getting a job—perhaps a better job—afterward at the Labor Office. By the time he discovers whether there is a better job for him upstairs, the one downstairs will be long gone. These days the matter is often academic, since there are hardly any jobs at either place, but the bipartite system is certainly not in the interests of the workers.

During my spell in Kotobuki, the Labor Center was supplying more jobs than the Labor Office, by a ratio of roughly 70:30. Typically there would be twenty to thirty jobs at the former and a dozen or so at the latter. Employers seemed to prefer the free-for-all system, and the Center also allowed them to nominate (shimei) workers whom they knew to be efficient. However, by 1999 even the Center was only supplying about a half-dozen days' work a year to the average Kotobuki man (table 13), with job availability at the office approaching zero (table 14).[14] Sad to say, by 1999 the main function of the two employment exchanges was in fact to provide employment for their own officials. When I visited on 10 September 1999, the office employed twenty-one officials and the Center thirteen. Between them these thirty-four officials had supplied a day's work to eighteen day laborers that day. Surely it is only bureaucratic inertia that has prevented the abolition, or drastic reform, of both places.

The bubble burst early in Kotobuki, suggesting that casual labor statistics may be a leading indicator of impending recession. Persondays of labor arranged through the Labor Center collapsed from a peak of 154,574 in 1986 to a trough of 50,806 in 1993, a fall of 67 percent in seven years (table 13). Period contracts were worst affected, falling 75 percent in this period while one-day contracts fell by 44 percent.[15] Consequently, the two kinds of contract accounted for roughly equal numbers of employment person-days arranged at the Center in the mid-1990s, whereas three times as many days were worked on period contracts as on single-day contracts ten years before (table 13). Apparently employers were cautious of taking on obligations even of just ten or fifteen days during the recession. By 1999, one-day contracts were providing somewhat more employment than period contracts, while the overall level of job supply had collapsed to even more disastrous levels.

The Street Labor Market

The stated objective of the Kotobuki Labor Center is to provide free job introductions for day laborers, and thereby to "stabilize employment, normalize the paths to employment, eliminate the open-air labor market *(aozora rōdō shijō)* and improve working conditions" (Kotobuki Labor Center 1996:1). However, twenty-five years since the launch of the center, the great majority of jobs are still arranged not at the public labor exchanges but on the street.[16]

The legal status of street labor markets in Japan is rather complex. Street recruiting is legal only for construction work and only in designated areas, corresponding closely to the yoseba in each city. The president *(shachō)* of the employing company may do it himself freely, but if one of his employees does the recruiting, a direct recruitment permit *(chokusetsu boshū kyoka)* from the Ministry of Labor is required. Recruiting by anyone who does not belong to the employing company is strictly illegal. Applicants must be enrolled in the day laborer unemployment and health insurance programmes, and can lose the license if found guilty of "intermediary exploitation" *(chūkan sakushu)*, that is, pocketing part of the day wage (a practice known colloquially as *pin-hane*).

Such is the theory. In practice the system is widely abused. Often the tehaishi (recruiter) is not a member of the employing company but a freelance operator; he may not be licensed; he may be illegally recruiting men for dock work, etc.; and pin-hane is commonly practiced. The authorities generally turn a blind eye.[17]

Jobs are negotiated between recruiters and day laborers. It is widely believed that the recruiters are all yakuza gangsters or in the pay of them, but the reality seems to vary from one yoseba to another. In Kotobuki most of the tehaishi appear to be independent operators, or representatives of large employers.[18] The yakuza get their share of the business indirectly, by charging a monthly fee *(shoba-dai;* see glossary) to permit tehaishi to recruit in Kotobuki. One recruiter for a longshoring company told me his firm paid ¥100,000 a month to the Sōai-kai, and that this was a standard figure, irrespective of company size or numbers recruited. His own company had only about ten regular employees, and hired up to seventeen day laborers on particularly busy days.[19] Some employers would deliberately park their cars just outside Kotobuki, or show up on a Sunday to take men for a whole week, apparently to avoid paying shoba-dai.

Day laborers get up very early, often before 5 A.M., and stand at strategic positions in the street, often at crossroads. Certain groups of people are associated with particular locations: the burly young Koreans congregate in front of the Ōkura snack bar at the central crossroads, for instance (see map 3.1). Likewise, some recruiters have a well-known stamping ground. When jobs are plentiful, recruiters will walk busily around, looking for good workers; when they are scarce, the workers will anxiously prowl the streets looking for recruiters.

Once a recruiter has agreed to employ a day laborer, he may well put him straight on a minibus. Every morning before dawn a dozen or so minibuses and a few larger coaches park in and around Kotobuki. Sometimes the driver will double as the recruiter. Alternatively, if the workplace is nearby or the number of men needed is small, the recruiter will give the man directions and sometimes his bus or train fare.

Here is an account of some prominent Kotobuki tehaishi by an experienced day laborer, Nishikawa Kimitsu:

> Mr. A is that small chap, with the close-cropped hair thinning on top. He works for a longshoring firm, mainly recruiting stevedores to unload the banana boats. The money is very good: ¥17,000 a day, the best you can get for unskilled labor . . . for two reasons: firstly, the longshore union at Bankoku-bashi, where the banana boats unload, has fought to improve wages there; and secondly, that company's oyakata is such a bastard that people won't work for the firm at ordinary wages. He is very quick-tempered and will beat a man up as soon as look at him if slacking is suspected. This all happens in the hold of the ship, where no one can see or interfere. When the man goes drinking in Kotobuki he is very friendly and buys everybody drinks—but he's a devil in the workplace.
>
> Mr. B is a veteran longshoreman himself, now recruiting for three companies. He specializes in young Koreans and Chinese and seldom takes on Japanese.
>
> The buses from company C take men to work in warehouses loading up trucks. The money is very bad: ¥11,000 a day. The men are kept working by a big supervisor with a tattoo on his arm.
>
> Mr. D specializes in plant maintenance, and in good times he arranges employment for fifty to one hundred men, sending them to numerous destinations. Even now he sends twenty or so. He is

getting on in years, and sometimes when he feels tired or indis-
posed he stays in bed and entrusts the business to an assistant.
Once the assistant did a runner, carrying about ¥1 million. I reckon
Mr. D will knife the man if he ever finds him.

Mr. E recruits for another longshoring firm. The work is mostly
unloading banana boats—also the emergency imports of rice[20] now
coming in.

Mr. F recruits for a firm that specializes in unloading refriger-
ated ships: frozen fish, octopus, squid etc.[21]

The kind of relationship a day laborer establishes with the recruiters is of crucial importance to his economic prospects. Successful day
laborers such as Kōhei (pp. 78–79) lay great stress on the importance
of cultivating more than one recruiter:

> He now works for about eight different companies—though times
> are hard and he can only nail down about 14 days work a month.
> He says that most experienced day laborers like to play the field:
> avoid over-dependence on a single tehaishi; maintain good rela-
> tions with many. Maintaining a subtle balance in one's network of
> tehaishi is the key to keeping enough work when times are bad—
> as they are now. "In good times, you can hold your head up high:
> the tehaishi will beg you to work for them. In bad times, you have
> to grovel to them. And the more of them you've helped out in the
> good times, the better your chances in the bad times."[22]

Many day laborers tell of how recruiters would beg them to work
for them, literally fighting over the better men, during the peak period
of the bubble economy. They tell of being woken up by a recruiter
banging at their door or pulling them out of bed to work. There is of
course no guarantee that favors rendered in good times will be recip-
rocated in bad; many recruiters simply stopped showing their face in
Kotobuki after the bubble burst. Still, the successful day laborer will
have a subtle understanding of the sense of obligation and degree of
reciprocity likely to be felt by each recruiter, and will play them accordingly. In hard times the recruiters often choose men on the principle of
kaozuke—employing only those whose faces they know. Men such as
Kōhei make sure that their face is familiar in all the right places.

For the older, weaker men, this ideal strategy may not be practi-
cable. Such men are likely to end up developing a client relationship
with a single recruiter or employer, sacrificing much of their independence in order to develop stronger bonds of obligation which they
hope will outlive their usefulness to the other party. That was
Masayoshi's approach.

Aged 58 . . . in Kotobuki several decades. Started in construction, then switched over to dockwork. Better paid. But ran out of work there and moved back to construction. Now can't even find work there.

He used to play the day laboring game: working for various companies, through various tehaishi, going where the terms were best. But in recent years has found it more effective to stick with a single company, a single boss (oyakata). Every summer, at the Obon gift-giving season, he gives the oyakata some beer; at the year-end gift-giving season, he gives the oyakata some sake or tangerines. In the last year or two, the oyakata has been unable to provide him with much work, but he does his best to take care of Masayoshi: for example, he will put employment stamps in his handbook and rubber-stamp them, even when no actual employment has occurred—enabling Masayoshi to claim the day laborer dole.[23]

In this decidedly informal economy, each day laborer has to work out his own employment strategy. Kōhei and Masayoshi represent extremes; others mix elements of both approaches.

Other Methods

The men in Kotobuki use many other methods of finding employment besides the recruiters and labor exchanges (table 15). Some establish a semiregular arrangement with a single employer, a practice called chokkō—"going directly." This is especially common among the more skilled, reliable men in the longshoring sector. Some of the minibuses arriving at Kotobuki before dawn were picking up the same men every time. Two or three buses were making a regular shuttle journey between Kotobuki and the port at Kashima, a drive of some three hours, carrying thirty to sixty men a day. The buses set out at 6 A.M., and the men had an informal rotation to decide who should rest on days when smaller numbers were needed. When I asked Shūzō*, a well-paid crane operator and regular on the Kashima bus, why he didn't get an apartment in Kashima, he insisted that he preferred the social life in Kotobuki. He was a gambler. Besides, he and his friends enjoyed drinking shōchū in the bus on the journey home.

Another man with one of these semiregular arrangements was Saburō*:

Short, longish hair, middle-aged (40s), glasses, cheerful. Says he works for a large shipping company. Gets ¥15–17,000 a day, depending on the skill, labor-load and danger entailed in each job. He always works for the same firm, though he has no contract.

Sometimes they send him to a job at the Tokyo docks, too. There is a system for noncontract regulars like him. Their names are put up on noticeboards, saying who is needed the next day and where.

I put it to him that the arrangement cost him his freedom to pick and choose where he worked, without giving him any security or rights in exchange. But he wasn't bothered: he said he could take a holiday any time—one month at a stretch was OK, a day off here and there also OK. He still enjoyed significantly more freedom than the company's payroll employees (sha'in), and had no wish to become one himself.[24]

Other day laborers sometimes use personal connections to get work, attaching themselves to a man with a good reputation and asking to be taken along. The first man gains a certain amount of prestige and may eventually become a sort of minor boss or recruiter. This pattern is prevalent among the foreign migrant laborers, where a man with connections and language skills may become a leader. I saw this happen with Kim Sang Chon, a sixty-eight-year-old political dissident who came over from Inchon to work as a day laborer in Kotobuki and soon parlayed his pleasant manner and Japanese language skills into an informal position arranging work for a dozen or more men every morning. Ventura (1992) describes similar cases.

Another way of getting work is through the job adverts in the sports newspapers. These go on sale around 5 A.M. every morning in Kotobuki, from a small wooden barrow in front of the Center building. It is not practical for companies to advertise single-day contracts in the papers, so most of these jobs are for periods ranging from ten days to a month or more.

Pay and Conditions

The pay and conditions for jobs at the casual labor exchanges are written on the panels above the windows. Here are a few examples from the Kotobuki Labor Office:

23 February 1994

Employer: Keihin Dōro (Keihin Roads)
Location: Uraga (about 20 miles away)
Workers required: 2
Content: Constructing access road for condominium
Hours: 8:30 A.M. to 5:30 P.M.
Pay: ¥10,000
Lunch: Yes

Travel expenses: Yes
Insurance:[25] Accident: Yes Employment: Yes Health: Yes
Limitations: None

25 February 1994

Employer: Nichi'ei Sōko (Nichi'ei Warehousing)
Location: Hanezawa Warehouse (nearby)
Workers required: 4
Content: Container loading
Hours: 9 A.M.–5 P.M.
Pay: ¥10,000
Lunch: Yes
Travel expenses: No
Insurance: Accident: Yes Employment: Yes Health: Yes
Limitations: None

7 June 1994

Employer: Yano Kōgyō (Yano Industries)
Location: Isogo-ku (about 5 miles away)
Workers required: 1
Content: Laboring; construction
Hours: 8 A.M.–5 P.M.
Pay: ¥12,000
Lunch: No
Travel expenses: No
Insurance: Accident: No Employment: Yes Health: No
Limitations: Age up to 53

I never saw a job that paid less than ¥10,000, although in other parts of Japan they are all too common. A few effectively paid less than ¥10,000 because of non-payment of travel expenses, etc. ¥15,000 seemed to be the top rate for unskilled labor, with the average around ¥12,000. Skilled work involving driving, carpentry skills, etc. paid up to ¥18,000 a day, and dangerous high-altitude work (done by *tobi,* the aristocracy of day laborers) might reach ¥20,000 on a good day. Many day laborers told me of good old days when skilled work would pay as much as ¥25,000 or even ¥30,000, but there were no such jobs when I was in Kotobuki.

The day wage *(dezura)* is considered highly sensitive to economic trends, but data collected by the Kotobuki Labor Center (table 16) suggests that the Heisei recession hit job numbers much harder than wage levels (cf. Epilogue n7, p. 236). Broadly speaking, day wages in the formal market rose by almost 50 percent during the six years from 1985 to 1991 and then stagnated from 1991 to 1998, with no job category registering a serious decline during the post-bubble recession. The best-paid class of worker (tobi) earned roughly 50 percent more than the worst-paid (oddjob-man; *zakkō*) throughout the period 1985–1998, though the gap tended to widen in good years and narrow in bad. Informants say that wages in the informal market are broadly similar, though they tend to be higher at the top end of the scale and lower at the bottom end.

Jobs obtained through the recruiters seldom carry the range of safe-guards that come with some of the formally arranged jobs. Some employers using the street labor market do provide insurance stamps (which helps to explain why hundreds of day laborers claim the dole at the Labor Office every day though only a handful get jobs there[26]), but informants insist that many others do not.

Jobs arranged through the exchanges are paid for, in cash, by the employing company at the end of the day's work. Tehaishi jobs are paid sometimes by the company and sometimes by the tehaishi. In the latter case, the tehaishi may show up at Kotobuki to meet the return-ing minibuses, bearing a sheaf of brown envelopes containing the cash, which he hands over to the workers with a flourish. Occasionally he may even give the men their money before they set out to work, if he believes them to be trustworthy. The actual role of the tehaishi varies considerably. He may be a simple middle man, finding the labor and being paid a flat rate per head; or he may have his own capital and pay the men himself, billing the company at the end of the month. The latter system is said to be far more common in Osaka than in Tokyo-Yokohama, but I found one clear instance of it happening in Kotobuki.[27]

No one can agree on the percentage of the wage taken by the tehaishi as pin-hane, but most estimates are in the area of ¥3,000 per man-day. If so, this would represent something like 25 percent—less than the cut taken by legal temporary staff agencies, which take 30 percent or more, but which are seldom accused of pin-hane because of their dif-fering cultural context.

Casual wages are often better, measured day against day, than wages for regular employees doing similar work. The general rule is that employers pay a little bit extra for the convenience of having no long-term responsibility for the worker.[28]

Because the yen was so strong in 1993–1995, day laborer wages seemed quite good when translated into other currencies: for a while it was well over $100 a day for unskilled work. They seem less good in 2000, now that the yen is at lower levels on international currency markets. Remember, too, that Japan has a high cost of living; and that for most day laborers, earning power steadily declines with age, whereas for people in steady employment it tends to rise. Day wage levels have virtually no relation to age (cf. Koike 1995:8), but ability to get work falls steadily. Many employers now specify an upper age limit in their advertisements, often fifty or fifty-five—a practice deeply resented by the aging day laborers of Kotobuki.

Employing Industries

Nowadays, the construction/civil engineering industry probably accounts for roughly two-thirds of all work done by Kotobuki day laborers, and longshoring/warehousing for the other one-third. More than 90 percent of employers registered at the Labor Center are in construction (table 17), which accounts for roughly three-quarters of one-day contracts and virtually all period contracts in the formal market. The longshoring industry accounts for the remaining one-quarter of formal one-day contracts; it has a bigger role in the street market and employs other Kotobuki men such as Saburō (pp. 57–58) with semiregular arrangements. Thus, despite the decline of longshoring, Kotobuki remains somewhat less dependent on construction than other yoseba.

Manufacturing industry used to be a major employer, but these days the manufacturing and service sectors seldom patronize the yoseba. I knew men who got work for Coca-Cola and the Japanese domestic telephone company NTT, but these were rather exceptional.[29]

The Labor Center occasionally surveys employers to see if its workers are doing a good job. The 1994 and 1998 surveys were inconclusive, with "good" and "bad" each accounting for about a quarter of responses and "ordinary" covering about a half (table 19). These surveys are part of a long-running campaign by the Labor Center to facilitate communication between employers and workers, and to persuade more companies to recruit at Kotobuki.

Period Contracts *versus* One-Day Contracts

The Labor Office handles only one-day contracts,[30] but the Labor Center deals in period contracts (*yūki keiyaku*), usually lasting seven, ten, or fifteen days, as well as one-day jobs. Some men specialize in these longer-term jobs, but the majority seem to avoid them as far as possible. Even in the teeth of the Heisei recession I sometimes noticed period contracts that nobody wanted, and Labor Center statistics show consistently lower take-up rates for period contracts. In the years since 1991 virtually all one-day contracts have been snapped up, but between 5 and 24 percent of period contracts have been spurned in each of those years (table 13).

Partly this is because of the poor reputation of the work camps (hanba) where these jobs are mostly done, and the makeshift dormitories where hanba workers usually stay. These work camps are known for exploitative work arrangements and lax safety measures, and during my fieldwork period there were at least three fatal fires resulting from inadequate safety precautions at hanba.[31] Other abusive practices at hanba include lending money at high interest at the start of a contract and deducting it from wages; selling cigarettes and alcohol at a hefty premium; and refusing to pay for work done if a man quits in mid-contract, which is not uncommon (table 20). Bad hanba are called *ketaochi hanba* or *han-keta* (see glossary).

Still, not all hanba are hell, and period contracts obviously offer greater certainty and regularity of income than one-day contracts. Wage levels tend to be lower on period contracts, but not by much. Hanba work also obviates the need to get up extremely early in the morning to find a job. Katō (1991:304) refers to the early-morning period (roughly 5 A.M. to 7 A.M.) as "a fixed period which [the worker] must allow to be consumed in order to sell the product which is his labor . . . and which lengthens the period for which he is under duress *(kōsoku jikan)* each day." That is only half the story. Katō omits to mention that this is also the most sociable time of day in the yoseba, when men share their experiences and useful information about recruiters and employers. Even men who obviously are not planning to work, being still in their pyjamas or hobbling around on crutches, often appear on the streets around 5 A.M. or 6 A.M. Partly no doubt this is from force of habit, but perhaps it also reflects a desire for community. So getting up at 7 A.M. instead of 5 A.M. is not necessarily as attractive as one might imagine.

Several other factors are involved in preferences for one-day or period contracts. One is health. Period contracts may be attractive to a strong, fit man, because he can do enough work to maintain dole eligibility on a single fifteen-day contract and have the rest of the month off. Hard work and often remote locations tend to prevent one from spending too much money and enable one to save up a stash. Some middle-stage alcoholics use a spell at a hanba to dry out and restore finances before returning to Kotobuki to enjoy the fruits of their labor, usually with more drinking. However, older men and more advanced alcoholics cannot cope with the prolonged gruelling labor at a hanba and have little choice but to seek single-day contracts.

Another factor is the worker's residential situation. Hanba jobs generally include accommodation, which is an advantage to the day laborer with few possessions who can clear his room at the drop of a hat and cut out the cost of renting a doya room while in the hanba.

Photo 3.2 Kotobuki: A Doya Building. As this picture clearly shows, the better doya have electricity and TV in every room. Photo by Morita Ichiroh, 1994. Reprinted by permission.

But it is much less appealing to the man who has been living in the same room for years and has acquired a vast clutter of possessions. He will have to pay for his doya room even when not living in it.

Seasonal factors also play a part. The worker may seek period-contract work in late autumn to build up funds for the winter (cf. pp. 111–112).

Finally, let me note that the distinction between one-day and period contracts is not as clear cut as it appears. Quite often a man will use a one-day contract to check out a work site while the employer checks him out. If both parties approve, the worker may well come back the following day or for quite a few days after (table 21).

Residence

Some of the doya in San'ya and Kamagasaki are little wooden buildings, covered with ivy and resembling quaint country inns except for the minuteness of the rooms. But in Kotobuki the doya are almost uniformly large and functional, with no frills. Only a handful of wooden ones remain; the great majority are multistory ferro-concrete structures.

The number of doya in Kotobuki has fluctuated with economic trends. From 1984 to 1994 there were about ninety; by 1998 this had risen to ninety-nine. The number of rooms available held steady at around 6,100 from 1984 to 1994, rising to about 6,700 in 1997.[32] Some 95 percent of rooms are occupied by single males (table 6).

Here is a description of a room I stayed in:

> Nice room, 2.5 mats, no cockroaches. Walls: greyish, mottled. Phone numbers ballpenned on, stickers from newly-bought clothing affixed. Furniture: 1 rickety coffee table. 3 or 4 shelves, boards of wood resting on bits of wood nailed in, held together with skeins of string and yet more nails. . . . Count 85 nails protruding from walls. One strip light, middle of ceiling, operated by switch in ball hanging from it. Nasty damp patch in corner, evidence of many botched attempts to cover it up: bits of cardboard, sheets of newspaper, torn-off calendar pages, masking tape etc. Damp still coming through. Greasy, damp tatami mats. Lank futons. Nailed to the wall, a light brown bakelite bathroom fitting with mirror and little shelf for soap etc. Faded floral border. English phrase in curly writing: *Hi, Bonny Pet.*[33]

The recent shortage of day laboring jobs does not appear to have damaged the business of the doya owners unduly: most of the doya seem to be full most of the time, and more are being built. This resilience to recession has several causes: some people who could no longer afford better have moved down to doya; there was big demand from Korean migrants for several years; and most importantly, the Yokohama city government is housing more welfare recipients in doya rooms. Most doya owners welcome this arrangement, since the city government is a far more reliable source of rent payments than the uncertain income of a day laborer. In 1990, some 40 percent of doya rooms were occupied by people on welfare. By 1999, that figure was approaching 80 percent and it was getting very difficult for a travelling day laborer to find a room in Kotobuki.[34]

Doya rooms range widely in standard, from vilely filthy to spotlessly clean. The better ones have TVs and sometimes even fridges and air conditioners. Rents vary accordingly, roughly from ¥1,000 to ¥3,000. Rents have risen steadily in recent years: from an average of about ¥1,300 in 1989 to just over ¥1,800 in 1997. In that period, the number of rooms costing ¥1,500 or less fell from 73 percent to 21 percent, the latter figure representing 1,667 rooms.[35] This figure is important because the lodging coupons issued by the Yokohama city government are only valid for rooms costing ¥1,500 or less.

Not even the best rooms have private toilets or even washbasins. Occupants must pay to use one of the three public baths or numerous coin showers around Kotobuki—or queue for the free showers at the Seikatsu-kan—if they wish to get seriously clean.

Another thing all doya rooms have in common is that they are extremely small, mostly ranging in size from two to four tatami mats (3.3 to 6.6 square metres) in area.[36] They are very efficient devices to maximize the return on land in an area where land is at a premium and the rent-paying population poor. They are also well adjusted to the day laboring lifestyle: rent is payable by the day rather than the month, making it easy to come, go, and be kicked out. Each resident is given a small card with the name of the doya and his room number on it. It displays a grid, very like the one used to record employment in his white handbook, in which the concierge (chōba-san) will stamp the seal of the doya for every night's rent paid.

This system adds another dimension to the day laborer's life strategy. Some will generally pay an entire month in advance, others will aim to stay just a day or two ahead of the game. Yet others will be perpetually falling slightly into arrears, and will let it slide to the point where they risk eviction, before doing a few days' hard work to retrieve the situation. Officially, arrears are not permitted at all; in practice, most chōba-san will be patient for some time. The grace period tends to be roughly in proportion to length of residency: a newly arrived tenant will get no quarter, whereas a man who has stayed for many years may be allowed to fall as much as a month or two behind before the chōba-san reluctantly gives up on him.

Compared with any other kind of hotel, doya are very cheap, but compared with cheap apartments, they are quite expensive. The doya room I described above cost ¥1,100 a night, or roughly ¥33,000 a month. For that, or not much more, one could get a modest apartment, with six mats rather than two, certainly with running water and probably its own toilet. But moving into an apartment in Yokohama usually entails paying about six months' worth of rent up front (two months' deposit, two months' nonreturnable gift to landlord, one month's worth for the agent's fee, plus one month's rent in advance). It also entails supplying the landlord with the name of a guarantor—a citizen of good standing who will vouch for the good character of the tenant and, in the worst case, take financial responsibility for rent defaults or damage to property. Few day laborers can supply either the large initial sum or the guarantor. Like poor people everywhere who cannot afford to buy in bulk, they pay a premium for their housing because they lack the resources to pay large amounts up front. Doya owners require no deposit and ask no questions about social standing or proof of identity. This flexibility and anonymity enables them to charge over the odds.

Many doya in San'ya and Kamagasaki operate a curfew *(mongen)*, and lock their doors around 10 P.M. Kotobuki doya have no curfew, and residents may come and go much as they please. This freedom of movement, much appreciated by the day laborers, reflects a more relaxed management style on the part of the Korean owners (cf. Saitō 1994:132).

Men who cannot afford to stay in a doya, or who are barred for bad behavior, can easily end up on the streets. I discuss homelessness in chapter 6.

Play and Other Nonwork Activities

Gambling

Nowhere in Japan have I ever seen such a concentration of gambling facilities, legal and otherwise, as in Kotobuki.

I have already mentioned the twenty-odd illegal off-course book-makers where you can bet on horse, bicycle, and speedboat races.[37] These are located in lock-up shops, sheds, or tents; some are just trestle tables standing in the pavement. They are equipped with satellite TV and radio, transmitting odds and live coverage of races, and they are well patronized. The Yokohama police have a reputation for being soft on the yakuza who run these places, merely making a few token arrests two or three times a year.[38] These illegal book-makers are called *nomiya,* literally "swallowing shops." The same word, written with a different character, means a drinking shop, but in Kotobuki a nomiya is one of the few places where you cannot generally get a drink.

Nomiya do not allow complicated multirace combinations, or simple win or place bets on single contestants. Invariably one must predict the first and second place finishers—a bet called a forecast in Britain, a quinella in North America, and a *baren* ("consecutive horses") in Japan. On a few of the big classic races, one may identify two horses by their own numbers, but in most horse racing and all bicycle and speedboat racing the contenders are placed in eight brackets (six for speedboats). So supposing there are twelve runners, the first four brackets will each have two runners and the last four only one each. Selecting a bracket containing two runners gives one two chances of success. However, imbalances between brackets are faithfully reflected in the odds, which are calculated at the course by computerized totalizer. This variation on the forecast bet is called a bracket quinella in North America and a *wakuren* in Japan. In the first few races of the day the wakuren is reversible—so that a bet on say, 3-5, will win on a result of 5-3 as well as 3-5. A red line is drawn across the results chart, and in the later races under the line the bet is not reversible.

The bracket quinella is a very impersonal bet. Gambling conversations at the nomiya sometimes discussed horses and jockeys, but mostly the talk would be along the lines of whether 4-7 or 3-7 offered the best prospects. Day laborers would study the form very intently, but in the end many seemed to rely on numerology in making betting decisions.

The traditional bookie, drawing up his own odds on the strength of his own knowledge and ingenuity, is not to be found in Kotobuki—or, as far as I know, anywhere else in Japan. The tote leaves nothing to chance: the odds on each combination are automatically calculated to allow a generous 25 percent margin to the race operator (a body licensed by central or local government). This betting tax covers running expenses, prize money, etc., and the residue goes into the public coffers. In Kotobuki, the yakuza use the same odds, electronically broadcast from the track, but pocket the 25 percent margin themselves. It is a very easy way to make money, and helps to explain why yakuza in Kotobuki drive brand-new white Mercedes-Benzes while most of the workers go around in beaten-up sandals. However, since the nomiya's odds are calculated on bets placed at the track, rather than by its own patrons, it can, very occasionally, go wrong. Yakuza and gamblers alike love to tell stories, possibly exaggerated, of these rare events when a nomiya got taken to the cleaners. But this would only be a serious problem for the yakuza if day laborers consistently outperformed the punters at the track. Evidently, they do not.

There are also several mah-jongg parlors in Kotobuki, one of them next door to the biggest yakuza office, and several arcades and coffee shops where one may play video one-armed bandits for illegal cash prizes. Then there are dice games, their number and location varying in response to periods of firmness and laxity on the part of the police. My friend Shūzō took me to one that was run in a yakuza safe house:

> The game was going on in a brightly-lit, all-white room on the ground floor of an ordinary apartment building. The room had a bamboo screen pulled diagonally down in front of it, forming a kind of lean-to, which I suppose was to give a little extra privacy. The game was going on in low, hushed tones. Shūzō was greeted in the polite manner he'd led me to expect. ("We are their customers; they have to treat us well.")

There was a table, about the dimensions of a small billiard table; a white cloth stretched across it. I guess the bright light, the brilliant whiteness and the complete absence of cigarette smoke—unthinkable in gambling joints in most parts of the world—had something to do with purity, with fairness, with nothing-up-my-sleeve; that it was analogous to the white gloves worn by Japanese politicians at election time.

There were about 14 to 16 people assembled round the table, of whom three or four were yakuza running the game. There were two dice, kept in an old fruit can; the participants took it in turns to cup a hand over the can and shake it. Then they would turn the can upside down and slap it down on the table with a flourish, so that the dice remained concealed under the can. Only then would bets be placed, when the dice had already settled but were still concealed. Wads of blue ¥1,000 notes were placed on the table, sometimes in long sheaves, sometimes in little L-shaped snaffles. A few brown ¥10,000 notes were also in evidence; and some ¥100 coins.

The House wins on evens and the punter on odds. Shūzō took out about ¥10,000 in ¥1,000 notes and started betting. He clearly didn't believe in the cautious approach: he would usually stake at least half his stash, and once he'd started losing he put his last ¥5,000 down in one go and promptly lost that too. He asked the House to stake him; an unfriendly grey-haired yakuza gruffly said they weren't doing that tonight. A friendlier young yakuza, with a Hawaiian shirt and a look of great long-suffering, folded up three blue notes and tossed them across the table to Shūzō, who won once, then lost everything on the next two throws of the dice. We took our leave; we can't have been there more than 10 minutes. Shūzō had lost over ¥10,000, the best part of a day's income.[39]

Finally, there are three massive pachinko halls in Kotobuki, called MAX I, MAX II, and MARINE. Pachinko is by far and away the biggest form of gambling in Japan, an industry with an annual turnover estimated at ¥20 trillion in 1995. Pachinko is often called "Japanese pinball" but it is more like a highly sophisticated bagatelle. Players sit in front of upright machines and attempt to catapult ball bearings into targets which will trigger the machine to disgorge more ball bearings. Winning players have their baskets of ball bearings counted by automatic weighing machines. They are supposed to be exchanged for prizes (legal), but most players prefer to collect their winnings in cash (illegal). The player takes a chit out of the hall and exchanges it for cash at a small, shabby booth nearby. In Kotobuki, the MAX payout booth was on the ground floor of the multistory car park attached to the hall, while the MARINE booth was a tiny window in a nearby doya.

The Kotobuki pachinko halls are under ethnic Korean ownership, like the great majority around the country. In recent years pachinko has become a diplomatic issue between Japan and the United States, with the latter claiming that pachinko profits remitted to Pyongyang have been propping up the government of North Korea.[40] Meanwhile, my visits to the Kotobuki pachinko halls suggest that this is the most addictive form of gambling in the area, and the most rapid way of losing money. Kotobuki men rarely seem to bet more than a couple of thousand yen on a race, and must wait some time for the result—but a modern pachinko machine can swallow a day's wages in twenty minutes. Several day laborer narratives included a battle with pachinko addiction, and some seemed to be losing that battle.

Drinking

Japanese academics of the social pathology school have tended to characterize doya-gai as breeding grounds of alcoholism (e.g., Ōhashi 1972; Ōyabu 1981). Certainly a lot of heavy drinking goes on in Kotobuki, but Murata Yoshio, who has been working with alcoholics in the area for more than thirty years, firmly refutes this view. His personal estimate is that some 30 percent of Kotobuki residents (roughly 2,000 men) have some kind of alcohol problem, just over half of whom (roughly 1,200) he would classify as "alcoholics." At the same time 20 percent are teetotal (double the national average of about 10 percent). He estimates that perhaps 90 percent of the alcoholics acquired the habit before they arrived in Kotobuki. Far from breeding alcoholism, he sees Kotobuki as a sanctuary for people whose lives have been disrupted in other branches of Japanese society. He finds that many of the alcoholics have mothers or fathers who were also alcoholics, which points to childhood environment rather than current doya-gai environment as a factor in alcoholism. He also says that alcoholics in Kotobuki show a much broader social profile than day laborers in general; all classes are represented, with a split of roughly 7:3 between working-class or under-class types and middle-class types.

The Alcoholics Anonymous group run by Murata has a success rate of "about 20 percent" in breaking people out of this downward spiral and enabling them to live relatively normal lives. The process generally takes more than three years. In 1999 there were three AA groups in Kotobuki, with a total of about sixty participants. Murata says that many former members have left Kotobuki and succeeded in getting steady jobs.[41]

Drugs

Alcohol is by far the biggest drug in Kotobuki, but there are others to be had. In the summer of 1993 I met a dealer there who said he was selling heroin (*pe* in street slang) at ¥10,000 for three hits, and also a little opium. He operated on the street, sending customers to a regularly changed doya room to do the transaction with a partner. He said he was not a yakuza but had to pay off the yakuza for protection. The rate had recently gone up from ¥50,000 a month to ¥100,000, and he was refusing to pay. He was thus at risk from the yakuza as well as the police. After this one early meeting, I never saw him again. Nor did I meet any other obvious dealers, although there was talk of men using amphetamines (*shabu*, or *hirapon* in older slang). I never saw or heard of any use of marijuana. The volunteers of the Kotobuki medical team reckon there is a small minority of amphetamine addicts; my dealer estimated the drug-taking population of Kotobuki at "about 30 'patients' (kanja), or 1 percent of the population."[42]

Several people told me that in the small hours of the morning wealthy young people would motor into Kotobuki to score drugs, though I never saw this myself.

Sex

Kotobuki seems to be an area of extremely low sexual activity. As stated, very few men there have wives or regular partners. There is the alternative of visiting the prostitutes in the long row of brothels under the Keihin elevated railway line that runs through Kōgane-chō and Hinode-chō (about a twenty-minute walk from Kotobuki), but day laborers are seldom in a position to pay ¥10,000 (roughly one day's wages) for twenty minutes of intercourse. Many of the Kōgane-chō women are foreigners, from the Philippines, Thailand, Taiwan, etc.

A few foreign prostitutes live in Kotobuki, but they do not work there. They use it as a low-rent base from which they set out around dusk, usually to work the street corners of nearby Wakaba-chō. This accounts for the female majority in Kotobuki's tiny Thai population (table 7).

Several men told me that after decades of drinking they no longer had any interest in women, nor the physical ability to express such an interest. Others had rooms littered with pornographic magazines, which are on sale from vending machines and convenience stores in Kotobuki, as everywhere in Japan. Masturbation is probably the most common form of sexual activity in Kotobuki, and is often joked about.

Homosexuality seems to be quite common, though little talked about. I myself was discreetly propositioned half a dozen times, by men who scratched the palm of my hand while shaking hands—a secretive message of sexual interest in Japan as in Britain. One gay rights activist who knows Kotobuki well said that it was mostly "opportunity homosexuality" (kikai dōsei-ai), stemming from the availability of men and unavailability of women in this mostly masculine community.

There are a couple of transvestite bars in Kotobuki, but they appear to be patronized for novelty value rather than as pick-up venues. In Japan as elsewhere, there are gay men with an interest in construction workers, and despite the deteriorating physical condition of the Kotobuki population, I hear that there are still a few such men who come into Kotobuki.

Fighting

There is quite a lot of fighting in Kotobuki, mostly drunken brawls. Many men carry scars from past fights, and some are constantly threatening violence. There are a few bullies who take pleasure in humiliating and injuring weaker men. But the number of murders has been around one or two a year of late,[43] quite a low figure in view of the circumstances. Personally I never saw a knife or a gun drawn in anger, nor did I observe yakuza bullying workers other than verbally. This supports a common view in day laboring circles, that the Kotobuki yakuza are easier to get on with than those in San'ya or Kamagasaki.

Nor did I witness any interethnic fighting. Fights were between fellow Japanese or fellow Koreans. Some Japanese day laborers do blame the Koreans for taking jobs away, but the Koreans' youth, strength, and ethnic solidarity are strong deterrants to racist attacks.

Bureaucratic Systems

The Labor Office has the important function of administering the Ministry of Labor's special unemployment insurance system for day laborers. When day laborers register at an employment exchange they are given a white handbook, with grids of squares representing days of the month. Employers are supposed to stick an employment stamp (inshi), which costs ¥176, on each square representing a day they have employed the holder. The employer and worker are supposed to share the cost of the stamp equally, but in practice the sum of money is so trivial that the employer seldom bothers to collect the worker's ¥88 contribution. This heavily subsidized system generally pays out ¥7,500 per day without work to any man who has stamps to prove he has worked at least twenty-six days in the last two completed calendar months.[44]

In a 1994 survey of one hundred Kotobuki day laborers, only sixty-nine admitted to knowing that it was illegal to work without the white handbook. However, the advantages are clear, and ninety were in fact carrying it (Kotobuki Labor Center 1994:4, 6). On 17 September 1996 there were 3,513 registered day laborers at the Labor Office, which expected this number to rise by about one thousand as day laborers got registered in order to take advantage of the Ministry of Labor's end-of-year bonus payment to day laborers. This payment, known informally as *mochi-dai*, money to buy the rice cakes traditionally eaten at New Year, was ¥33,000 in 1995, rising slightly to ¥34,600 in 1998. To qualify, a worker must have at least three stamps per month in his handbook for every month since the start of the financial year (April), or since registering as a day laborer. Hence, anyone registering in November only has to get three stamps to qualify for the payment, a loophole that has not gone unnoticed.

Since 1989 there has also been a system of health insurance for day laborers under article 69, part 7 of the Health Insurance Law (*Kenkō Hoken-hō*), but this is far less widely used than the unemployment insurance, mainly because it is far more expensive. Again, there is a handbook; for a man paid ¥12–14,500 a day (typical for Kotobuki), the daily stamp costs ¥1,410, of which ¥870 is payable by the employer and ¥540 by the worker. The system is also very bureaucratic, and quite unsuited to most day laborers since they are mainly solitary men and the expensive premium covers a huge range of dependent relations.

The scheme is supposed to be compulsory, but many employers ignore it. Until 1996 the Labor Center refused to supply workers to employers not enrolled in the scheme, but the Labor Office (much to the chagrin of the Labor Center) turned a blind eye.[45]

On 1 April 1996 the Labor Center finally scrapped the requirement for employers to be enrolled in the scheme, and stopped insisting even on unemployment insurance. Accident insurance has never been compulsory. So nowadays, out of the three kinds of day laborer insurance mentioned on official job descriptions, the Office only insists on unemployment insurance and the Center on none. The trend-breaking 12.5 percent recovery in jobs transacted at the Center during FY1996 (table 13) must be seen in the light of this ad hoc, ground-level deregulation. On the other hand, 1996 was also the one relatively good year for the Japanese economy during the 1990s.

In the 1994 survey, only forty-nine men out of one hundred were carrying the health insurance handbook; and of those forty-nine, only twenty-three had enough stamps to use the insurance. Some men preferred to use the standard national health insurance *(kokumin kenkō hoken)*, which has cheap premiums for those on low incomes, but pays only 70 percent of medical costs against 90 percent for the special day laborer system. Others pay their own medical expenses in full or rely on social services (table 22).

Men who cannot support themselves by working must turn to the local social services. Assistance comes in two broad categories: social welfare *(seikatsu hogo)*[46] and extralegal assistance *(hōgai engo)*. Social welfare pays room rent plus roughly ¥80,000 ($800) a month for a single man. In theory it is payable to anyone without means of support; in practice, welfare officials in most Japanese cities have insisted that recipients must be physically unable to work, and require a doctor's letter to that effect. Lengthy negotiations between the day laborer union and the local authorities have gradually eased the latter's interpretation of welfare eligibility; hence, in part, the recent marked increase in welfare recipients in Kotobuki (tables 5, 9).

As the name suggests, extralegal assistance is help which the authorities are not legally obliged to give; it *may* be given as a favor. In Yokohama, this assistance takes two forms: food vouchers *(pan-ken)* and lodging-house vouchers (officially *shukuhaku-ken*; unofficially, *doya-ken*). In 1999 the former were worth ¥690 (¥724 including 5 percent consumption tax), and were exchangeable for goods (except alcohol or cigarettes) at a few selected shops in the Kotobuki region; the latter had a face value of ¥1,500 in 1999 and were good for one night's accommodation at one of the cheaper doya in Kotobuki. About a quarter of the doya accepted them. The fact that both kinds of voucher are only usable in Kotobuki naturally tends to attract poor people from other parts of Yokohama into the doya-gai.

Until financial year 1991, the staff at Naka-ku ward office were issuing about thirty accommodation vouchers a day. By FY1993 they were issuing more than two hundred a day, and by FY1997, more than three hundred and fifty a day (table 23). The predictable result is that the doya that accept them are nearly always full, and many of the vouchers are unusable. They are called *kara-ken* (empty tickets). The best you can do with a kara-ken is sell it to a yakuza who will then attempt to defraud the local government of the ¥1,400. The yakuza used to pay ¥500 for a dud accommodation voucher, but during the Heisei Recession the market was flooded and the price sank to ¥300—supply and demand in action again. As for food vouchers, their rate of issuance climbed thirteen-fold, from about fifty a day in FY1991 to six hundred and fifty a day in FY1997 (table 23).

Yokohama's food and accommodation vouchers are wholly inadequate, but still considerably more generous than anything Tokyo or any other big city has to offer. Add in the relative willingness of Yokohama to put people on welfare, and the result is that people who are unable to support themselves tend to gravitate toward Yokohama. This factor, as well as the impact of the Heisei recession, has caused the massive increase in welfare cases and voucher issuance. It is a source of friction between city governments and has put an immense strain on the program.

Health

Kagoshima Masa'aki, a leading figure in the union, estimates that roughly 150 people die every year in Kotobuki, and that life expectancy for men who have spent their entire working career in yoseba is around sixty, almost twenty years below the national male average for Japan.[47]

The people of Kotobuki are prone to various ailments, of which the most common is back trouble and the most disturbing is tuberculosis (table 24). Saiki Teruko, the doctor in charge of the Kotobuki Clinic and something of a Yokohama celebrity (see Saiki 1991 [1982]) told me early in 1994 that she was seeing roughly three cases a week of TB, up from about one a week a couple of years before. "And these are really awful cases, often at a very advanced stage," she added. This she ascribed to the impact of recession-induced poverty. She guessed that TB was responsible for at least 5 percent of all deaths in Kotobuki.

Day laborers who lack medical insurance or money to pay the full cost of treatment cannot be seen at most clinics and surgeries. The Kotobuki Clinic is an exception. Those who cannot pay are given "special treatment" (tokubetsu shinryō) and are required to fill in a form, addressed to the mayor of Yokohama, asking the city to lend them the price of their medical treatment. This is simply a matter of form: no effort is made to get the money back. The patients are simply encouraged to pay back what they can, when they can. In 1993 ¥18 million was "lent" in this way, of which ¥380,000 (about 2 percent) was paid back. In recent years the special cases have fallen in number, as more and more men have been granted welfare, which makes them eligible for free treatment (table 25).

There is nothing like this special system for the uninsured in Tokyo or Osaka. Dr. Saiki says the Yokohama approach reflects the lingering influence of progressive policies adopted by the Socialist city administration of the 1970s. She admits that some people abuse the clinic, especially yakuza looking for sick-notes to facilitate bogus welfare claims, but after two decades in Kotobuki, she reckons she can spot them.[48]

There is also a volunteer group called the *Iryō-han* (Medical Team) operating in Kotobuki. Once a month Iryō-han members set up a table and conduct simple on-the-spot medical examinations. In a serious case, they will pass the patient on to a professional doctor (also a volunteer) or call an ambulance and accompany the patient to hospital (cf. Stevens 1995a; 1995b; esp pp. 247–248). On 1 April 1996, two Iryō-han doctors opened a clinic, open 6:30 to 8:30 P.M. daily, mainly for the foreign workers in Kotobuki.[49]

The Union

The Kotobuki Day Laborers' Union (Junichirō), is based in the upstairs part of the Chōnai Kaikan, for which it pays ¥20,000 a month in rent. Junichirō prides itself on its human face. It has an extra character in its Japanese name which slightly distinguishes it from unions in other yoseba: they are "day labor unions" but Junichirō is a "day *laborer* union." It has a very informal organization, with no official leader. Anyone who turns up at a meeting may participate in decision making. During my fieldwork period, Junichirō had only one paid worker (and he only intermittently), Kondō Noboru. Another unionist, Kagoshima Masa'aki, also had a paid job helping to run the Seikatsu-kan as an indirect employee of the Yokohama city government. A third, Hanada Masaru, was in charge of running the coin lockers in the Center, and the other dozen or so activists mostly survived by day laboring. The situation was much the same in 1999.

Union activists mentioned four main objectives:

1. to represent members in negotiations with employers over abuses such as nonpayment of wages, failure to compensate for industrial accidents, etc.;
2. to negotiate with the city, prefectural, and national authorities for better employment and welfare measures for day laborers;
3. to help organize the summer festival and winter survival campaign (see pp. 134–140); and
4. to raise political awareness among day laborers and encourage them to fight for their rights, by organizing demonstrations, etc.

Members are effectively defined as any day laborer in the Kotobuki area. Officially there are monthly dues of ¥500, but hardly anyone pays and Junichirō makes little effort to enforce payment beyond gentle reminders. Most men in Kotobuki have a positive attitude toward the union, but few do anything to actively support it. They only go to the union when they need help, typically in an industrial dispute. It struck me several times that Junichirō was operating more like a charity than a union. There is one other union seeking to represent day laborers, the Kanagawa City Union, based in the neighboring city of Kawasaki but with branches in Yokohama and Yokosuka (Saitō 1994:141–142). This union fights discrimination by accepting any worker as a member, including illegal foreign workers. Some of the Koreans in Kotobuki are members, but the union has no visible presence in Kotobuki.

Junichirō is a member of the National Federation of Day Labor Unions *(Hiyatoi Zenkyō)*, attends the annual Hiyatoi Zenkyō conference, which rotates among member cities, and sometimes sends personnel to support struggles in other yoseba. The union is also fiercely internationalist, and seeks to support illegal foreign workers as well as Japanese workers. In May 1987 the union joined with citizens' groups to form the Association in Kotobuki for Solidarity with Foreign Migrant Workers *(Kotobuki Gaikokujin Dekasegi Rōdōsha to Rentai Suru Kai)*, better known as the Kalabaw Association.[50] This group offers legal advice, language lessons, shelter, and support to migrant workers. Kalabaw has links with citizens' movements in Korea, the Philippines, etc., and has published an important book on the "foreign worker problem" (Kalabaw no Kai 1993 [1990]).

There is some controversy among the unions as to whether it is ethical to extract fees from workers who have been helped in extracting unpaid wages or compensation payments from employers. Junichirō goes no further than encouraging donations from workers it has helped in this way. The Kalabaw Association provides a similar service for foreign workers, free if the matter can be resolved through a telephone call to the employer. Kalabaw used to charge expenses plus a small donation where it was necessary to visit the employer, but Kalabaw has no full-time paid staff, and in recent years has tended to pass on the difficult cases to the Kanagawa City Union, which generally charges around 15 percent of the amount won in negotiations.[51]

I got to know many activists from Junichirō and other day labor unions. There is a general consensus within the movement that Junichirō is less ideological and more practical in its approach than others. It organizes few purely political events, preferring to empha-

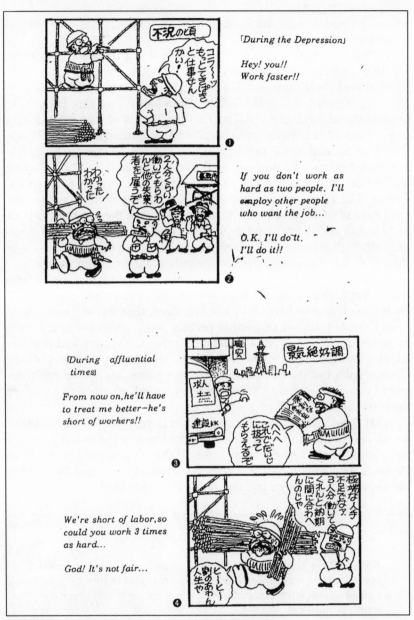

Cartoon 3.1 Day Laboring in Good Times and Bad. Kamayan, a cartoon day laborer from Kamagasaki, learns that in a recession he has to do the work of two men to avoid losing his job to another man; while in a boom he has to do the work of three men so the construction company can meet its deadline. Cartoon by Arimura Sen (Arimura 1989:112–113). Reprinted by permission.

size negotiations with local authorities, in which it has won several important concessions.

In 1993 Junichirō responded to the deepening recession by joining together with two voluntary associations, the Old People's Club *(Rōjin Kurabu)* and the Kotobuki District Center *(Kotobuki Chiiki Sentaa),* to form the *Kotobuki Takidashi no Kai.* The objective of this body is to organize food handouts *(takidashi)* on the streets of Kotobuki during those times of year when need is greatest. Initially the takidashi "season" was defined as the five-month period from November to March, but from 1997 to 1998 this was extended to November to July. During the season, meals are served every Friday afternoon in front of the Center. The menu always includes *zōsui* (gruel), usually with some kind of fruit or vegetable sidedish. Several times the team of thirty or forty volunteers has served more than one thousand meals at a sitting—though the number of men using the service is somewhat lower than that, since coming back for seconds is far from unknown.

To sum up: At first glance, Kotobuki looks like a paradigm of free-market capitalism, a labor market where men can be freely used, parted from their wages at bars and gambling dens, then left to die when no longer needed. Closer inspection reveals many and various attempts by government and private citizens to soften the system and regularize employment, health, and welfare. In recent years the loss of day laboring jobs and the relaxation of welfare policy has gone three-quarters of the way to turning Kotobuki from a worker's town to a welfare town (cf. Stevens 1997).

What these widely differing institutions have in common is that they are all part of the fabric of a distinctive community that is not based on the nuclear family. At the same time, all these contrasting community elements tend to emphasize Kotobuki's stigmatized status. By making life easier to bear, they may also make the place harder to leave.

Kōhei

Kōhei was a short, thin man, grey haired with silver-rimmed spectacles. He was fifty-two when I first met him in July 1993. He looked almost elfin, especially when he wore his pointy green cap with ear mufflers.

I last saw him in February 1995. Most of our meetings were very early on weekday mornings—job-hunting time. This was because Kōhei was a businesslike worker. He had a profession, as

(continues)

(continued)

a ship's carpenter, and specialized in building the timber frameworks used to prevent cargoes from shifting with the movements
of the sea.

He said he worked for about eight companies, via some fifteen
tehaishi. He would strategically manipulate the recruiters to maximize job security (see his comment on p. 56). He took care to
ascertain pay and conditions before agreeing to any job proposi-
tion. He showed a professional respect for the recruiters and
strongly denied that they were a bunch of gangsters.

He was a day laborer by choice: he had worked at the Nissan
factory in Atsugi for four years in his youth, but got fed up and
left in 1967 to travel the world on his motorbike. He toured the
United States four times and Europe once. He later discovered
that he could make better money working freelance on ships than
as a tied worker in a car factory. He'd been working out of Kotobuki
for twenty-five years, but no longer lived in the place, having
rented an apartment nearby. He commuted to Kotobuki on a smart
and sturdy bicycle. He also said he owned seven large Honda
motorbikes, but this was a hobby: he did not ride them to Kotobuki.

He claimed to have a life-strategy. He did not drink, smoke, or
gamble, and deliberately avoided making friends. In Kotobuki, he
said, friends were a serious liability. Nor had he ever married or
had children—he couldn't afford it. He saved money obsessively,
and said he had substantial reserves. He was planning to retire in
the year 2000 and return to his native town of Kagoshima, in southern Kyushu. Both parents were still alive and living there in 1993.

As a lone wolf, Kōhei apparently had no use for the union. I
once rattled a Junichirō collecting tin under his nose when he had
just collected his year-end benefit; he gave me a broad smile but
no money.

The Heisei recession was a damaging blow to Kōhei, but he
seemed to be weathering it. Almost every time I met him he would
say that he had failed to get a job that day, but this may have been
because he would be out of Kotobuki very early on successful
days. By his own account he managed twenty-three days' work in
September 1993, about twenty in October, seven in November,
thirteen in December, about eleven in January 1994, and about
fifteen in February. After that I lost track of him for about a year,
but in February 1995 he told me he had "plenty of work" because
of the Kobe earthquake, which had diverted a lot of shipping
from Kobe to Yokohama.

Resourceful and phlegmatic, Kōhei always gave the impression that he could cope.

4

Ethnography of Other Doya-Gai and Yoseba

D AY LABORERS, or at least those registered with the Ministry of Labor, are very unevenly spread around Japan (table 26). All the major day-laboring prefectures are in relatively warm regions, with none to be found in the northeast or along the Japan Sea coast, and there is a marked concentration in western Honshu. The top eight day-laboring prefectures all have major cities in them, while predominantly rural prefectures have very few registered day laborers: nine prefectures had none at all in FY1996. In 1996 only Kumamoto prefecture was anywhere near supplying regular work for its registered day laborers through employment exchanges; elsewhere, informal labor markets apparently dominated.

San'ya (Tokyo)

Location and History

Some 70 percent of Tokyo's yoseba day laborers live in and around San'ya.[1] The place name is written with characters meaning "mountain-valley," yet the place is flat as a pancake. It is located in Northeast

Tokyo, near Minami-Senju station on the Hibiya line. There is a broad street, generally known as San'ya-dōri (San'ya Street), running through the middle of the district, lined with pachinko parlors, bars, restaurants, and doya. San'ya-dori crosses Meiji-dori at a broad, nondescript crossroads which marks the entrance to the main drag. This is called Namidabashi, the Bridge of Tears, though there is no bridge nor any sign of a river.

However, this name is the first clue to the inauspicious history of this part of Tokyo. The main Edo execution ground was located here; it was called Kotsukappara,[2] and it is thought that some 200,000 people were killed here during the last two centuries of the Edo era (1667– 1867), by methods including beheading and crucifixion (Asahi 1986 Vol.2:7–8; Kaji 1977 Vol.1:11). The condemned would bid their loved ones farewell at Namidabashi. Near Minami-Senju station there still stands a large statue of Kannon, the Buddhist goddess of mercy, where people would pray for the souls of those executed.

San'ya-dori used to be known as Kotsu-dōri, a name still used by some people to describe the portion to the north of Namidabashi. There are rival theories to account for this name, which appears to mean "bone street." One says it is simply an abbreviation of "Kotsukappara-dōri"; the other is that it refers to bones lying around the cremation ground which was located at present-day Minami-Senju 5-chome from the Edo period until 1887. The name Kotsukappara itself may derive from a tumulus in the region dedicated to the tempestuous and wayward Shinto god, Susanō (Asahi 1986 Vol.2:7–8).

Amid these reminders of San'ya's brutal past, a couple of place names stand out in intriguing contrast. Tamahime Kōen (Jewel Princess Park) and the adjacent Hōrai Chugakko (a middle school named after the island of eternal youth in Chinese myth) form a kind of island in central San'ya. The small park, a traditional gathering place for off-duty day laborers, has had three-quarters of its area fenced off for use as a sports ground by supervised children. The only gate is kept firmly locked outside hours and there is a wire-netting roof as well, forming a fairly secure cage.[3] On a mild afternoon one may often see old men sitting on benches, or hanging onto the fence, watching children play baseball inside the cage.

San'ya has a close association with Burakumin outcasts, reflected in the considerable number of meat, leather, and footwear wholesalers to be found in the area. San'ya's Tamahime Inari shrine holds semiannual footwear festivals in which a couple of dozen local retailers set up stalls in the shrine grounds.

San'ya also has a close association with prostitution. When the famous Yoshiwara pleasure quarter burned down in the great Meireki fire of 1657, the houses of assignation were temporarily moved to San'ya before being being permanently relocated at nearby Asakusa. Even after that the names of San'ya and Yoshiwara were almost synonymous, with *San'ya-gayoi* ("San'ya visiting") becoming an established slang term for patronizing the Yoshiwara. Though the exact location of the Yoshiwara varied over the next three centuries, it was never very far from San'ya. During the Edo era San'ya served as an adjunct to Yoshiwara: there were cheap Hinin prostitutes, known as *yotaka* (night-hawks) for those who could not afford to patronize the Yoshiwara, and it was also a "nest of pimps" *(zegen no su)* who supplied women of outcaste or poor peasant origins to the Yoshiwara itself (Kaji 1977 Vol.1:3).

The Yoshiwara was officially closed in 1959, but the modern Yoshiwara, with its neon-lit massage parlors and fantasy brothels, has skillfully bypassed the law and is just next door to San'ya. However, the San'ya-Yoshiwara boundary is very clearly demarcated, and like Kotobuki, San'ya itself is not a center of prostitution.

Until World War II, the most notorious slum district in Tokyo was located around Fukagawa and Honjo, on the far side of the Sumida river from San'ya and slightly farther south. Kon Wajirō, writing in 1925, describes the Sumida river as a kind of class boundary: the east bank is "a country of different ways," a great seamless slum (Kon 1971 [1930]:120), a hundred times more crowded than the average residential district, with human dwellings little bigger than dog kennels (121). Day laborers were living three to a three-mat room at flophouses charging them thirty sen a night (122). Many could not afford even this and just stood around in the street. None had families. There were bars everywhere.[4]

By 1939, San'ya, or "Namidabashi," was Tokyo's second-biggest residential center for free workers after Honjo-Fukagawa (Imagawa 1987:122). As a casual labor market it was third behind Honjo-Fukagawa and Shibaura (where dock workers gathered), but day laborers still made up only 60 percent of doya inhabitants. The other 40 percent were people using the area as a cheap base for visits to prostitutes in the neighboring Yoshiwara; worn-out prostitutes who could no longer make it in the Yoshiwara; and travelling street players and peddlers on their way into and out of central Tokyo (Imagawa 1987:123).

The 1939 study cited by Imagawa was made by a government official, in order to suggest ways of harnessing the wild and unreliable day laborers to the war effort against China. Interestingly, he concluded that recruiting through the casual labor exchanges in the yoseba would be ineffectual, and that "although it is somewhat feudalistic, we should use the *oyakata*" (Imagawa 1987:124). These oyakata, or small-time bosses, were similar to the tehaishi who still recruit in yoseba today. San'ya was then controlled by a yakuza gang called the Akibagumi, and this report effectively calls for the government to treat the gangsters as partners.

During the war the allied firebombing of Tokyo destroyed all the doya-gai. San'ya was razed to the ground on 10 March 1945 (Kaji 1977 Vol.1:1). As the city rebuilt, Fukagawa-Honjo was gradually turned into a respectable residential district. As for San'ya, it served as a temporary prostitution zone while the Yoshiwara was being rebuilt, just as it had done after the great fire of 1657. This was actively encouraged by the Japanese government, under direction from the allied occupation authorities. San'ya was a "special comfort facility for the occupying forces" *(shinchū-gun tokushū ian shisetsu)* (2–3, citing Kanzaki 1955).

Kaji Daisuke, a day laborer himself and San'ya's most famous modern historian, says that San'ya started to revert to its prewar status as a day laboring center around 1948 (Kaji 1977 Vol. 1:18), by which time the Yoshiwara was up and running. Again, government policy played a big role, since the Tokyo Welfare Bureau *(Minsei-kyoku)* built barracks in San'ya to house single men whose homes and families had been lost in the war. Some were prewar residents returning to San'ya; others were soldiers hailing from other parts of Tokyo. From the following year, however, a growing number of migrant laborers from impoverished peasant families came into San'ya after failing to find anywhere better to work in Tokyo (19–20).

After the war, doya landlords started subdividing room space into ever smaller units to maximize profits, for instance by installing bunk beds in their tiny rooms. Some of these landlords became wealthy and influential men, controlling large chains of doya (Kanzaki 1974:2–10). Their families still dominate San'ya. As of 1991, out of 189 doya in San'ya,[5] the Tamura family owned twenty-three, the Satō family nineteen, the Kaeriyama family fourteen, and the Ueno family twelve.[6] These families were all well represented on the board of the doya owners' union. We thus have a mixed picture of free-market capitalism within which a small number of wealthy clans negotiate influence. Twenty years earlier, Kanzaki listed the ten wealthiest people in San'ya (2–10). Satō Hiromichi, a member of the doya-owning Satō family, came top with an annual income of ¥32.78 million in 1971.

With such a wide and obvious gap between rich and poor, San'ya has been a theater for class warfare for most of its postwar history. The district had its first major riot on 22 October 1959, and a dozen more followed during the 1960s, peaking in 1967–1968. The largest one, in 1967, followed protests about unfair treatment of a day laborer involved in a traffic accident. Some two thousand men rioted, throwing stones, setting fire to shops and pachinko parlors, and assaulting the police station.[7]

Contemporary San'ya

Some of the small doya in the warren of back streets off San'ya's main drag look positively picturesque, with ivy climbing all over them, or jumbled collections of potted plants around the front door. But many of the larger doya were renovated in business-hotel style during the years of the bubble economy (the late 1980s), and room charges have risen to average about ¥2,500, well above Kotobuki levels. There is even one "deluxe doya," which charges ¥4,100 a night and has a stone rooftop jacuzzi. On the other hand, San'ya still has a few "bedhouses," where several men (often around six to eight) share a single room. In the late 1990s, bedhouse prices were ¥800–1,100 a night—comparable with an individual room at the very cheapest Kotobuki doya.

There is a distinct change in atmosphere as one crosses San'ya-dōri from Kiyokawa (the east side) to Nihonzutsumi (the west side). Most of the narrow alleys and pretty doya are in Kiyokawa. The roads are wider and dirtier on the Nihonzutsumi side, and it is here that the homeless men of San'ya tend to gather. One road in particular has a look of bleak desolation to it. I often saw thirty or forty men lying around on the pavement there. At night the area is less popular because it lacks shelter, and homeless men prefer to sleep in the Iroha covered shopping mall, or under the shopfront awnings of Asahikai-dōri, a nearby shopping street.

The major landmarks on the Nihonzutsumi side are the Jōhoku Welfare Center and San'ya Labor Center, housed together in a large concrete building roughly corresponding to the Labor Center at Kotobuki; the San'ya Workers' Welfare Building (*San'ya Rōdōsha Fukushi Kaikan*); the Iroha shopping mall; and an exceptionally large police box, known simply as "the Mammoth" (*Manmosu*). On the Kiyokawa side we find the Palace Hotel bedhouse; Tamahime Park; Tamahime

Photo 4.1 San'ya: The Suzumoto Inn and Its Proprietors. Shida Masayuki and his wife have been running this picturesque doya in San'ya for thirty-five years. In 1999 a room was ¥1,500—as it had been since 1983. The Suzumoto is always full, mostly with elderly long-term residents. Mr. Shida has a pair of stout truncheons to deal with troublemakers, but has not had to use them for many years. Photo by Morita Ichiroh, 1995. Reprinted by permission.

Inari shrine; Hōrai Middle School; and, importantly, the headquarters of the Kanamachi-ikka (Kanamachi Family) yakuza gang.

The fact is that San'ya-dōri, an ordinary, busy main road, also serves as the site of San'ya's street labor market, and as a line dividing San'ya into mutually hostile spheres of influence. Broadly speaking, the Nihonzutsumi side is the territory of left-wing activists supporting the day laborers while the Kiyokawa side is yakuza territory. Government institutions of welfare and control are also on the Nihonzutsumi side. The mammoth police box has actually crossed the road—its predecessor was on the Kiyokawa side of San'ya-dori.

In Kotobuki, it is not unknown for day laborer unionists passing a yakuza in the street to nod or in some modest way acknowledge the latter's existence. One San'ya activist told me that such a thing would be unthinkable in San'ya. He and his comrades avoid the Kiyokawa side, and the yakuza keep out of the Nihonzutsumi side.

Relations between day laborers and yakuza have been far more confrontational and violent in San'ya than in Kotobuki. In San'ya the informal labor market is largely controlled by a single yakuza gang, the Kanamachi, which has a strongly right-wing political coloring[8] and is engaged in a bitter, long-running feud with the main left-wing union-type organization, the *San'ya Sōgidan* (San'ya Dispute League), founded in October 1981 after a byzantine sequence of rifts and mergers involving more than twenty left-wing groupings, dating back to the early 1960s (Funamoto 1985).

Two Sōgidan activists, filmmaker Satō Mitsuo and union leader Yamaoka Kyō'ichi, were murdered by Kanamachi yakuza in the mid-1980s. Tensions were running very high after the murders, with large early-morning anti-yakuza street demonstrations almost every day. They continued for months on end, and are still occasionally repeated today. I participated in one held to mark the tenth anniversary of one of the murders.[9] Another indirect consequence of the murders was the decision, by the Sōgidan and various Christian support groups, to build the San'ya Workers Welfare Building as a more secure headquarters.

The Welfare Building was constructed by day laborers themselves, with funds raised by support groups (San'ya Rōdōsha 1992). The project was an inspirational event in the history of San'ya, proving that day laborers could be organized into a major self-help operation. Unfortunately, in November 1995 a far-left sect, claiming to be saving the day laborers from corrupt leadership, stormed and occupied the building—another episode in the interminable sequence of ideological schisms that have plagued the yoseba movement and

Photo 4.2 San'ya: A Yoseba Street Demonstration. Hiyatoi Zenkyō has the power to muster day laborers and activists from all over Japan on occasion. A banner from Kamagasaki is visible in this San'ya street demonstration protesting against the murder of two San'ya Sogidan activists by the Kanamachi yakuza. Photo by Morita Ichiroh, January 1991. Originally published in Morita Ichiroh: *Tokyo Streets*. Tokyo: San'ichi Shobo, 1993. Reprinted by permission.

every other left-wing movement in Japan. Fortunately, the occupiers were eventually removed.

These left-wing feuds are increasingly irrelevant to the day laborers of San'ya. They are rather subdued these days, and as in the other yoseba, most are now well over fifty. The yakuza have also gone very quiet in the late 1990s, reflecting the steady dwindling of the financial rewards San'ya has to offer them.

Administration

During the 1960s San'ya's reputation for filth and violence became an embarrassment to the metropolitan authorities, which made rather pathetic attempts to legislate the place out of existence. The name was struck off the map in the course of boundary changes, with Kiyokawa-chō and Nihonzutsumi being expanded to cover the area that had belonged to San'ya-chō and the other central precinct, Tanaka-chō. To further obscure matters, the local welfare center and the landlord association now use the name Jōhoku ("North of the Castle") in their titles. This archaic name, dating from the Edo period when it designated the part of the city to the north of the shogunal palace, is another euphemism.

Administratively San'ya is now divided between the precincts of Kiyokawa-chō, Nihonzutsumi, and, north of Namidabashi, Minami-Senju. Minami-Senju is in Arakawa ward, while Kiyokawa-chō and Nihonzutsumi are in Taitō ward. Responsibility for employment and social welfare in San'ya is thus divided between three precincts and two wards, besides the city of Tokyo and the national government, giving ample potential for bureaucratic chaos and buck passing.

As in Kotobuki, there are two casual employment exchanges. The San'ya Labor Center *(San'ya Rōdō Sentaa)* is run by the Tokyo Metropolitan Government, via an external organization. Its shutters go up at 6:30 A.M. weekdays, and as at the Kotobuki Labor Center, the principle is first come, first served. There is only one set of shutters, however, and the men do not wait for them to go up. The technique is to press one's head as hard as possible against the slowly widening gap until it gets through, then force the rest of the body through and sprint to the clerks' windows. The tactics differ from those used at the Kotobuki Labor Center (p. 52):

> Kotobuki: Wait/jostle, sprint, wait/jostle, scrum.
> San'ya: Wait/jostle, limbo, sprint.

Such are the varied body techniques required of the modern day laborer.

San'ya's other employment exchange is a ten-minute walk away, on the far side of Tamahime Park. Jobs are given out at 6:45 A.M., so one has to hurry to try both places. This one is run by the Ministry of Labor, and uses the same fair shares rotation system as its sister exchange in Kotobuki. But whereas the Kotobuki officials express tired indifference, in San'ya there is an air of urgency and razzmatazz. A bell rings out and a young man calls the numbers rapidly and with great excitement, as if he were auctioning art treasures rather than offering casual labor contracts. Other young men in jeans and tee shirts rush around the bay in front of the job advertisements, grabbing handbooks from applicants and slamming them into wooden trays like basketball players making a slam dunk.

There tend to be somewhat more jobs available than in Kotobuki, mainly because of a modest government job-creation program. In spring 1994, for instance, there were two programs running. For a two-month period there would be thirty jobs a day weeding and cleaning at Yabashira Rei-en, a large municipal cemetery; and thirty-five jobs weeding, cleaning, and trimming trees at landfill projects in Tokyo Bay and along the verges of Tokyo roads. Both projects paid ¥9,000 after deductions. Since several thousand men use the employment exchange, one could rarely hope to get more than one day's work a month on these schemes. Several men told me that very little work was actually done, and that the programs were thinly disguised handouts.

It is very hard for those without jobs or homes to get accepted for social welfare in San'ya, and extralegal assistance is severely limited. In 1994 the Jōhoku Center had contracts for sixty beds a night at welfare institutions and boarding houses around Tokyo, for which it was getting several hundred applications a day. Instead of food vouchers the Center gave out emergency rations of four slices of bread and 200cc of milk, but not to the same man two days in a row, arguing that they were meant for strictly *temporary* relief. Relief measures elsewhere in Tokyo varied: some wards supplied simple food and clothing, others nothing.[10]

Recent Developments

By the mid-1990s, the smartly redecorated doya were mostly half-empty. Short of work and unable to afford the increased rents, a growing number of men were sleeping rough; in 1994 there were some four hundred men sleeping on the street every night. Another three hundred or so were sleeping a few miles away at Ueno station, and many more at Shinjuku station on the other side of Tokyo. Another factor moving men from the doya to the street was the city government's reluctance to house welfare recipients in doya. In the late 1990s the line began to soften, however. At the same time, the union of doya owners changed policy to deliberately target welfare recipients. Thus, some of them cut room rents to meet the upper limit paid by the city's welfare authorities: ¥2,100 a night.

These changes have greatly changed the San'ya population. There were some 9–10,000 day laborers based in San'ya in the 1980s, but veteran San'ya activist Nakamura Mitsuo estimated in September 1999 that there were some six thousand men living in the San'ya doya, roughly half of them on welfare and the rest day laboring. Some 2,500 men were collecting enough employment stamps to claim the day-laborer dole in San'ya, and these two factors formed the basis of his estimate that 2,500–3,000 day laborers were based in and around San'ya. Most of them were going directly to the worksite (*chokkō*). No more than five hundred would gather in the streets each morning,[11] and half of them would be homeless men left over from a night sleeping rough. Another six hundred men were living in shacks on the bank of the nearby Sumida River, and the total number of homeless people in the broad area around San'ya he estimated at 1,500–2,000. Virtually the only jobs left at the Tamahime employment exchange were on government job-creation projects, which had provided a fairly steady fifty thousand man-days of work a year for the last few years—enough for two or three days' poorly paid work a month for the average man.

Nakamura felt that the increase in homelessness could not entirely account for the declining doya population. Many men had also disappeared into work camps away from the yoseba where they would be fed and sheltered even when there was no work. He called these work camps "hanba," but they were similar in function to the *ninpu-dashi* of Western Japan (pp. 104–108). They were located in the prefectures around Tokyo (Kanagawa, Saitama, Ibaraki, Chiba), and sent men in minibuses to work at construction sites in and around Tokyo. Some hanba were very abusive and generated complaints of nonpayment of wages. Others were better, and once one left such a hanba it was very difficult to get one's place back: hence, men who went there tended to end up staying away from San'ya permanently.

Kamagasaki (Osaka)

Location and Landscape

> I hear that in the past, there were a number of outsiders who were separated from their guides, became deeply lost in the interior of this densely crowded district, and were never seen again. (Osaka magazine article on Kamagasaki, quoted in Takeda 1933)

Kamagasaki, sometimes referred to as "Nishinari" or "Airin," is located in Nishinari ward, central Osaka. It enjoys excellent communications, being right next to the Japan Railways Shin-Imamiya station, and with four more stations of private lines dotted around the district. Used by some twenty thousand day laborers, Kamagasaki is the biggest yoseba/doya-gai in Japan, with a fearsome reputation to match.

However, on my own visits to Kamagasaki I have been struck by how *small* the place feels. It is roughly square in shape, with sides of around six hundred meters (Genki 1989:3), making it about four times bigger than Kotobuki. You can comfortably walk across it in ten minutes. Even so, the relaxed, shambolical atmosphere may reflect a sense of safety in numbers. Kamagasaki feels somehow maternal, and its denizens like sons.

There are yakuza offices all over Kamagasaki; informants told me the whole district was carved up between seven or eight gangs, all affiliated to the Yamaguchi-gumi (Japan's biggest underworld syndicate, based in neighboring Kobe). The biggest gangs are the Kano-gumi and Azuma-gumi. They do the usual gambling and drugs business, and take protection money from stall holders in Kamagasaki's lively street market. But informants disagreed as to how heavily they were involved in the labor market.

History

Yamada Minoru, leader of *Kamanichirō*, the Kamagasaki Day Labor Union, the largest of several Kamagasaki unions, said in an interview on 7 August 1994 that institutionalized casual labor in Osaka dates back at least to the Tokugawa Era, when it was used by the *Bugyōsho*— the shogunal government in Osaka. People would flee from rural poverty in the surrounding villages and end up working as day laborers in public works, manufacturing, or as porters. Many lived in kichin yado at Nagamachi, near the present Nihonbashi, on what was then the southern edge of Osaka (cf. Leupp 1992:149).

The city authorities used a licensing system to concentrate the flophouses and their clients in one part of the city (Honma 1993:25). But the subsequent Meiji Era modernization necessitated a large labor pool and the Nagamachi slum grew rapidly. The city government vacillated between its traditional policy of tolerating and concentrating the flophouses and a new one of sweeping them away. The city's first experiment with slum clearance came in 1886 but failed (25).

Then in 1911, when the great Industrial Exhibition *(Kangyō Hakurankai)* was held in Osaka, the Nagamachi slum was demolished because it happened to lie in the route to be taken by the emperor on his way to the exhibition, and most of the population was relocated to Kamagasaki (Genki 1989:81).[12] By this time Kamagasaki also had a match factory on its turf, providing hazardous employment.

World War I and the rapid industrialization that followed turned Kamagasaki into a major yoseba. Most of the newcomers were single men, who soon came to outnumber the existing family households (Honma 1993:26). Kamagasaki was bombed to oblivion during World War II, but made a rapid recovery afterward, supplying casual dockers and building workers to the rebuilding of Japan. There were numerous men with families as well as solitary males.

The Kamagasaki Riots

In 1961 Kamagasaki had its first major riot—a legendary event to day laborers there. The following is an eyewitness account given to me by Shin'ya Noboru, a veteran day laborer of Kamagasaki:

It was August 1, 1961. I was walking along the main street in front of Kamagasaki . . . (when) I happened to witness a traffic accident. A man, a worker of Kamagasaki, was hit by a passing car and seriously injured. He was knocked sprawling, and he was bleeding all over. The driver didn't stop—he put his foot down and escaped. Well, I called an ambulance. But in those days, ambulances didn't like going into Kamagasaki . . . and besides, there was the question of who was going to pay for the medical treatment . . .

Anyway, I stood there next to this poor guy for an hour before the ambulance finally showed up. It wasn't moving very fast, and it didn't even have its siren going. It pulled up and a couple of ambulance men got out. They took one look at this man and said "Oh, he's already dead." They got out a *mushiro*, that's a kind of thick mat which they use to put over dead bodies . . .

But the thing is, he wasn't dead. He was still moving, anyone could see he wasn't dead. So I said "Hang on, he's still alive!" They ignored me and carried on wrapping him up in the mushiro. They weren't going to take him to the hospital, they were going to take him to the morgue, that was it. So I got angry, and I took a swing at one of them. Well, there was quite a big crowd gathered by now, and a lot of the others got angry too, and started shouting at the ambulance men, who got frightened and ran away. Then we turned over the ambulance, like this, heave-ho, heave-ho (*yoi-sho, yoi-sho*) until it went crash (*dokkan*) onto its side. We set fire to some newspapers and shoved them through the window and set the thing on fire.

By this time there was such a big crowd that the traffic couldn't get through. The first car to stop in the crowd, we smashed in its windows, the driver ran away, then we set fire to that as well. It's true, as you say, that the driver had nothing directly to do with the affair, but you have to remember that in those days . . . if you had a car it meant you were pretty rich. It was one of these rich people in his car who had knocked down that man in the first place, and hadn't bothered to stop; and because people in Kamagasaki were poor people, the ambulance hadn't shown any interest in saving the man's life. Do you see what I mean? It was the gap, the gap between rich and poor.

In the end we destroyed about twenty cars. Then the police came in and cordoned off the area . . . There was a Christian church near the station, called the Kyūrei Kaikan, which the cops used as a base, to treat their wounds, have a rest and a cup of tea, etc. To this day you'll find that most men in Kamagasaki hate that church, though in general they don't mind Christians.

We threw stones at the police for about a day and a half. We tore up all the paving stones and used up all the stones we could find lying around the area, and then people started going up the stations and collecting the stones they put under the rails as bedding.

People were selling stones, for ¥5 each. Ten for ¥50. Twenty for
¥100. In those days a navvy's daily wage was ¥500, and a room in
a doya was about ¥50, so ¥100 was a lot of money to pay for a bag
of stones, but somehow it didn't seem like much. And even if just
one of them hit a policeman, you got a lot of satisfaction out of it.

After a day and a half, we finally ran out of stones. For the next
day and a half there was a staring match *(nirami-ai)*. We workers
stood facing the police with just a few meters between us, in the
middle of the road, all silent . . . until the evening of August 3, and
then it started to rain. The workers were getting awfully wet, and
one by one they drifted away. Eventually I looked over my shoul-
der and saw there was hardly anyone left behind me, so I legged
it too, before the police arrested those who were left.

And that was the end of what came to be known as the First
Kamagasaki Riot. Though we didn't even know the word *riot*
(bōdō) in those days.

"What about the man in the original accident?"

"He did die. There was a riot going on all around him as he lay
there. Well, it was his fate to die. They'd even got the mushiro out
for him . . . It was his fate."[13]

I have heard and read several other accounts of this famous riot
(e.g., Arimura 1992:57–68; Honma 1993:57–59), differing in detail but
confirming the broad outline of Shin'ya's version. Everyone remem-
bers the traffic accident, and the detail about the stones for sale. The
riot was a defining moment in Kamagasaki history, and the first of
many. Riots are carefully counted in Kamagasaki, and have totalled
twenty-three to date. The chronological distribution has been very
uneven:

> 1961: First riot
> 1965: Second riot
> 1965-1973: Nineteen riots in eight years
> 1973–1990: No riots in seventeen years
> 1990: Twenty-second riot
> 1992: Twenty-third riot

The 1990 riot thus drew on a tradition that had been dormant for
some seventeen years. It was provoked by a leaked report to a local
newspaper to the effect that a senior police officer had been tipping
off the Kamagasaki yakuza about police raids on their gambling dens.
It was a major riot, lasting from October 2 to 7 and televised around
the world.[14] Press reports mentioned fifty-five arrests and 189 injuries,
including 150 policemen.[15]

The 1992 riot was triggered by the abrupt suspension of a special city government loan program to help jobless day laborers, on the grounds that the budget had dried up just nine days after the program was launched. Kamanichirō organized a sitdown protest at the welfare office by about 750 men, and fighting broke out when police tried to move them on. Rioting lasted two days; 2,500 police officers were mobilized.[16]

The police responded to the revival of Kamagasaki's rioting tradition by building a bigger, more central police station. There are also fifteen closed-circuit surveillance cameras dotted around the district. They were installed in November 1966, during the main rioting period. Significantly, none of them point at yakuza offices. In July 1990 a group of twelve residents filed suit at the Osaka District Court, demanding removal of the cameras and ¥14.4 million in compensation for gross violation of privacy. On 27 April 1994, the judge ruled that just one of the cameras—the one trained directly on the union offices—was a violation of privacy and ordered its removal. The other fourteen were deemed necessary for crime prevention. No compensation was awarded.[17]

Administration and Employment

The day labor market in Kamagasaki differs from those in Kotobuki and San'ya in two important respects.

Firstly, the dualistic approach found in the other yoseba, with separate labor exchanges run by central and local government, is greatly modified in Kamagasaki. Both institutions are housed in a massive concrete structure called the Airin Labor Center (*Airin Rōdō Sentaa*), built in 1970 at a cost of ¥2.3 billion. This building was the model for the smaller one in Kotobuki. However, in Kamagasaki the office run by the Ministry of Labor makes no attempt to supply jobs—it merely processes the day laborers' white handbooks and pays out the unemployment insurance.[18] The legal job market is handled by the local office, which, as in Kotobuki and San'ya, is an external organization of local government.

The day laborers generally hate the office run by the Ministry of Labor, and assaulted it in the spring of 1994 as part of a campaign for better employment and welfare measures to deal with the recession. In contrast, they feel fairly positive toward the locally administered Center, the staff of which includes Sumida Ichirō, a prominent Burakumin activist, and Arimura Sen, the cartoonist whose creation, Kama-yan, is the dominant fictional representation of day laborers.[19]

Photo 4.3　Kamagasaki: The Airin Labor Exchange. Note the recruiters' mini-buses parked in the lee of the building, and the crowds of men milling around in hope of jobs. The taller building behind the labor exchange is a hospital. Photo by Nakajima Satoshi, 1994. Originally published in *Teiten Kansoku: Kamagasaki* (Fixed-Point Observation: Kamagasaki). Osaka: Yōbunkan Shuppan, 1999. Reprinted by permission.

Secondly, employers in the other two yoseba must choose between regulated recruitment at the exchanges and informal recruitment on the streets; but in Kamagasaki they may formally recruit on the streets, under a system called the "face-to-face formula" *(aitai hōshiki)*. The employer registers with the center and promises to honor his respon-sibilities for unemployment stamps, health insurance, etc. He is then given a permit that allows him to recruit in Kamagasaki. Typically, he sends along his own recruiter in a minibus that will carry the workers to the site. The minibuses gather around the Center and the recruiters display the terms of the jobs available on official yellow placards taped to the minibus' windscreen. They stand near the minibuses and nego-tiate with the workers directly.

For the employers this system has the great advantage of en-abling them to pick and choose workers taken on each day. The reason the Ministry of Labor's office does not handle job introduc-tions is that it would be legally obliged to hand them out fairly using the rotation (*rinban*) system. With 2,600 handbook-carrying day laborers over the age of sixty,[20] employers would not accept the unfavorable odds against getting a fit, strong man. The Ministry of Labor's withdrawal from the labor market, and the invention of the face-to-face formula (in the 1970s), both happened in response to street-level realities.

For the workers the system affords a greater degree of legal protection than with unlicensed recruiters, and gives some kind of framework for the union to use when negotiating with employers. In 1994 members of Kamanichirō told me with some pride that they had established a minimum day wage in Kamagasaki, which usually went up by ¥500 each year. The recession prevented any raises after 1993, but for five years the union managed to defend the 1993 level of ¥13,000 a day for unskilled labor. By 1998, conditions had deteriorated and a small but growing number of employers were paying less than ¥13,000, despite an energetic union campaign to defend the minimum wage.

But the face-to-face system also has a serious disadvantage for the worker. It makes it easier for employers to dump men who are viewed as too old or too weak, or as potential troublemakers. The divide between viable and nonviable workers is wider and deeper in Kamagasaki, and it was here that I encountered many of the most and least successful day laborers. One of the most successful was Ogata Haruo:

> He is short and slight of build, with glasses. Ogata is forty years old, hails from Saitama prefecture, and first came to Kamagasaki some ten years ago. He is a second son, with one older brother, a younger sister and two younger brothers. He is a determined libertarian, who says he favors day laboring because it enables him to work on his own terms.
>
> A skilled house-carpenter, he commands ¥20,000 a day or thereabouts. He has built and owns no fewer than three houses: one in Wakayama prefecture, one in Yamaguchi prefecture (both rural districts of western Japan), and one in the Philippines, in a small town about an hour's drive out of Manila. He has been spending over half the year in the Philippines for the last five years, avoiding the colder months in Osaka. He says he generally spends three to six months in Kamagasaki and then uses the money amassed to spend six to nine months in the Philippines, where the yen is strong and the cost of living much cheaper.
>
> He has a Filipina girlfriend who lives in the house near Manila and teaches at a local school. He says he is seriously considering marrying her.[21]

Photo 4.4 Kamagasaki Day Laborer Prepares for Work. Photo taken in a Kamagasaki doya room by Nakajima Satoshi. Originally published in Nakajima Satoshi: *Tanshin Seikatsusha* (People Who Live on Their Own). Osaka: Kaifu-sha, 1990. Reprinted by permission.

Men like Ogata displayed a confidence and *joie de vivre* that I rarely noticed in eastern Japan. At the other extreme, Kamagasaki also had far more homeless street dwellers than any other yoseba. In the spring of 1994 the union had succeeded (by violent direct action) in getting the city government to leave the shutters at the Airin Labor Center open overnight so that men could sleep there for a few weeks. Every night there were some five hundred men lying on dirty futons and bits of cardboard at the Center, watched over by union members. By 1998, the Center was being kept open for longer periods and there were up to one thousand men sleeping there. In 1999 the Center stayed open at night until the end of February and was then reopened from April to July after intense negotiations. In September 1999 the city authorities attempted to house the Kamagasaki homeless in giant tents nearby. On the first night it rained and the tents were found to leak. An authoritative survey by sociologists from Osaka City University found 8,660 homeless people in Osaka in early 1999—the highest official figure recorded in a Japanese city in decades.

When day laborers lose their ability to support themselves, they find themselves in a much harsher bureaucratic environment in Osaka than in Tokyo or Yokohama. The city government will not allow people to go on welfare unless they are clearly physically unable to work and have a doctor's letter to prove it. The sad irony, that welfare policy encourages people to make themselves ill, is at its strongest here. Nor is there much in the way of food handouts or job-creation programs.[22] Kamanichirō leaders told me that for them, welfare was a secondary issue. Handouts were humiliating; the key slogan was still "Give us a job!" (*shigoto yokose*).

Parallels with San'ya and Kotobuki

Though it happened earlier, the shift from Nagamachi to Kamagasaki parallels the Honjo/San'ya and Sakuragi-chō/Kotobuki shifts in Tokyo and Yokohama. There is a consistent picture of yoseba being placed, tolerated, controlled, and shifted around town to suit the authorities. Like San'ya, Kamagasaki is located on the site of a former execution ground (Genki 1989:79) and again like San'ya it has had its name removed from the official map, though again much earlier, in 1922 (Genki 1989:82; Honma 1993:27). Honma reckons that the name was abolished to punish a district that had been at the heart of the 1918 rice riots (Honma 1993:28). In a postwar development, the city government has officially renamed the doya-gai "Airin-chiku," which roughly means "District of Neighborly Love." The new name is heartily loathed by most inhabitants.

Again like San'ya, Kamagasaki has a historical association with the Burakumin outcasts, though some think the relationship is subtly different. Mizuno Ashira, a day laborer and activist of Kamagasaki, remarks that San'ya "was originally a Buraku town," whereas in Osaka the two groups have tended to be adjacent rather than overlapping. Today one of the biggest Burakumin centers in Japan is at Tsurumibashi, just the other side of Route 26 from Kamagasaki. Mizuno says he prefers the Kamagasaki layout because "Burakumin have always discriminated against day laborers."[23]

Yet again like San'ya, Kamagasaki is located next to a celebrated red-light district, in this case Tobita. Tobita was one of Osaka's seven cemeteries in the seventeenth century and became Osaka's main red-light district in 1919, after its predecessor, at Minami, burned down (Constantine 1993:20). In 1994 Tobita was still surrounded by the remains of a high wall, which Mizuno told me had once functioned to prevent women from escaping. Within this symbolic boundary, Tobita still affects the air of an Edo-period licensed quarter, with brothels designed to look like quaint rural tea houses.

Kamagasaki has a street market bigger than San'ya's. Many are run by ethnic Koreans, though Koreans play a smaller role in Kamagasaki than in Kotobuki.

Sasashima (Nagoya)

Sasashima is located in the major central Japanese city of Nagoya. It is a yoseba without a doya-gai. There are doya-type hotels in Nagoya, but they are scattered around several different districts and there is no residential center, no permanent place of community, for the day laborers here. By day Sasashima is an ordinary commercial district, a couple of wide streets with small shops and offices in the lee of the gigantic Sumitomo Life Insurance Building. The only clue to Sasashima's early-morning identity is the Naka Public Employment Exchange, located across the road from Sumitomo Life. It is a general employment exchange, mostly catering to people looking for long-term jobs. But round the back, fronting onto a narrow side street, is an inconspicuous door, which most people only ever see closed by blue-grey metal shutters. This is the casual labor exchange.

From about four o'clock every weekday morning, several hundred men gather in the pitch-black streets, warming themselves at bonfires, looking out for minibuses, heading off for work. Then the sun comes up and the remaining men slowly disperse. The bonfires are doused, a few men selling old clothes and bric-a-brac pack up their stalls, and by the time the smartly suited employees of Sumitomo Life show up for work the yoseba has disappeared, leaving only a few blackened areas in the gutter.

Activists and police used to concur that some three thousand day laborers used Sasashima. In a September 1999 interview, Ōnishi Yutaka of Sasanichirō, the local day laborer union, estimated that roughly 2,500 men were still using the yoseba. Some 1,500 turned up on the average morning, about a third of them actually finding work. There were just over a thousand homeless people around Nagoya station and Sakai, the areas covered by Sasanichirō's twice-weekly patrols. Ōnishi reckoned there were perhaps 1,500 people homeless in Nagoya as a whole.

Employment at Sasashima is almost entirely in the informal sector. During the several days I spent at Sasashima in November 1994, there were never more than two jobs on offer at the exchange itself, and usually there were none at all. To the day laborers the exchange is simply a place to collect the daily dole. It is run by the Ministry of Labor and there is no alternative locally run exchange of the kind found at the larger yoseba.

Officials I interviewed at the exchange insisted that the minibuses that recruit on the street were licensed, under the Kamagasaki-type face-to-face formula. However, there were no licenses on the mini-buses. The officials said there were eighteen companies licensed to recruit in Sasashima, but Ōnishi, leader of Sasanichirō at the time, had a list of about one hundred employers using Sasashima. This meant the vast majority were unlicensed. The officials admitted they had never checked the minibuses. They appeared to be pursuing a policy of willful neglect.

Licensed or not, Ōnishi says employing companies have to pay off the local yakuza, the Inabachi-gumi, at ¥30,000 a month for the privilege of recruiting in Sasashima. Officially, the money is paid to an Inabachi front called the Nagoya Construction Friendship Association *(Meiken Shinboku-kai)* as a "membership fee." In 1994 the Inabachi were the only gang in Nagoya not yet absorbed into the massive Kobe-based Yamaguchi-gumi syndicate.[24] As in Kotobuki, the casual labor racket appears to be too small to interest the big fish. Even so, in late 1994 the employment exchange was paying out a total of ¥170 million a month to some two thousand claimants of the day laborer dole.[25]

Union activists say that unlicensed recruiters seldom supply unemployment insurance stamps, and even the labor exchange officials admitted this was a problem. Employment stamp fraud seems to be widespread; four arrests were made by Nagoya police in October 1994. The offense, "forging a seal on an official revenue stamp" *(yūin shubi gizō)* carries a maximum penalty of five years in prison, though one year is typical.[26]

The struggle between capital and labor appeared to be fought out in Sasashima with less state intervention than in the larger yoseba. Many people said it was extremely difficult to qualify for social welfare in Nagoya, and there were no food handouts or job creation programs. This was still the case in 1999. Ōnishi ascribed this lack of concern among the authorities to the fact that the lack of a doya-gai at the yoseba meant there was no center for the eruption of riots—the ultimate sanction of day laborers.[27]

However, the day laborers of Nagoya showed great spirit. In conversations around the bonfires of Sasashima I rarely heard pessimistic or self-pitying talk about the recession. Even those who were living in cardboard boxes seemed to be coping,[28] and several of them enjoyed relentlessly arguing about history and politics. It was tempting to draw the Thatcherite conclusion that the absence of the nanny state had made these men more independent-minded than some in Kotobuki; alternatively, the separation between residence (doya) and employment (yoseba) perhaps meant that despairing day laborers were away from Sasashima.

History

Like the other yoseba, Sasashima has had its official name changed. Today it appears on the map as part of Mei'eki Minami 1-chōme (Nagoya Station South, 1st precinct). The name "Sasashima" is attached only to a bus stop and a small police box on the corner of the yoseba. But the name also appears on several large office buildings in the area, suggesting that it is less stigmatized than "San'ya" or "Kamagasaki." I believe the reason for this is that "Sasashima" ("Bamboo-grass Island") is itself a euphemism. The district occupies a small part of what was Nagoya's most notorious prewar slum district, Suisha ("Water-wheel").

Hasegawa (1994:2) has traced this place name all the way back to 1670,[29] when there really was a water wheel there. Workers started to congregate at Suisha with the construction of Nagoya's railways from about 1877, and by 1890 there was a major slum there. By the time of World War II there were some ninety kichin yado at Suisha, about one-fifth of which belonged to a Taiwanese chain called "Kiraku," but the whole district was firebombed to extinction by the allies (Yamamoto 1986:1, 49). After the war Suisha was taken off the map, and unlike their counterparts in Tokyo, Osaka, and Yokohama, the Nagoya government tried to plan the doya-gai out of existence in fact as well as name.

After the war, a lively slum-type environment developed around Nagoya station, with a black market, a Burakumin ghetto, and numerous boarding houses for day laborers (ninpu-dashi; see pp. 104–108). But the authorities finally broke up the district around 1962, and today the day laborers of Nagoya are scattered around the city, except for the early morning when they gather at Sasashima. The city has only one other casual labor exchange, at Atsuta, and officials at the Sasashima exchange told me that only about fifty workers regularly used it. Another one, at Ozune, was shut down in 1988 and there are no others anywhere in Aichi prefecture.

Sasanichirō estimates that 98 percent of all one-day, cash-in-hand jobs are negotiated at the yoseba in Sasashima. But for period contracts the split is about fifty-fifty between the yoseba and recruiters who pick up unemployed men at parks and stations. The union says the day-wage starts at ¥10,000 at the yoseba, but some of the contracts arranged outside the yoseba pay as little as ¥6,000 a day, reduced to ¥2–3,000 after deductions for room, food, etc.

Day Laboring in Fukuoka Prefecture

Although most day labor in this industrial area of northern Kyushu is informally arranged, even official statistics show it as the top day-laboring prefecture in Japan in FY1990, well ahead of second-placed Tokyo in terms of person-days of work supplied by casual labor exchanges (table 26). This reflects the rapid decline of the coal and steel industries in northern Kyushu. As late as 1994, nearly 90 percent of jobs at the prefecture's casual labor exchanges were being supplied by public agencies to people covered by the "unemployment counter-measures" program (p. 30).[30] This program was scrapped in April 1996, with a doubtless severe impact on five to six hundred people. Hence in part the drastic decline in Fukuoka's figures for FY1996 (table 26).

Chikkō (Fukuoka City)

Chikkō is the smallest yoseba I have visited. It consists of a portion of a single street leading to the central wharf at Hakata, Fukuoka's main port. The location reflects its original function, as a place for hiring dock workers, and even today dock work accounts for 40 percent of demand for casual labor (union estimate), since containerization has progressed relatively slowly here. The other 60 percent of demand comes mostly from construction. Perhaps two hundred men use Chikkō fairly regularly.

As in Sasashima, residential and employment functions are separate. There is only one, very run-down doya in the Chikkō district itself; there are five more at Dekimachi, more than a mile further south. Inevitably the name "Dekimachi" is no longer on the map—it is now part of Hakata Eki-mae 1-chōme ('Hakata Station Front, 1st Precinct').

In Fukuoka, the disintegration of the day-laboring lifestyle has gone a step farther than in Sasashima, for even the formal and informal labor markets are far apart. The only casual labor exchange is run by the Ministry of Labor at Ginsui, a good two miles southwest from Chikkō. In July 1994, the Ginsui exchange—a shabby little bungalow set in a garden of weeds and rubbish—had almost ceased to function as a supplier of jobs. In the first quarter of 1994 it transacted an average of 147 person-days of casual labor per month, barely enough to sustain ten day laborers. This was down from a monthly average of 971 person-days in 1992 and 448 in 1993.[31]

The Fukuoka Day Labor Union (*Fukunichirō*) has long and fruitlessly campaigned to have a casual labor exchange set up at Chikkō. The one small concession the union has won is to have the Ginsui exchange open a little later in the morning—at 7:30 A.M.—to give day laborers time to cycle over there after first trying their luck at Chikkō. So the men look for work with the tehaishi at Chikkō, and then trek to Ginsui to claim their dole payment if they fail and are eligible. With no employment officials at Chikkō, the tehaishi can do much as they please.

Fukunichirō says the biggest yakuza gang in Fukuoka is the Izugumi, but it has no interest in day laborers. The Chikkō yakuza belong to the Hagoromo-kai, a Korean-led gang. They are fairly well-behaved *(otonashii)*. Another gang called the Umezu-gumi is run by Burakumin.

Workers' Boarding Houses in Fukuoka

The main alternative for day laborers unable to make a living with these thoroughly unhelpful arrangements is to enter a workers' boarding house or *rōdō-geshuku*, also known colloquially as *ninpu-dashi* ("navvy-supplier").[32]

The workers' boarding house is a highly significant institution in the world of Japanese casual labor. It combines the functions of the doya (cheap, low quality accommodation) with those of the tehaishi (introductions for casual work). The worker relies on the owner of the boarding house for shelter, food, and employment. The wages are typically paid by the owner of the boarding house (who later settles up with the employer). Rent, meals, and sundries are deducted from the wage.

The boarding house system concentrates enormous power in the hands of the owner, who combines the roles of employer and landlord. Compared with yoseba day laboring, it leaves the worker with far less freedom. Whether he enjoys greater security in recompense will depend on the character and economic circumstances of the owner of the boarding house. Day laborers seem to prefer the street-corner approach when work is plentiful, tending to retreat into a boarding house when it is not. However exploitative the arrangement may be, at least the man will have a roof over his head and three meals a day for some time.[33]

In Fukuoka city, the boarding houses dominate the casual labor market. Ōtō Katsu, a leading activist in Fukunichirō, estimated that there were about ten thousand day laborers in the city, but only two hundred of these were to be found at Chikkō. The others were mostly in boarding houses. He said the recession had forced many men into boarding houses, which tended to attract older men. Broadly speaking, yoseba workers tended to be in their forties and boarding house workers in their fifties and up.[34]

Geographically, Fukuoka's key day-laboring locations are linked by the Mikasa River. The Chikkō yoseba stands just to the west of the estuary; the main boarding house districts are a little further upriver, also on the west bank, with the main Burakumin and North-affiliated Korean districts on the opposite side; and the Dekimachi doya-gai is another mile upriver, again on the west bank. The Ginsui labor exchange is on the west bank of the next river along, the Nakagawa. Rivers run through just about all day-laboring districts in Japanese cities, perhaps because of historical associations with sanitation problems and bad building land.[35]

The boarding houses vary greatly in style. Some are shabby little buildings resembling doya; others are smart new multistory buildings, with covered forecourts for minibuses to park. Clearly some people are doing very well out of them.

Wages are low in Fukuoka. The going rate for unskilled construction work was ¥9,000 in 1995, and even trusted semiregulars seldom made more than ¥13,000. Ōtō said that men who lived in boarding houses were lucky if they still had ¥6,000 in hand after paying for board and lodging.[36] This assumes that the proprietor has supplied a day's work; even if he has not, board and lodging are still deducted from the worker's account. Add in the fact that wages are often withheld for several weeks, during which the management of the boarding house will lend money at interest, sell alcohol and cigarettes at inflated prices, charge extra for showers and TV, etc., and one has a recipe for exploitation. Many informants accused the boarding houses of deliberately taking on too many men, forcing them to take days off in rotation, or even giving them so little work that they ended up owing the boarding house money. The system destroys solidarity, for the owner may well find more jobs for obedient workers and fewer for "troublemakers."

Until 1985, these labor-supplying boarding houses were illegal, though the police usually turned a blind eye. But in that year the new Labor Dispatch Business Law *(Jinzai Hakengyō-hō)* legalized the practice of agencies taking money from an employer and paying their own, lower wage to the worker.

I had not even heard the terms "ninpu-dashi" or "rōdō-geshuku" until I arrived in Fukuoka. I subsequently learned that there is a big boarding house district at Taishō in Osaka, quite near to Kamagasaki and used by some seven thousand people, that they exist in Kyoto too, and that they are the dominant form of casual employment in Fukuoka's neighboring city of Kitakyushu (see pp. 106–108). The pattern seems to be fairly clear: ninpu-dashi are strong in the west of Japan and yoseba in the east.

Ōtō suggests that the reason why boarding houses are prevalent in northern Kyushu may be because of the area's connection with the coal and steel industries, which have a tradition of tight control of workers through the naya system (see p. 22), which Ōtō sees as the forerunner of the modern ninpu-dashi.[37]

Most informants agreed that the boarding houses were gaining ground steadily, thanks to legalization, plus the recession and the aging of the day laborer population. This signified a shift among day laborers toward security at the expense of freedom. In the worst cases, I was told, men got so heavily into debt with the boarding house that they were reduced to virtual slavery.

Workers' Boarding Houses in Kitakyushu

A one-hour drive east of Fukuoka lies the sprawling industrial city of Kitakyushu, home of Nippon Steel, the world's biggest steel maker.

Casual labor in Kitakyushu has closely followed the fortunes of the steel industry, its principal twentieth-century employer. The prewar yoseba was in a famous slum district called Harunomachi (Spring-town), next to the Yahata steelworks. But since the 1960s the industry has declined and Nippon Steel has gradually run down Yahata.[38] In the 1970s the main yoseba was at Senbō, just next to Nippon Steel's Tobata works, which are still functioning. However, when I got to Senbō in the summer of 1994 I found that the yoseba had virtually withered away, with no more than a couple of dozen men standing in the street.[39] Even these men were not necessarily looking for a recruiter. Many already had work arranged and were just waiting for the truck or minibus to pick them up. They were living in boarding houses, which dominate the casual labor market in Kitakyushu even more than in Fukuoka.

Kamata (1971) insists that large-scale use of casual workers was a consistent policy of Yahata Steel (which merged with Fuji Steel to form Nippon Steel in 1970) from its inception at the turn of the century. Originally, when the firm was still a public enterprise, the casuals were kept in massive dormitories called "thousand person huts" (sennin koya; Kamata 1971:72, 120); later, when the firm had been privatized, the relationship was made indirect and the boarding houses came into their own. After the war the institutions were made illegal under article 44 of the Employment Security Law, remaining illegal until 1985 (see pp. 30, 105).

Illegality just made the boarding house business more brutal. Kamata has a vivid description of the violence and coercion of postwar casual employment at Yahata Steel.[40] The boarding houses peaked around 1960, when there were 150–160 of them at Yahata, supplying three to four thousand workers a day, and another fifty at Tobata, supplying about three thousand a day. By 1970 there were only forty left at Yahata, supplying six hundred workers (Kamata 1971:70). Initially some workers shifted to Tobata, where new plant was being constructed, but by the time Kamata wrote his book (1971) the Tobata boom was over and the boarding houses were struggling along by gradually shifting from steel work to construction.

Amid his horrific accounts of workers being beaten up for trying to escape from their boarding houses, Kamata is careful to mention that "these were not all violent boarding-houses dominated by underworld gangs. It is said that there were also some extremely homely *(katei-teki)* places run by Japan-resident Koreans" (Kamata 1971:70). By the time I reached Kitakyushu in 1994, the entire boarding house industry appeared to be in Korean hands. Both Chongryun and Mindan (see glossary) had branches near Senbō, and the former was a sumptuous new building. No one I asked could name a Japanese-run boarding house.

I was fortunate enough to have several interviews with a Korean widow who runs a boarding house in a district of Tobata called Torihata.[41] She viewed the term "ninpu-dashi" as insulting and preferred "rōdō-geshuku." Her son was still more sensitive: He thought "rōdō-geshuku" was also discriminatory, and preferred *jinzai hakken-gyō*, meaning "personnel dispatch business."

Her company had a name ending in *Kōgyō* (Industries), making it sound like a construction company. One worker said it was embarrassing to admit to fellow workers that one was with a ninpu-dashi, and better to simply mention this respectable-sounding name. It was a sizeable operation, dispatching ninety to one hundred men to work sites in Kitakyushu and neighboring cities every weekday morning, in a fleet of twenty vehicles. It was semi-residential, with thirty men living on the premises and another sixty-odd showing up for work. The company paid ¥8–10,000 a day, rising to ¥12,000 for more skilled work. It charged ¥900 a night for a three-mat room (including a ¥100 TV charge), and an extra ¥300 for breakfast (optional). The final employers were billed monthly in arrears, and the company's margin was "¥1–2,000" per person-day.

When work was short, some men might be asked to "rest" for a period. The widow said that residents of the boarding house would generally be given preference in job allocation, but if they were laid off for some time and ran short of cash, they would be allowed credit against their room bill. She also said that she looked after ill workers and helped them to get compensation and social welfare in serious cases. She stressed that the business was run like one big family *(katei-teki)* and was providing shelter and gainful employment to men who would otherwise be sleeping in the street. Certainly I noticed only one possibly homeless person while in Tobata.

Wages were paid in cash, at the end of each day's work. I observed this happening. The widow said this was the usual practice in Tobata, but mentioned some larger, more impersonally run boarding houses in nearby Kokura where wages were withheld for a week or ten days. She had heard of many cases of abuse at these places, such as deliberately forgetting about overtime, or refusing to pay a worker's wages if he wanted to leave before payday.

She confirmed that the entire industry was run by Koreans. Asked if there were also Koreans in the work force, she said there were very few: the Koreans in Tobata could get better work. She said the recession had damaged her business, but there seemed to be plenty of activity, and her father appeared to be driving a Bentley in British racing green. Both Chongryun and Mindan, the equivalent organization for Japan-resident Koreans supporting South Korea, had major offices in the region.

Men working for this boarding house confirmed most of the above, and said it was one of the better places. One of them claimed, however, that the cozy, family-style relationship between employer and workers only lasted for as long as the latter were fit enough to generate income for the former. The boarding house would dump anyone who was reckoned to be past it. The widow did say that she never employed old people, and that the average age of her workers was about forty-five.

She repeatedly described her workers as diligent *(majime)* and obedient *(sunao)*. She contrasted them with the workers in Senbō, who she said were sometimes very badly behaved.

Other Yoseba

Tokyo-Yokohama Region

In Tokyo, as well as San'ya there are smaller concentrations of day laborers at Takadanobaba and Kamata, and another casual labor exchange at Tawaramachi. There used to be a sizeable day-laboring district at Nakamura-chō in Yokohama, but it has gone (see pp. 173–174).

Kawasaki, a major city between Tokyo and Yokohama, has a sizeable yoseba at Harappa, used by several hundred workers. It combines a street labor market with a Ministry of Labor casual employment exchange, but as in Sasashima, there is no doya-gai. Nor is there a union in Harappa, but the Kotobuki union, Junichirō, frequently sends teams of activists to Kawasaki, and there is a volunteer homeless patrol there on Wednesday nights. Unionists, volunteers, and day laborers forced a series of intense negotiations with the city government of Kawasaki during 1994, with important results. The city started to provide emergency food rations to homeless men, along the lines of the Yokohama system, and arranged temporary accommodation in a municipal gymnasium for the New Year period. This has now become established practice. However, the city government threatened to cut off the food rations in 1999, citing budgetary constraints.

Osaka-Kyoto-Kobe Region

In Osaka, Fukada says that Kamagasaki has been acting like a "black hole," drawing in workers from peripheral yoseba. The two smaller yoseba within Osaka, at Tendoku and Chidoribashi, have both disappeared, as have several medium-sized yoseba in Osaka's neighboring cities. Matsuzawa (1988a:175) mentions five hundred men using the yoseba at Deashiki in Amagasaki city (Hyogo prefecture), but unionists and workers in Kamagasaki confirmed that the place was a shadow of its former self.[42] By contrast, a *hanba-gai* (boarding house district) at Hatsushima, also in Amagasaki, is reportedly thriving.[43]

The yoseba at Kyoto is called Uchihama. It is very small, and day laborers are widely dispersed. Many are homeless and a volunteer group called *Yomawari no Kai* (The Night Rounds Association) is working to help them.[44]

The city of Kobe used to have a nationally notorious slum at Shinkawa, luridly described by Axling (1932:39–40). The district is associated with the crusading Christian Socialist Kagawa Toyohiko (1888–1960), an early campaigner for the rights of day laborers, who is the subject of Axling's book.

A postwar English-language account of longshoring at Kobe harbor in the early 1960s (Mori 1962) estimates that day laborers were doing 70–80 percent of the work (38). Mori describes brutal, inhuman treatment of *ankō* ("drifters and day laborers who hire out as dock-hands") by the local tehaishi, and an ongoing battle by the local authorities to put the tehaishi out of business and control the labor market through the Kobe Harbor Employment Security Office. Interestingly, Mori also says that the daily wage for casual dock work at Kobe harbor was in the region of ¥1,000, at a time when many workers around Japan were making less than ¥300: " . . . the *ankō*'s daily wage, therefore, represents a labor victory . . . the *ankō* who sell their labor strictly on a money basis represent a 'capitalistic' form of laborer seldom seen in Japan. It is ironical, but to be deeply pondered, that such hard-headed bargaining can take place so successfully at the very depths of Japanese society" (Mori 1962:42).

Day laborers in Osaka say that most day labor in Kobe is now done by men travelling from Kamagasaki, an hour's train ride away. Kamagasaki was the base from which day laborers set out to help clear up the wreckage left by the Kobe earthquake.

Hiroshima

According to Professor Aoki Hideo,[45] there is no doya-gai in Hiroshima, but there are two small yoseba—one near the station (mostly for construction work) and the other near the docks (for dock work). Only about fifty men use each yoseba. Of course there are more than one hundred day laborers in Hiroshima, but most of them are in semiregular employment with employers who "know their face" (*kaozuke*).

Since the labor market is small and there is no doya-gai, long-term migrant workers are rarely drawn to Hiroshima. Instead, most of the day laborers are from towns and villages within the prefecture, working to supplement inadequate farming incomes. When work is not available, they tend to go back to their homes rather than onto the streets. Hence, there are relatively few homeless workers in Hiroshima—about thirty in 1994–1995 by Aoki's estimate.

The Deep South

Ōtō[46] says that Kagoshima has a small yoseba at a district called Tenmonkan. There is also a minor yoseba, said to be used by about fifty men, at Shūri, in Naha, the prefectural capital of Okinawa. Though few in number, the day laborers of Naha support a branch of Hiyatoi Zenkyō (the National Federation of Day Laborer Unions). They are seldom able to send delegates to conferences, but always send fraternal messages.

The North

I have not come across surviving yoseba or doya-gai in any northern city. This may reflect the cold climates of these cities. Matsuzawa (1988b:147) says there used to be yoseba in Sapporo, Aomori, Sendai, and Kanazawa—four cities with harsh winters—but my informants insist that there are no yoseba in those cities today.

Summary

To summarize, the yoseba/doya-gai in Tokyo and Osaka have much longer histories than Kotobuki's, with intensely polluted associations. In Nagoya and Fukuoka, yoseba are ad hoc spaces with no residential dimension. The worker's boarding houses dominate casual employment in western Japan, especially Kyushu. The bureaucratic approach to day laborers is different in every city. Even so, all the cities I visited had a recognizable day laboring scene. Ultimately the similarities between yoseba are more striking than the admittedly numerous differences.

Noriyuki

I first met Noriyuki on a street corner in Kotobuki, very early in the morning of Tuesday, 19 October 1993. I last saw him two days later. He was short, stocky, weatherbeaten, looking tough and leathery but getting on in years. Minus a few teeth.

Noriyuki said he was born in Hokkaido on 11 February 1939. He used to work in the famous Akabira coal mine until it closed in the late 1970s. After that he was a yakuza for five years, but got fed up with that and became a touring day laborer: Kamagasaki, San'ya, Kotobuki, Takadanobaba, Sasashima. For most of 1993 he was struggling along on about two days' work a week.

Every year he conducted his own winter campaign. In early November, he would look for a big construction project with a work camp (hanba) away from the city, and work very hard through November and December. Hanba life being inexpensive and devoid of amusement, he could usually save ¥2–300,000. Come the year-end festivities, he would choose a nice sauna[47] and live there through the New Year and January: a kind of hibernation.

He said he never went for period contracts at other times of year. It was too tiring and boring. But, "New Year is completely different. Spending New Year in a yoseba is just too miserable." Apparently that unpleasant prospect gave him extra energy.

During the summer months, Noriyuki said he sometimes took to the country, doing seasonal work and living off the land. He ate snakes, mice, and dogs—but not cats, which tasted vile. He loved exotic foods (getemono); dogs were his favorite.

He had not been back to Hokkaido in ten years. His parents were long dead. He was the sixth and youngest son. He had brothers and sisters in Hokkaido, but "that's no reason to go back." He liked children, but had never married or had any of his own.

He could not use the Ministry of Labor employment exchanges because he had had his handbook confiscated for forging

(continues)

112

(continued)

employment stamps. When I met him he was struggling to get work in Kotobuki, although he said he got up earlier every morning—at 3:30 A.M. on the day I last saw him. He said he was dreading asking his chōba-san (landlady) to wait another day for the rent, but knew from experience that morning was the best time to do this: chōba-sans grew steadily more hostile as the day wore on. If he left it till evening he was likely to find that the room had been emptied and his possessions were lying around the stairwell.

I lent him ¥2,200 for a day's rent. He was staying at a relatively expensive doya because he could not bear to be without TV. He accepted the money with an enormous smile and promised to pay me back the following week: he had a couple of days' work lined up on a demolition job the following Monday and Tuesday. But I wasn't able to be in Kotobuki on those particular days . . . and I never saw him again.

5

Who Are These Men?

"T HE SOLITARY WORKERS of Kamagasaki and San'ya did not grow on the branches of trees," observes Funamoto. "It follows that somewhere there is a 'factory producing low-wage workers.' That factory is located among the disintegrating farming and fishing villages, among the Ainu settlements, in Okinawa, in the unliberated Buraku, in the rationalized coalmines, in the Korean settlements" (Funamoto 1985:169). As we shall see, my own findings only partially support Funamoto's observation.[1]

Geographical Background

Geographically, the overwhelming majority of the Japanese day laborers in Kotobuki come from rural backgrounds,[2] with concentrations in the rural northeastern prefectures and the Kanto region (table 27). A 1992 survey by Junichirō found that nearly 60 percent of the population came from these two regions, and my own very small sample concurs. However, all districts are represented to some degree, and locally born people are decidedly the exception. The Junichirō figure for Tokyo and Kanagawa combined is only 21.4 percent and my own is 17 percent. Adding in the other major urban prefectures of Osaka and Aichi still gives only 25 percent in the Junichirō survey and 17 percent in mine.[3]

The only major divergence between Junichirō's figures and my own concerns the Okinawan community. My figure of 22 percent is certainly too high—a result of associating with a couple of Okinawans who introduced me to their friends—but the union's figure of 0.8 percent is certainly too low. There is a distinct Okinawan community in Kotobuki. Its members tend not to use the free prefab accommodation set up in Kotobuki during the Winter Survival Campaign (pp. 138–140), which is where Junichirō annually collects its information.

Occupational Background

On occupational background, my sample is too small and haphazard to say anything authoritative. However, rough patterns do emerge from the fifty-six men who told me about their working life before coming to Kotobuki (table 28).

The range of previous occupations is very wide, a reminder of the truth that just about anybody might wind up in the yoseba. But only about ten of the fifty-six informants mentioned middle-class occupations—including four in the ambiguous category of "engineer." The vast majority have not fallen from any great height, and some are simply doing the same kind of work as before but on a casual basis. The Japanese media like to tell riches-to-rags tales of elite businessmen who have taken to the street, but such people seem to be a minute minority.

Another popular yoseba stereotype, this time favored by academics and activists, is that people from declining heavy industries are often forced to become day laborers by changes in the macroeconomy. However, I only found a couple of ex-miners who fitted this stereotype, and nobody from iron and steel or shipbuilding.[4]

The figures on father's occupation are even skimpier, with just fifteen informants, but the fact that eight of them are sons of farmers or fishermen may be added to the prevalence of rural backgrounds in support of a third yoseba stereotype, that of the migratory worker from the country who never quite went home.

Age

The extent to which the Kotobuki population has aged is clear enough from my age statistics (table 10), which broadly concur with those compiled by the Kotobuki Labor Center (table 8). Nearly everyone is in the forty to sixty age range, whereas Caldarola's 1964 survey of several doya-gai found that "their (day laborers') age usually ranges from 20 to 40 years" (1968:513). The Labor Center's progressive figures show how the population has aged continually, though at varying speed, through the intervening years.

The mean of the ages told to me was 53.2, which coincides almost exactly with Junichirō's estimate of fifty-three for the overall day laborer population of Kotobuki, as of the winter of 1994–1995. Evidently the great majority of day laborers in Kotobuki are in their forties or fifties. The almost complete absence of day laborers under the age of thirty-five confirms that the yoseba is an institution in decline, while the almost complete absence of any people over sixty-five gives an ominous credibility to Junichirō's assertion that the average age at death is fifty-six.[5] The population has been aging at close to one year per year since 1975 except for the first half of the 1980s, when the construction boom associated with the bubble economy temporarily made day laboring a more attractive style of work to younger newcomers. This spectacular rate of aging, with almost no under thirties and just 10 percent under forties in the population, strongly supports my own impression there are very few newcomers and that essentially the same group of men is getting steadily older.

Marital Status

Nearly everyone I met in Kotobuki seemed to be living alone, with the exception of six men, mostly living outside Kotobuki and using the place for job connections. The question of why people are living singly is a delicate one that I seldom asked. However, two men said they were widowers and eight said they were divorced or separated. Another twelve said they were bachelors, and forty-eight more I knew to be living singly from having visited them at home (table 29).

Caldarola's 1964 survey found 23 percent of day laborers married, against roughly 4 percent for my informants. That may be explicable by the thirty years between us, during which time high economic growth and rising material expectations must have made marriage to a day laborer steadily less attractive to Japanese women.

Sibling Group Size and Sibling Birth Order

When I arrived in Kotobuki, I guessed that many of the day laborers would be second or third sons. This appeared likely because of the well-known Japanese tradition whereby the eldest son inherits the house and other major assets such as the farm or fishing boat, while younger sons are often obliged to leave home and seek employment elsewhere. In his three-volume survey of rural poverty in the period just after World War II, Kondō (1953–1995) argues that the problems of second and third sons were especially acute in this period, during which many of my informants were in their teens.

The intense poverty of that period must not be forgotten. Kondō quotes a Ministry of Labor report documenting 674 cases of families selling children into bondage during a one-year period from 1950 to 1951, and guesses that the true figure would probably be "ten or twenty times higher" (Kondō 1953:19). Many of these would be cases of daughters sold into prostitution or service, but Kondō says that second and third sons were sometimes sold too, especially in the northeastern prefectures of the Tohoku district.

Kondō describes a widespread fear for survival among rural households on his travels through farming, fishing, and mountain villages. He adds: "The eldest sons, who inherit their fathers' land, are relatively well-off, but there was something thought-provoking in the dark expressions of the second and third sons" (Kondō 1953:13).

Kondō identifies eldest-son inheritance as a key factor sustaining prewar Japanese capitalism. It ensured a steady supply of junior sons to work in industry, and provided them with a refuge if they became unemployed in the form of the parental household in the countryside, which would be maintained by the eldest son when the parents died or became incapable. This, Kondō argues, enabled capitalists to get away with paying low wages and was a key factor limiting social unrest and revolutionary sentiment in prewar Japan (Kondō 1953:14). Under the 1946 reform of the inheritance law imposed on Japan by the American-led occupation, it became illegal for eldest sons to inherit the father's entire assets, but since most farmers owned too little land to be divided and still bring in a living, the reform was sometimes ignored. Many junior sons formally renounced their newly received inheritance rights at local courts during this period (15).

In the mid–1960s, Caldarola found that "a good number of them (doya-gai dwellers) were the youngest children who were thereby exposed to discrimination in the typical old-fashioned Japanese families" (1968:517). In the mid–1990s I too found many youngest children in the yoseba—but to my surprise, I also found a large number of eldest sons (table 30).

The key terms here are *chōnan* and *suekko*. They are not opposite in meaning or even mutually exclusive. "Chōnan" means "eldest son"— or more literally, "chief son." He is not necessarily the first born, as he may have older sisters. He may even be the *last* born of an otherwise female sibling group. "Suekko" means last born, irrespective of gender. These are important conceptual categories in Japan. The first-born son matters because he usually inherits and has responsibility for the parents in their old age; the last-born child because he or she is subject to a unique mixture of stigma and romance—in times past the child most likely to suffer infanticide, in latter times the one most likely to be sold into prostitution or servitude, the one least likely to inherit and most likely to have to leave home and village, but also, in stories and perhaps sometimes in reality, the one most likely to have a special place in the parental affections.[6]

The terms *jinan* and *san'nan* mean second and third son, and they may also include some suekko of course, where there are no younger siblings. In addition, a few men just said they were "in the middle" (*naka*). Of course, they could possibly have been chōnan if all their older siblings were female.

Assuming that jinan and san'nan are middle children (and thus probably underestimating the suekko population), and that "naka" children are not chōnan (thus probably underestimating the chōnan population), I can now speculatively rearrange my data as in table 31, counting Jinan + san'nan + naka as "middle"; and counting *hitorikko* (only children) and chōnan-who-are-also-suekko as one-half chōnan, one half suekko. This admittedly rough-and-ready approach, applied to an admittedly very small sample, divides the population of 105 into three groups, with forty-three "eldest sons," forty-two "last children," and twenty "middle children," some of whom may themselves be eldest sons or last children.

Even is this is anything like an accurate picture of the yoseba population, any significance it may have depends on family size and gender distribution. In present-day Japan, where the average married couple has about 1.5 children, most sons are chōnan, more than half of all children born are suekko, and the intermediate categories are much rarer. But whereas the "total special birthrate" for 1992 was 1.50 children per woman, it was more than three times higher at 4.54 in 1947 (the peak postwar year) and was above 4 throughout the war years.[7] The mean sibling group size for my informants was 4.75.[8] Excluding the informants themselves, who were all male, roughly 60 percent of siblings were male and 40 percent female.[9]

Assuming a mean of 4.75 children per sibling group, including 2.85 males (4.75 times 60 percent), we would expect to find the following proportions if the day laborer population were randomly distributed in terms of birth order:

$$\text{Chōnan} = 1/2.85 = 35 \text{ percent}$$
$$\text{Suekko} = 1/4.75 = 21 \text{ percent}$$

Given that the actual figures are just over 40 percent for each category, we appear to have twice as many suekko, and slightly more chōnan, than in a random distribution. However, the chōnan figures are more striking than this suggests, since their presence in the yoseba is not supposed to be governed by random distribution in the first place: eldest sons are supposed to be the ones that stay at home.

The smallness of the sample means that the above calculations are no more than suggestive. However, it was striking that several informants expressed the view that eldest sons were particularly numerous in the yoseba. Early in fieldwork, my assumption that there would be few of them was flatly contradicted:

> I said (to Noriyuki [pp. 111–112], a suekko) that I had the impression there were rather a lot of younger/youngest sons in Kotobuki, and relatively few first sons. He disagreed. *"Kekkō iru yo!"* (There are quite a few you know!) Seemed surprisingly sure on this point. . . . [10]

Later, when I started to think it might be the other way round, the suggestion would be enthusiastically confirmed:

> I told him (Kimitsu [pp. 168–170], a chōnan) about my eldest son theory. In Kimitsu's English, "chōnan" is rendered not as "eldest son" but as "top brother"—interesting terminology. He thought the theory was spot on. "That's right! There are so many. Like me!"
>
> I asked him why.
>
> "Something deep behind it. Need careful study of Japanese traditional family system." (Peering through microscope gesture) "Must open the door." (Door-opening gesture)
>
> "Eldest son stays at home, so. . . ."
>
> "That's right. Top brother has rights. Top brother has power. So we are soft. We are spoiled. When we graduate from home . . ." (resigned shrug of shoulders). "When I look for work, I have no . . . confidence. My whole life, I try to find why I exist."[11]

I tentatively conclude that birth order is an important factor influencing people's careers, including those in the yoseba, and that both eldest sons and youngest children may be overrepresented in the yoseba population. By contrast, Bahr (1971), analyzing birth order on the Bowery (New York's skid row district), finds "only children" to be the only category overly represented.[12]

Midway through fieldwork I started asking day laborers what they thought about the idea that there were a lot of chōnan and suekko around. Everyone seemed to find the theory plausible; the most common explanations were psychological, like Kimitsu's above. His idea is that chōnan are first pampered, having no male rivals for their mother's affection, and then loaded with responsibility as they get older—a fatal combination. Shigehirō (pp. 188–190), another very articulate chōnan, quoted to me the Japanese proverbial expression *sōryō no jinroku*—"the foolishness of the eldest son"[13]—and said that wealthy chōnan had a reputation for squandering the wealth bequeathed to them by their fathers.

> On the other hand, where the family is poor, there is a lot of pressure on the eldest son. He has to somehow keep the family household alive, and make sure there is enough money for his younger siblings to be fed, clothed, and schooled. The eldest son is a sort of second father *(dai-ni otōsan)* in the family, and when the father dies, he has to take over responsibility for everything. Sometimes they crack up under the pressure, and end up escaping to Kotobuki or San'ya. I too have noticed a lot of eldest sons among my acquaintances in both places."[14]

In contrast, several other men argued that *last-born* children were the ones that got spoiled. They would still be children after the others had grown up, and often had a special place in the parental affections—especially the father's. But once they grew up, economic reality would take over and they would be turfed out to fend for themselves. For some it seemed almost axiomatic that *suekko* (youngest child) = *amaembo* (spoilt brat):

> He (Sakashita) tells me he is a "suekko," the last-born of five. This, he says, accounts for his character: he is an "amaembo," a spoilt child.[15]
> Matsubara says he is a typical suekko, i.e. an amaembo. He says he is from a family which has traced itself through the female line *(jokei kazoku)*; it has a tradition of strong women and weak men; this plus two older sisters he offered to account for his being an amaembo.[16]

The word "amaembo" derives from *"amai,"* roughly meaning "presuming on another's indulgence," a word made famous by the psychiatrist Doi Takeo, who sees it as not much less than the key to understanding the Japanese character (Doi 1973). Some of my informants thought they had been "spoiled" (amaekasareru) in childhood, in part because of being either a chōnan or a suekko. This may be a catchall excuse for not achieving great social heights, but it is not entirely implausible. What the two categories have in common is a period of relatively undivided parental attention, followed by a predetermined role that is not necessarily easy: maintaining the household, or being cut loose to fend for oneself. The psychological argument favored by some of my informants says that some people cannot bear to perform these ordained roles. They cut and run, sometimes to the yoseba.

Once there, how do they get on? This is a very subjective matter, but my fieldnotes suggest that among my informants roughly three-quarters of "middle" siblings were fairly successful at getting work and staying well fed and housed, against two-thirds of suekko and only one-third of chōnan (table 32). This impression, too, was supported by my informants. Several of them took the view that life in the yoseba was harder for chōnan because they were brought up with the expectation of staying at home and not having to cast about for an occupation.

Kojima's (1989) statistical analysis of the Eighth National Fertility Survey confirms the chōnan expectation of staying at the parental home. He finds that for the 1940–1944 birth cohort, 65.1 percent of married eldest sons co-resided with their parents before marriage, against 42.6 percent for non-eldest sons (1989:36). Even in 1982, 76 percent of unmarried eldest sons aged thirty to thirty-four were still living with their parents against 58 percent of unmarried non-eldest sons (35), whereas in the United States eldest sons were the ones *least* likely to live with their parents (37). In the Japanese data, the gap in coresidential probability between eldest and younger sons was widest in larger (38), rural (41–42) families such as those of most of my informants.

Several of the most successful day laborers I knew were suekko, and gave a strong impression of having some kind of plan or guiding principle for their working lives, but I also noticed that the two worst bullies in Kotobuki were both suekko (including Ron-chan, pp. 122–124)—and that the more philosophical day laborers tended to be chōnan (e.g., Sakae pp. 10–12; Kimitsu pp. 168–170; Shigehiro pp. 188–190). In general, I felt there was a tendency for chōnan to be passive and accepting of their lot, while suekko were more active and determined to stamp their own will on their surroundings, whether by controlling their own working careers or by wielding power over those weaker than themselves.

The War and the Big Move

This data on birth order must be viewed alongside the other demographic material. The picture that emerges is of a body of men mostly born in rural prefectures during World War II or shortly before or after.

The role of the last-born has always been difficult in rural smallholding families practicing inheritance by primogeniture; the role of the oldest son can be easy or hard, depending on material circumstances. Defeat in World War II meant that for a generation of chōnan the role was a burden more than a privilege. Undoubtedly the war experience was a major influence on my informants. They seldom spoke of their fathers, but their ages, and the massive losses sustained by Japan, make it likely that some of them, especially oldest sons, literally had to take the role of "second father" mentioned by Shigehiro, following the father's death in the war. Some eldest sons may have ventured out to one of the big cities in a bid to support a large number of younger siblings in a struggling rural household, by shi-okuri—sending money home.[17] It may not have been intended as a permanent move. Perhaps some of them failed to send money home; perhaps others succeeded, but got into the yoseba habit and never got out of it; and perhaps some of them didn't fancy rural life once they had tasted the excitement of the city.[18]

I write in this speculative fashion because most of my informants were reluctant to speak of their youth and how they became day laborers. Occasionally, however, I would get a fleeting glimpse of the distant past:

> When I was a kid there were six of us. . . . My childhood wasn't particularly happy. Family affairs were complicated. Besides, there was the war: from 1942 to 1949 we had eight very tough years. There was nothing to eat. We were living on radish leaves and potato skins.[19]

> In those tough days just after the war, they never had enough food. Food for a day would be two loaves of bread between six . . . the children would have four slices each usually.[20]

> At the end of the war, he and most of his family spent two years living in "a hole in the mountainside." His dad was killed fighting in Siberia; Fukuoka was destroyed by incendiary bombs. His mother led the children into the mountains, on foot, with wet futons over their heads as protection against the incendiary bombs. "We ate things I can't describe."[21]

For many chōnan, this kind of traumatic childhood would then have been followed by heavy responsibilities toward the family at a time (the aftermath of defeat) when their legally enshrined privileges were being swept away by the Occupation. This was a sea change from prewar Japanese society, when oldest sons had been exempted from military service because of their special role at home (Kondō 1953:12), and when most of the emigrés to Manchuria, Latin America, etc., had also been younger brothers (Guelcher 1994). In short, the privilege of the first-born son was rigorously protected by the prewar government of Japan; and then abolished almost overnight by the occupation government which replaced it.

I suspect that the combination of clearly established traditional sibling roles, plus the abrupt economic, legal, and social changes that followed Japan's defeat in World War II, may jointly account for the preponderance of eldest sons and youngest children which my admittedly limited sample seems to reveal in the yoseba population.

Ron-chan

In the Tokyo-Yokohama area at least, the diminutive suffix *chan*, when used with a man's name, tends to demarcate him as somewhat out of the mainstream, an object of patronizing affection. I found seven men with "chan" nicknames in Kotobuki and ten more in the other doya-gai. The Kotobuki "chan" men included two who were unusually small of stature; one who was mentally retarded; one who was old and homeless; and three who perhaps liked to think of themselves as good-natured rogues and used the "chan" suffix mutually. One of these was Ron-chan.*

I first met him in September 1993: a youngish man in shorts and tee-shirt with spiky hair, handsome dragon tattoos on both arms, and a cynical smile of worldly ennui. He was well built, but running to fat and generally letting himself go.

He said he hailed from Tachikawa, on the western outskirts of Tokyo, and was the youngest of five siblings, all brothers. The others all went to university; one became an architect, another an aerial surveyor. But Ron-chan never went to university. Instead, he joined the local yakuza gang and got his beautiful tattoos done. His parents disowned him, but these days he goes and visits them sometimes, invited or not, he says.

Ron-chan had a romantic notion of the yakuza as "defenders of the townsfolk," but soon discovered that twentieth-century reality

(continues)

(continued)

was very different. The gang in Tachikawa was led by a "bad yakuza," a Korean who just wanted to make money any way he could, and ruthlessly exploited the local community. He said he quit after three years, coming to Kotobuki about ten years before I met him. He had very mixed feelings about yakuza. Sometimes he would talk of going back to the yakuza life, insisting that there was some nobility in it; later on he grimly denounced yakuza for making trouble for respectable people. His attitude may have varied with the treatment he got from the Kotobuki yakuza; I suspected he was running errands for them.

Ron-chan's account of his brothers' academic success may help explain his snobbish interest in the relative status of universities (Cambridge far outscores Tokyo University; he saw the rankings on TV) and his intense hatred of Koreans. He insists that they are intellectually inferior to Japanese, because "the veins in their brains are narrow" *(nō no kekkan ga hosoi kara)*. By contrast, he reckons British people are even cleverer than Japanese.

I met Ron-chan many times, and never once saw him make a serious attempt to get work. He seemed to live mostly from government and volunteer handouts, patronage from more successful mates, and bullying weaker men into giving him food and money. Many people told me he was a thief, and I did see him gleefully snatch a bottle of saké from a stranger in the street once. He seldom washed and would lounge around with his hand in his pants, obviously playing with himself. He would squeeze one nostril and blow skeins of liquid snot onto the pavement from the other. On two occasions I saw him kick weaker men to the point where I was concerned for their lives. In both cases the kicking was justified as punishment—one of the men had allegedly stolen some money from a mentally retarded girl, the other had apparently failed to show respect.

His attitude to me was ambiguous and changeable, with elements of deference, contempt, and suspicion. He tried to assault me once when drunk, but was restrained by a friend. On another occasion he treated me to several drinks and gave me ¥2,000, which he told me to spend on food for myself.

I found him sleeping in a filthy futon in front of the labor exchange early one morning; I also heard tell of him sleeping on other men's floors. Many spoke ill of him, but there were always those who would help him, whether out of sympathy or fear or regard for a certain boyish charm. He attracted women, and I

(continues)

124

(continued)

spent one bizarre evening touring bars with him and an elegant but eccentric non-Kotobuki woman, middle-aged with a toy dog, whom he seemed to know well.

Ron-chan liked to describe the day-laboring life as a piece of cake. He could get work any time he felt like it, for good money too. He claimed he often helped out his buddies by using his connections to fix them up with work. One day he planned to open a little bar or restaurant—it would only cost ¥5 million or so, all he needed was a wealthy sponsor or a bit of luck on the gambling—easy.

But for all the bragging, Ron-chan was insecure. He declined to tell me his real name, saying, "It's not a name of any consequence." In a philosophical discussion with me, he insisted on the existence of hell. Moreover, hell was subdivided into different levels: the worse you were, the deeper into hell your spirit would be plunged, the worse would be its torment, and the more millions of years it would take to get out.[22] I wondered if at the back of his mind he thought that he, too, might be heading that way.

6

The Meaning of Home

Why Mr. Shinohara Sleeps in the Street

SHINOHARA YŪKI HAS BEEN A well-liked character around Kotobuki for a quarter of a century. Slight and thin, with battered black glasses and bandy legs, Shinohara often hangs out around the union offices. He is not really an ideological activist: he just likes a party, likes a festival, likes a bit of camaraderie. He vociferously joins in when the union conducts negotiations with local officials, and can be relied on to join any demonstration. He sometimes joins in the volunteer patrols that check on the well-being of homeless people—which is ironic, since he himself is more or less permanently homeless.

Friends estimate that Shinohara spends eleven months in the year sleeping rough, and the rest of the time mostly on friends' floors; he can rarely afford a doya. He is ashamed and embarrassed about it, but if he does get spotted by the homeless patrol he will try to make a joke of it and ask for a blanket or a cup of soup. Sometimes he complains that the union men refuse these requests; perhaps they just fail to recognize when Shinohara is being serious.

Why does Mr. Shinohara sleep in the street? Fate, character, and the sociopolitical context are all involved. From birth he has had a mild disability: weak legs, afflicted by some kind of partial paralysis. He walks with an uneven, crabby motion. So when Shinohara does get a day's work on a building site, he tends to be rather slow. He gets jeered at, or criticized for slowing the work up. Having a reputation as a slowcoach makes it harder to get work; and the abuse saps Shinohara's willingness to keep trying. But at the same time, his disability is classified as minor, so that he only qualifies for a very small disability allowance. It is a classic hole in the safety net: the disability is too serious to allow the man to generate much income, but not serious enough to persuade the state to fill the gap. Moreover, Shinohara has an alcohol habit, doesn't particularly enjoy hard manual labor, and likes to have a laugh with his mates. Put all these factors together, and that is why Mr. Shinohara sleeps in the street.

Shinohara's family has not entirely abandoned him. He still visits his folks occasionally, but cannot imagine staying with them permanently. Shinohara was around forty-eight in 1995; a friend reckoned he had about another five years to live. He was still in good spirits when I renewed our acquaintance in 1999, however.

In his pocket, Shinohara always carries a scrap of paper with his sister's address and telephone number on it. He hopes that if he dies in the street, somebody will find it and get in touch with her. That way he can be given a proper funeral and avoid the fate of becoming a *muen-botoke*. This term, literally meaning "unconnected Boddhisatva," is applied to people who die with no known relatives (see p. 15). Day laborers seem to fear isolation in death more than in life. It is not uncommon for the family of a long-lost man to learn of his death via a scrap of paper like the one carried by Mr. Shinohara. In Kotobuki, muen-botoke are given the Buddhist equivalent of a pauper's funeral by the monks of Tokuonji temple. Tokuonji is a temple of the Shingon sect, located some 15 miles away from Kotobuki. There are hundreds of temples closer by, but Tokuonji is the only temple in Yokohama willing to look after the ashes of penniless, nameless day laborers. (Gill 2000a:108–109)

Though Shinohara is a unique character, there are many other men who, for their own combinations of personal and structural reasons, may often be found sleeping rough around Kotobuki.

Homelessness: Narrow and Broad Definitions

For many years academic debate on homelessness has had a problem with defining the term. In Somerville's (1992) terminology, does homelessness mean "rooflessness" or "rootlessness"? The two terms interestingly echo the Tokugawa distinction discussed earlier (pp. 14–15) between "yadonashi" (without a roof over one's head) and "mushuku" (lacking affiliation). Most of the Euro-American literature seems to approximate to the latter position, classically summed up thus:

> Homelessness is a condition of detachment from society characterized by the absence or attenuation of the affiliative bonds that link settled persons to a network of interconnected social structures. (Caplow et al., 1968:494)

Or more recently and cross-culturally, thus:

> [T]erms such as the Spanish "descamparado" (without the protection or comfort from other people), the Japanese "furosha" (floating people), . . . or the American/English "homeless" imply the loss of family and social relationships. (Glasser 1994:5)

By contrast, my impression is that the prevailing Japanese view remains closer to the literal definition, or to put it another way, a *furōsha* (drifter) is not necessarily a *nojukusha* (homeless person). "Furōsha" does indeed imply "the loss of family and social relationships" but is not an appropriate translation for "homeless" unless one accepts the "rootlessness" definition.

> To the poor people who cannot afford a house, a single tatami mat in a flophouse is a sort of home. (Yokoyama 1899:67, my translation)

Under Caplow or Glasser's definition, almost all day laborers would be "homeless." Nor is this a recent development. Anderson (1923) frequently uses the word *"homeless"* to include men with regular rooms. As Kalvis (1995) rightly points out, "[O]ne can see the problem that this 'detachment' definition could have with other possible models that highlight the chance of a different order of interaction, of creative, positive social relationships and value systems on the street that preserve solidarity in adversity." There is an inherent assumption in the definition that there is a normative lifestyle associated with a narrowly-defined "home," and that anyone who does not live in that way is thereby deprived.

Just to give some idea of how loaded with value judgments the "detachment" definition can be, consider the paragraph that follows Caplow et al.'s definition quoted just above:

> At the extreme point of the scale, the modern skid row man demonstrates the possibility of nearly total detachment from society. . . .

> Homeless persons are poor, anomic, inert, and non-responsible.
> They command no resources, enjoy no esteem, and assume no
> burdens of reciprocal obligations. Social action, in the usual sense,
> is almost impossible for them. (Caplow et al. 1968:494)

This supposedly objective encyclopedia entry is in fact no more
than an expression of prejudice. A large swathe of people are defined
as homeless and then assumed to share a state of total, subhuman
apathy. It does not fit my experience in Japan, and is also criticized by
Giamo in his study of the New York Bowery (1989:178, 184–185).

Other American critics of the detachment definition include Hoch
and Slayton (1989) and Groth (1994). The former stress that there can
be a kind of community in the skid row hotels that are being torn
down and replaced with "homeless shelters" that connote failure and
expulsion from community far more than the old hotels; the latter
draws attention to a more general American tradition of living in
residential hotels, found among the very rich as well as among certain
segments of the poor.

In the case of the yoseba/doya-gai, there are many men who have
lived in the same doya room for years, acquired numerous possessions, enjoy stable relationships with some of their neighbors, and
would strongly object to being called "homeless." At the same time,
other rooms in the same doya may be occupied by transient men who
have virtually no possessions, work infrequently, and sleep rough when
they cannot afford the rent. Their rooms are almost totally bare. Even
they would probably argue that they are homeless only on nights
when they cannot get a room.

Those men who do not live in the doya also show a variety of
approaches and attitudes to the question of residence. Many say they
avoid the doya during the summer months because they get stiflingly
hot (which is true) and they prefer to sleep al fresco. Others, such as
Kuriyama (pp. 144–146), have built their own shacks (koya; lit.: little
house) on slivers of urban space around Kotobuki. The police mostly
turn a blind eye, doing the minimum required to deal with complaints
from locals. Some of these shacks are quite well built and have a
homely atmosphere. After all, the occupants may be professional
builders. There was a thriving shanty town of twenty to thirty residences near Kotobuki under the elevated railway track at Kannai station in 1993–1995, and the hedges lining the Nakamura River also
concealed several improvised homes.

Some men were living in shacks because they could not afford the
doya, others because they preferred the greater independence afforded.

Two men told me they were living in shacks because they had pet animals, which are not allowed in doya. Naturally they had no mains electricity, gas, or water supply, but they made do with battery-powered lighting, camping gas, bottled water, etc. Being moved on by the police was a perpetual threat, but it was rarely long before expelled shacks reappeared in their old places.

There were also a few people living in abandoned vehicles, although the police had a clear-out of these during my fieldwork period, and were taking a harder line against this form of residence.[1]

Finally, many men and a few women had nowhere to stay and were sleeping in the streets. There were usually two to three hundred people sleeping rough within a half-mile radius of Kotobuki while I was there (table 33), and numbers have risen since.[2] The two main areas were both near Kannai station: the semi-sheltered walkways running round Yokohama City Hall and its annex; and the underground shopping mall. The former was favored because the city officials would not kick or hose down the homeless people, whose presence was a daily reminder of failures in their own social welfare policies; the latter because it afforded total shelter from the elements, although station officers were far less tolerant and frequently moved people on.

Every evening a neat row of cardboard boxes would encircle city hall, with the same people regularly setting up on the same pitches. Many completely enclosed themselves inside the boxes, pulling the last flap down like Dracula retiring to his coffin. These were experienced rough sleepers, who hid their boxes and futons away by day and usually had plenty of warm clothing in the colder months. Nearly all were men, but I also saw a handful of single women and one elderly couple, who shared a double futon and had a small pet dog with its own futon.

The people sleeping in the underground mall were less experienced and less adept at handling homelessness. They chose the mall for protection from the elements, but had to endure harassment and bright lights. They tended to be worse equipped, too. Few had futons and many had nothing more than a scrap of cardboard between themselves and the concrete floor. There were more alcoholics and people with serious health problems.

Only the people sleeping in cardboard boxes would be unequivocally viewed by Japanese standards as homeless, and for the rest of this chapter I will use the word "homeless" in this limited, literal sense. Those living in shacks are not counted in the homeless tally maintained by the Thursday Patrol, a volunteer group that tours the main Yokohama homeless districts at night and hands out blankets, food, and advice on health and welfare.

Nowadays the English word "homeless" is rapidly gaining currency in Japan, transliterated as *hōmuresu* and meaning "living on the street." The orthodox term for homelessness is *nojuku* (lit.: "field living" or "living in the wild"), which a respected dictionary renders as "camping out; bivouac; sleep [pass the night] in the open (air); sleep on the bed of grass [under the open sky]" (Masuda 1974:1245). The slang term favored by day laborers is *aokan* (a contraction, some say, of *aozora* [blue sky] and *kantan* [simple]). Both terms convey a romanticized view of "rooflessness."

Before rejecting that element of romance out of hand, consider the following conversation I had with "Lazybones," a homeless day laborer in Nagoya. It was 8:15 A.M., long after those with jobs had left for the worksite:

> He is of average height, going to grey, dressed shabby but warm, bicycle. Smiles.
>
> I: Going to work today?
>
> He: Naah, not in the mood.
>
> I: Since when have you not been in the mood?
>
> He: Oh, since about twenty-five years ago.
>
> I: What sort of life are you leading?
>
> He: I sleep outdoors, under the overhang of a large building. It keeps the rain off. It's quite okay, I have futons, a pillow, everything I need.
>
> I: Don't you get cold?
>
> He: No, I have plenty of futons, so I'm nice and warm.
>
> I: But in winter, surely . . .
>
> He: Winter's the best time of the year. Not so many people wandering about the streets at night making a noise.
>
> I: What do you do about food?
>
> He: It's no problem—I eat stuff that's just past its sell-by date. The supermarkets have to chuck it out, but it's still quite okay. The only drawback is that they tend to chuck it out at three or four in the morning, and I have to compete with other homeless people to get the good stuff. But the food itself is excellent.
>
> I: Don't you use money?

He: Well if one doesn't have much money, why fuss about it? Better to have none at all.

I: How's your health?

He: I'm fine. I'm nearly fifty, and I expect to live another twenty years.

I: How about a drink?

He: No thanks, I don't drink at all. That's why I'm okay. The friends who joined me round this bonfire last winter are nearly all dead. Once you start drinking, that's it—you're dead in one or two years.

I: Might I know your name?

He: You don't need to know it. It's not a name of any consequence.[3]

I had a slightly similar conversation at new year 1995 in Yokohama, at the Naka ward welfare office. There I met a man dressed like a tramp, waiting for a food coupon.

He: I live off what I can get myself. I don't owe nothing to no one. I work when I can, I come and get the food vouchers—like today—when I can't.

I: Are you living in Kotobuki?

He: No, I'm homeless (*nojuku*). I sleep rough, but not where the other guys sleep. I have my own place.

I: And are you staying in the prefabs (temporary shelters) now?

He: No way! I'd much rather sleep on the streets. It's too noisy in the prefabs, all those guys get on my nerves. And I'm always getting into fights.[4]

Yoseba activists and left-wing academics will vigorously deny that homeless day laborers live the way they do because of their own personal weakness or laziness, or because they like it. These people are innocent victims of capitalism.[5] No doubt this is true of many people, but the conversations quoted above show that laziness, too, can be a political statement. The fact that "Lazybones" doesn't drink is very important, of course, and his unwillingness to reveal his name may hint at some concealed shame. Still, his narrative is a reminder that in a society as wealthy and wasteful as Japan, no one need die of cold or hunger if they keep their wits about them and are not too fussy about what they eat.[6] As for the man in

Yokohama, he was a self-avowed misanthropist, who denied any interest in companionship or community. It may be naïve to take narratives like these at face value, but it may also be naïve to assume that nobody could possibly be happy without an apartment and family.

Against these relatively positive homeless narratives, I must set the following extract from my account of a night on the streets with the Thursday Patrol.

> It was about 11 o'clock. We descended into the system of underground malls and passageways around Kannai station . . .
>
> We found four isolated sleepers around the brightly lit passageways, but the vast majority, at least thirty . . . were in a single short, relatively grubby and dimly lit passageway on the fringe of the subterranean system . . .
>
> Some raged. Inaba Masanori (a volunteer) got a flea in his ear from a thin and ragged man, tanned and short of teeth, who rubbed in the ineffectuality of the volunteers' work:
>
> Inaba: Got any problems?
>
> Man: For a start it's pretty strange that I'm in a place like this, eh? I've only had four days' work this month.
>
> Inaba: Hm, I see . . .
>
> Man: Whadyamean, "I see"?! . . .
>
> A few places further on we find a middle-aged man in an awful state. Eyes very bloodshot; hands and legs grotesquely puffed up. Something wrong with his liver: probably cirrhosis or hepatitis. Said he'd been going to the Ariga Hospital for a week as an outpatient, though he could hardly make it for the pain in his legs. Couldn't walk as far as his doya, fell over 4 times when he tried; he couldn't eat, had no appetite, could only swallow water; he couldn't get work . . . as he told us all this, the next man along constantly interrupted with sarcastic remarks implying that Swollen-Legs was really a mere idler.[7]

There are plenty of people who are in despair about being on-the-street homeless. However, they will not necessarily take advantage of shelter when it is offered. Compare the numbers of homeless people in the Kannai district on ordinary Thursdays (table 33) and during the period of the Winter Survival Campaign or *Ettō* (table 35). During the latter period there are prefabricated shelters set up by the city government in Kotobuki in which anyone may stay. But although hundreds of people do stay in the prefabs, hundreds more do not. Thus the average number of people found sleeping rough during the 1992–1993 Ettō was 111; the last Thursday Patrol before the Ettō found ninety-one homeless people and the first one after found 107. In the 1993–1994 Ettō the parallel figures were 122 just before the Ettō, 197 during it, and 138 just after it.[8] In both cases there were more people sleeping rough while the shelter was available than when it was not. Nor were the shelters full to capacity during the Ettō.

This is partly to do with the absence of employment opportunities and closing of conventional welfare services over the new year period (the original reason why the Ettō was started). Even so, the figures suggest that many prefab residents are not long-term homeless people but day laborers who are not usually homeless but take advantage of the free accommodation briefly available at New Year. Many homeless people, like the two men quoted above, decline offers of shelter. In the winter of 1995–1996, refusals of temporary housing by some of Tokyo's homeless people prompted a bemused headline in the International Herald Tribune: "Luxury Digs? Tokyo's Homeless Prefer Cardboard."[9]

There are sound reasons why some long-term homeless people decline to make use of temporary shelters. Often they have established a favorably located pitch which they fear may be taken by someone else while they are in the shelter, or the loss of their bulkier possessions which may not be taken into the shelter.[10] Often they also have a community on the street which they do not wish to leave. Such people may be roofless but not homeless in the "detached" sense. Sometimes they are attached to their own network of relationships.

Symbolic Representations of Home
Festival Time: Yoseba as Hometown

San'ya ni wa nannimo nai ga	There's nothing in San'ya
Taiyō to kūki to	But sunshine and air
Yūjō dake wa ippai da	And friendship aplenty
Dakara San'ya o ai shi	And so loving San'ya
San'ya ni ikite iku	We live on in San'ya
Watashitachi no machi San'ya	Our town San'ya
Watashitachi no furusato San'ya	Our hometown San'ya

—Anonymous poem, reproduced in Kaji 1977 Vol. 2:523

A number of times during fieldwork day laborers referred to the yoseba as a hometown or community. It sometimes seemed that what concerned them about their detachment from mainstream life was not so much being homeless as being "hometownless."

This impression was reinforced through my participation in the two major events in the Kotobuki calendar, the Summer Festival (*Natsu Matsuri*) and the Winter Survival Campaign (*Ettō*),[11] which struck me as more or less conscious attempts to replicate the community spirit of a close-knit village environment.

The Summer Festival

Summer festivals have become an established item on the calendar of the major yoseba. In 1999 Kamagasaki celebrated its twenty-eighth summer festival, San'ya its twenty-seventh,[12] Kotobuki its twenty-second, Sasashima its sixteenth and Chikkō its twelfth.

I participated in the sixteenth and seventeenth versions of the Kotobuki festival, in the summers of 1993 and 1994. The festival is organized by a committee grouping union activists, the Kotobuki Welfare Center, and other well-wishers, and is held over the closest weekend to *Bon*, the feast of the dead, which falls in mid-August in this part of Japan. It is customary to spend Bon with one's parental family, and yoseba summer festivals are designed to dispel the sense of isolation that may arise from being unable to go home at this important time of year. Accordingly, yoseba summer festivals feature traditional Bon singing and dancing, the wearing of loin cloths and happi coats, and the carrying of portable shrines (*omikoshi*) around the streets.

Another traditional element is the festival fan. These used to be made of splayed bamboo, but nowadays are mass produced out of plastic and paper. The fans are handed out free at the festival, and interestingly combine the evocation of rural tradition with overtly political sloganeering. The 1994 Kotobuki fan, for instance, features on one side a stylized ink-wash picture of a Chinese bellflower (*kikyō*), growing out of purple earth against a pale-blue summer sky. The other side has the following slogans written on it:

Hitori ga minna no tame ni	One for all
Minna ga hitori no tame ni	All for one
Shigoto o yokose!	Give us jobs!
Han o yokose!	Give us rice!
Neru tokoro o hoshō seyo!	Guarantee a place to sleep!
Oretachi wa danketsu no chikara de tatakau-zo!	We will fight with the power of solidarity!

—1994 Kotobuki Natsu Matsuri Jikkō Iinkai (Summer Festival Committee)

Photo 6.1 Some Participants in the 1999 Kotobuki Summer Festival. A mixture of day laborers, activists, and volunteers, these people have just finished carrying the *omikoshi* (portable shrine) around the streets of Kotobuki. Photo by Kagoshima Masa'aki, 1999. Reprinted by permission.

This is also one of the few times in the year when Buddhist monks are seen in Kotobuki. There is a small outdoor stone altar behind the Center, where monks from Tokuonji chant sutras and the people of Kotobuki come up and place lighted joss sticks next to a small statue of the Buddha, in remembrance of deceased day laborers. (Once every few years, a mass memorial service is also held for day laborers who died without known kin.) Thus, Shinto celebrations of life, such as the dancing and omikoshi carrying, mingle with Buddhist death ceremonies in the characteristic Japanese mix, and Christianity takes a back seat.

Most of these elements also feature in the summer festivals at other yoseba. Another much more modern institution common to all is the *karaoke* singing contest, which in a decade or two has permeated Japanese society from top to bottom. But there are also location-specific elements to the Kotobuki festival. One is the participation of children.[13] It matters to Kotobuki people that the place does not consist entirely of lonely old men. Hence, the couple of dozen children who still live

Photo 6.2   Children's Sumo Wrestling at the 1999 Kotobuki Summer Festival. My son Jake competed in the 1993 version of this annual event. Only a dozen children participated, and it was all over in twenty minutes. Photo by Kagoshima Masa'aki, 1999. Reprinted by permission.

in Kotobuki get star treatment at festival time. They lead the Bon dancing, shuffling around a ten-foot-high elevated stage while the rest of the revellers follow round at ground level, glancing up to check the steps. There are special events for children too, such as blindfolded melon smashing *(suika-wari)* and sumo wrestling. The festival organizers also make a conscious attempt to celebrate Kotobuki's special ethnic identity, chiefly by including performances of Korean, Philippine, or Okinawan folk songs. At the 1993 festival this backfired when a beer can was thrown at a Korean woman in mid-song.[14]

Ever since the second year there has also been a free rock concert, which dominates one day of the festival. It has become a trendy event of late, with well-known bands travelling long distances to play for free. It is the one day of the year when numerous fashionable teenagers may be seen in Kotobuki.

Most festival events are centered on a big stage, decorated with the red and white paper lanterns that are a traditional feature of Bon festivals. The stage is set up in the Center courtyard in a symbolically important act of communal labor (*butai-zukuri;* stage building) eagerly anticipated by some day laborers and union men. The stage is built on the morning of the first day of the festival and dismantled the day after the festival ends. It has several levels of significance for those who make it:

1. Its erection and dismantling symbolically mark the beginning and end of nonquotidian, festival time.
2. It is a sampler of the construction worker's craft. Whereas day laborers usually do their work far away from the yoseba, this is a rare opportunity to demonstrate skill on home territory.
3. It is an act of labor freely given for the sake of the community. Most of the time day laborers sell their labor to the highest bidder and have to struggle for every yen. But the erection of the stage is purely voluntary work. It recalls the communal house building and thatching still found in some rural districts of Japan, one of which, at Shirakawa, Gifu prefecture, I have earlier described. (Gill 1992)

When I participated in the 1993 stage building, I found the symbolism slightly muted. Certainly it attracted young and old (about fifty-fifty), male and female (about eighty-twenty). Artisans sporting leather pouches full of tools worked alongside students, housewives, and day laborers. But a close look at who was involved revealed an irony: Kotobuki is full of construction workers, yet very few of them actually helped with this simple construction task. For the most part it was the volunteers doing the work. I saw a pair of young salarymen, who had taken a day off from work especially to help build the stage, struggling with the scaffolding under the silent gaze of working men who surely could have done a better job.[15]

In other respects too, the symbolism of community was muted. A few day laborers danced with the youngsters during the rock concert, but others resolutely attempted to get their afternoon sleep stretched out on the upper levels of the Center while great waves of noise came crashing off the concrete walls. The 1993 festivals at Kotobuki, Kamagasaki, and Sasashima prompted a pictorial in the Japanese weekly edition of *Playboy* magazine entitled "There's a recession on—but grandpa's doing fine" (*Fukyō da ga—Otchan wa genki da*). A careful inspection of the pictures shows one or two day laborers amid a sea of youth. At Kotobuki I saw young women gingerly picking their way round the prone bodies of a couple of day laborers lying unconscious in a pile of rubbish, bleeding from untreated head wounds. The scene went unphotographed.

The Bon dancing and omikoshi do, however, generate a much more convincing community atmosphere. Held on separate days from the rock concert, they draw far fewer outsiders. Larger numbers of day laborers take part, everyone has plenty to drink, and the dancing is riotous. All the noise and merriment happens in the middle of an otherwise eerily quiet Yokohama: nearly all businesses and shops are closed for Bon, and half the population has decamped to visit elderly relatives in the country. After a few drinks and a few shuffles round the Center courtyard, with children belaboring the great *taiko* drum on the stage, it is just about possible to believe that, yes, this is a kind of hometown.[16]

The festival entails substantial costs—scaffolding, lighting, sound equipment, fans, transportation, refreshments, etc. Most of the money comes from donations. Hats are passed round at the rock concert; more formal donations are taken on the other two days, with the donor's name and the amount given being prominently displayed on a noticeboard, a common practice at Japanese festivals.

Formal donations to the 1994 festival exceeded ¥1 million (table 36), the median donation being ¥5,000. Just over half the doya contributed, although many with pathetically small amounts—¥2–3,000. There are two associations of Korean doya owners, one supporting Seoul and the other Pyongyang. The former gave ¥20,000, the latter ¥10,000. Bars and restaurants donated far more generously than doya. By far the biggest donation (¥100,000) came from the Kotobuki Mah Jongg Club.

Activists at other yoseba are rather shocked that Junichirō takes festival donations from local doya owners, shopkeepers, etc. Mr. Fukada of Kamanichirō told me that such people were class enemies of day laborers and that Kamanichirō would not take their dirty money. He said that the Kamagasaki summer festival was financed entirely through donations from the workers themselves.[17] It seems that Junichirō's concept of community is far more inclusive than Kamanichirō's.

The Winter Survival Campaign (Ettō)

I took part in the twentieth, twenty-first, and twenty-fifth Ettō, in the winters of 1993–1994, 1994–1995 and 1998–1999. The word literally translates as "wintering" or "passing the winter," but in context it has a somewhat grimmer ring to it, hence my translation.

Just as the Summer Festival coincides with Bon, so the Ettō is focused on the other great festival in the Japanese calendar, *Shōgatsu* (New Year). Again, the great cities fall silent as people struggle through appalling traffic jams to their parental or grandparental families in the country, while those who stay in the city hole up watching festive TV and eating rice cakes and dried persimmons.

No one questions the importance of company at Bon and Shōgatsu. The great difference, of course, is that Shōgatsu is a winter festival, and in yoseba the winter is associated with severe physical hardship and risk of death. Each year one of the Ettō slogans is that "not one person will die" (*hitori mo shisha o dasanai*), but this is not always achieved. There were four deaths around the time of the 1993–1994 Kotobuki Ettō: one man who died of exposure in front of the Center, another fished out of the Nakamura river, a third found dead in his doya room, apparently of natural causes, on new year's day itself; and a fourth rushed to hospital by the volunteer medical unit (*Iryō-han*), only to die later.[18]

In December 1969, the Kotobuki District Self-governing Association staged a Winter Festival. The experiment was not repeated until 1974–1975, by which time the oil shock recession was threatening the lives of underemployed day laborers. So the concept of the winter festival merged with the need to protect lives and campaign for jobs and welfare, producing the characteristic format of the Ettō.

The main events of the Ettō last from about 28 December to 3 January, for two reasons: first, this is the period when building sites, docks, casual labor exchanges, and welfare facilities are closed for New Year, depriving day laborers of their usual sources of income and support. Secondly, this is also the period when it is easiest to mobilize volunteers, since they too are off work.

The volunteers, some of them day laborers themselves but mostly students and other idealistic younger people, provide hot meals, blankets, and medical advice. They also organize karaoke contests, street theater, debates, etc. Most of the volunteers are either Christians or politically left wing. Some of the catering is done by the union, some by a senior citizens' self-help group called the Old People's Club (*Rōjin Kurabu*) and some by the monks of Tokuonji. Like the summer festival, the Ettō is an institution at all the major yoseba. The winter of 1998–1999 saw the twenty-ninth Kamagasaki Ettō and the twenty-seventh at San'ya.[19]

But alongside this voluntary operation, there is also an official, bureaucratic Ettō. Ever since the oil shock winter of 1974–1975, the Yokohama city government has taken measures, centered on Kotobuki, to keep the homeless off the street over New Year. These measures have gradually improved in response to prolonged campaigning by Junichirō and other groups over the years.

The biggest budget item is housing. Each year, the city government pays a private contractor to put up prefabricated dormitories in Kotobuki, to house several hundred homeless workers over New Year.

This is an expensive business—costing the public purse more than ¥80 million for the 1994–1995 Ettō—but ironically, the prefabs are dismantled a couple of weeks after being put up, while many of their inhabitants go straight back on the streets. Residence in the prefabs was permitted for just eleven days (29 December to 8 January) at the 1994–1995 Ettō, itself the longest period ever allowed.

These prefabricated dormitories are the symbolic center of the Ettō, just as the stage is the center of the Summer Festival. But whereas the building of the stage is done by the people of Kotobuki themselves, the prefabs are built by an external contractor that makes no use of day laborers. In January 1994 I interviewed the site manager, who said it was not uncommon for onlooking day laborers to shout out "give us a job!" (shigoto kure-yo) while his men were erecting and dismantling the prefabs.

Once the prefabs are up, however, Junichirō makes a big point of keeping their day-to-day management under worker control. "Autonomous Control in Force" (Jishu Kanri Jisshi-chū) proclaims a banner outside one of the prefabs. There are no policemen or bureaucrats keeping an eye on the men, in sharp contrast to Tokyo and Nagoya, where temporary winter accommodation for the homeless is strictly controlled, often with the use of private security firms.[20]

Junichirō is justifiably proud that it manages to maintain the Ettō prefabs as a commune rather than a prison. Bureaucrats who come to check up on the prefabs get a cool reception, and during the 1992–1993 Ettō a Junichirō member tried to refuse the police permission to photograph the interior after a man had died in one of the prefabs (Stevens 1995a:177). But there is a price to pay for this degree of autonomy: the union itself must deal with any behavior problems, and must shoo the men out into the cold January air on the last morning of "autonomous control"—with the coldest period of the Yokohama winter still to come.

The government argument is that workers should be able to survive by their own efforts or through orthodox forms of social welfare outside the holiday season, but during the recession-bound 1990s this became ever less realistic. The opening of a permanent shelter at Matsukage-chō in November 1994 was a belated recognition of this truth by the city government. The Matsukage shelter housed some seventy people around the year, doubling to 140 during the Ettō period. Permanent capacity was increased to over a hundred in 2000.

My own impression was that seasonal sentiment, similar to that behind Christmas bonuses to old age pensioners in Britain, was the main factor in the city of Yokohama's Ettō provisions in Kotobuki. There is a sense that at New Year at least, everyone should have a hometown.

Room as House

Many day laborers build houses and apartments, but cannot afford to live in one themselves. It is an enduring and keenly felt irony, symbolic of social injustice. However, the conceptual space of the Japanese home is reproduced in the most unpromising circumstances. Doya rooms, although in many ways more primitive than the worst in an American skid row hotel,[21] will always have a *genkan*, an entrance area where one takes off one's shoes. In a house or school (Tobin 1992:32–33), the genkan is a hallway, symbolically marking the transition from public to private space; in a doya room, it is a sunken rectangle of space set into the tatami-mat floor, just big enough to park a pair of shoes.[22]

Some homeless day laborers maintain this sense of space:

> There was just one homeless man in the park. . . . He had turned the area underneath a small slide into a cozy little home. He had draped a plastic car cover over the top of the slide to form a protective awning, and he was sound asleep (or faking it) in a futon underneath the slide. Near his feet was a larder, with a selection of instant noodles, bottled water, dry biscuits etc. He had even contrived a sort of genkan, by laying out a blue rectangular plastic bath cover at the entrance to the house. His battered boots were standing neatly together on the bath cover.[23]

Some improvised homes were communal, such as this one concealed under a disused motorway access ramp near Kotobuki:

> A small ladder led down to Nakasone's home, which was in a small fissure between the side of the road and a great wall of concrete a couple of meters away. There was a concrete overhang under which were the futons and sleeping bags of Nakasone and two other men, spaced at wide enough intervals to allow some privacy. There was a sort of communal al fresco living room in front of the overhang, with a low table, a homemade cooker created from a large salad oil tin with holes cut out of it, a mulch of cardboard and old newspapers on the floor, and a black rubbish bag which proved to be the larder, well stocked with bread and vegetables.
>
> The whole place was filthy. There was a *go* board, but the pieces were scattered all over the living room, along with empty cans, cigarette butts, plates with not-quite-finished meals decomposing on them, etc. Conveniently, there was a sewer grill set into the concrete in one corner of the living room; Nakasone and his friends would piss straight into it.[24]

See also my account of Kuriyama (pp. 144–146) for an example of how shack construction can entail cooperative enterprise and hierarchical exchange relationships.

My overall impression was that homeless yoseba men were resourceful and mutually cooperative in improvising places to live and ways of living. Other observers convey a similar impression:

> Walking around the area at night I saw homeless men camped out by the roadside, in a small encampment on a railway embankment, in the edges of doorways, in the tunnels underneath the overhead railway line at Shin-Imamiya, lying amid the bicycle racks around the underground stations, beneath road bridges in their own self-constructed cardboard and metal structures. Some have gone so far as to bring furniture out onto the street, so there are chests of drawers and tables—to visit them is as if walking into their pavement living room. (Kalvis 1995:21–22, in Kamagasaki)

Bonfire as Hearth

Another important symbol of community in Kotobuki is the bonfire *(takibi)*, which is kept burning most of the time during the colder months. There is a well-established location: an area of concrete about five meters square beneath the outside staircase leading to the upper level of the Center. At the lower end there is a concrete wall, at the higher end two metal stanchions create the meeting points of three more imaginary walls. The wall and the sloping ceiling are blackened by years of smoke, and the ground is strewn with dirty old futons, cardboard boxes, empty bottles and cans, etc.

If yoseba festivals replicate the idealized hometown, and individual dwellings the spatiality of home, the bonfire is a symbolic hearth, which preserves a homely atmosphere although the people keeping warm around it vary by the day and hour.

I mostly found the bonfire a relaxed and friendly place. It was home to the bottom layer of Kotobuki society, the yankara (see glossary), whose soot-blackened faces associated them with the bonfire even when they wandered away from it. But more successful day laborers would also drop in on their way to and from work, to warm their hands and converse. Anyone finding a piece of wood or cardboard in the vicinity would drop it off at the bonfire for fuel. The old man who ran the fruit and vegetable stall by the Center always donated his empty boxes.

There was a less homely side to the bonfire as well. The combination of drunk people and an open fire caused numerous serious acci-

Photo 6.3 *Yankara* around the Bonfire at the Kotobuki Labor Center. The graffiti on the pillar warns that a certain construction company has cut wages and doesn't even pay travel expenses. Photo by Tokuda Masahiro, winter 1983–1984. Reprinted by permission.

dents, one of which I witnessed;[25] and a fatal stabbing incident, which occurred at the bonfire on 18 April 1990, led to a day laborer named Nobuta Masao being convicted of murder.[26] Again, Dr. Saiki Teruko of the Kotobuki clinic told me of a case in 1992 when a man came in with hideous burns on his face and hands but with the rest of his body unscathed. He told her that some men had shoved his face and hands in the fire as punishment for persistently failing to provide fuel.[27] Clearly the bonfire was not such a free society as to dispense with rules altogether.

At one point during my fieldwork, a man named Morimura* turned the bonfire area into a restaurant, selling curried rice cooked over the bonfire at ¥400 a portion. Very few people actually paid this amount— friends were given free helpings, others exchanged drinks for food, and one or two made donations worth more than the announced price of the food.[28] The restaurant lasted less than a week. On one occasion I was left in charge of it. There were no customers:

> I looked into the embers. It was fully night by now, and I was alone in the heart of Kotobuki. I thought of the houses in Shinohata,

the village described by Ronald Dore, and the steady symbolic replacement of the timbers as the generations passed . . . [29]

The takibi has no timbers, of course. It is just a semi-sheltered space. And yet it has a hearth, indeed it is defined and colored by the hearth, like the "unreconstructed soot-blackened houses" of Shinohata.[30] It has a roof . . . and it too has housed many generations. But in Kotobuki the generations change over much more quickly; from month to month the crowd at the takibi may be quite different. Last month there was no Morimura; this month he is running a restaurant here. Next month, who knows?

And yet even if all their original timbers are replaced, the houses in Shinohata are still the same houses across the years, just as the human body may change all its cells but remain recognizably the same. And even the takibi, which may change all its constituent human elements in the space of a few months, is still the same social institution.

And for all its associations with poverty and death by fire, it is a homely place. Sometimes you may find a few umbrellas hanging from a clothes line; or some futons, or some clothes or cushions. Or there may be a big pile of firewood. It is a construction of home, in the midst of urban anomie.[31]

Of course, as Dore points out,[32] the oldest son in a village like Shinohata has a special role in maintaining the traditional household: he is in charge of generational transition, ensuring that the house endures even after his parents' death. Perhaps the blackened hearth at the heart of Kotobuki had a special significance for those who, according to custom, should have been presiding over a different hearth, in a different place.

Kuriyama

I first met Kuriyama* in January 1994. He told me had arrived in Kotobuki seven months before, after being thrown out of the house by his father. He was an only child, and at forty had still been living with his parents. He used to work as a cook, but kept getting fired for drunkenness and fighting. One night he came home late, drunk, and noisy once too often.

> When my father finally threw me out, he told me never
> to darken his door again. I know he meant it. He's a

(continues)

(continued)

> retired civil servant, from the Ministry of Posts and Tele-
> communications. He never makes jokes. He never
> smiles."[33]

Kuriyama was thin, with glasses and no chin. He talked fast and breathlessly, and gave an impression of infinite weakness. As well as alcohol, he said he was also addicted to saunas, and had spent several million yen on visiting them over a couple of years. He claimed that he had another ¥3 million in a bank account, but had left the passbook and seal at his parents' house and didn't dare go back for them. He fawned on me and others, and sponged somewhat, though I somehow believed him when he said that one day he would return favors.

How had this apparently mild-mannered man got into so much trouble? Perhaps it had something to do with the "great love" (dai-ren'ai) that he said he experienced when he was still a teenager. The girl was a teenager too. They wanted to marry, but their parents said they were too young. She was sent away to live with distant relatives. He lost touch with her, and says he's barely looked at a woman since.

Kuriyama had a tough time in Kotobuki. At first he stayed at the Atami-sō, but he couldn't keep up the rent payments and took to the streets. In the warmer months he slept in the covered area atop the stairs in front of the labor office, but in mid-January that got too cold and he moved into a home-made shack built on a flower bed concealed behind a hedge along the side of the Nakamura River. The old man in the shack next door helped him to build it. He referred to this man as his "grandfather figure" (ō-oyabun) and a slightly less elderly man in the third shack in the flower bed as his "father figure" (oyabun). He seemed to crave these paternalistic relationships.

When I knew him he was living in his shack, under heavy threat of police eviction, with a stray cat he'd picked up and named Shigeko.

Getting work was a struggle for Kuriyama. At one point he did night work, reeling up drums of cable for NTT, the telephone company. Later he found some semi-steady work at a construction site in Ōyama, a two-hour journey from Kotobuki. It only paid ¥10,000 a day and they didn't cover his travel expenses. Once they even sent him back to Kotobuki empty-handed because they didn't happen to have work for him on that particular day. Even so, he was grateful for the work, and pointed out that regular

(continues)

146

(continued)

work was better than single-day contracts even if the pay was lower. When he couldn't find work, he lived on food vouchers.

Kuriyama visibly aged and frayed during the three months I knew him. He was a sensitive man who hated suffering and tried to help others, seldom getting any gratitude. He would fetch a blanket to cover up a drunken acquaintance lying in the road, and try to stop people from catching alight at the bonfire. He saw much filth, violence, and degradation, and was asked to carry dubious packages by yakuza. He dreamed of buying an interview suit and escaping from Kotobuki, perhaps by getting a job at a pachinko parlor. These places are havens for hard-working people with difficult personal histories, but as Kuriyama discovered, they usually insist that new employees be no more than thirty-five years old.

The last time I saw Kuriyama, in March 1994, he was subjected to a vicious verbal assault by a sadistic bully, and scurried away in fear. I hope he disappeared from Kotobuki for positive reasons, but I do not know.

7

Marginal Identity
in the Yoseba

I N THIS CHAPTER I attempt to identify salient elements in the identity
of yoseba day laborers. I argue that marginality is the fundamental
condition of yoseba life, and that it implies two further conditions:
a degree of freedom over one's daily activities that is rarely found in
the mainstream, and a long-term likelihood of rapid decline and death.
These elements of marginality, freedom and fate are all reflected in the
philosophical outlook and behavior of yoseba men.

Marginality

The Marginal Condition

Marginality, a detachment from the institutions of mainstream society,
is the defining condition of life in the yoseba. Geographically, marginality is expressed in the drastic change of landscape on the very clearly
defined borders of the yoseba, which I discuss in the next chapter.
Socially, it is symbolized in the detachment of day laborers from the
two central institutions of modern capitalist society: the family and
the company. Whether that detachment should be described as

147

involuntary, in terms of exclusion, or as voluntary, in terms of escape, is a highly contentious issue within the yoseba.

Isolation from the Family

Nearly all day laborers are detached from their natal and marital families in a geographical sense, for the great majority live on their own, whether in apartments, doya rooms, wooden shacks, or cardboard boxes. In many cases, however, detachment is also social and permanent. Some day laborers say that they have been explicitly rejected by their parents (Kuriyama pp. 144–146) or siblings (Kimitsu pp. 168–170), others *assume* that they would be rejected or feel too ashamed to go home anyway (Shigehirō pp. 188–190). Yet others say they avoid their folks because they dislike them or see nothing in common. Similarly, some men say they have been thrown out by the wife, or simply that they are long separated. I also heard of a man whose parents did not reject him, but who had to make his infrequent visits home under cover of darkness so that the neighbors would not know that his parents were still seeing him.

It is tempting to read the apparent isolation of day laborers from their families simply as a reflection of a culture of exclusion. However, it would be wrong to assume that day laborers have always been detached from family life. Though seventeenth-century castle building was done largely by single men, later in the Tokugawa period most day laborers had families (Leupp 1992:149–150). From the Meiji era onward a split seems to have developed, with family men and solo operators coexisting and competing. Matsubara's 1888 account of the Tokyo poor has a brief chapter on the subject (Matsubara 1988 [1888]:158–160). He describes the miserable struggles of men trying to support families on inadequate wages, then states, "In contrast to this, it is the bachelors who have it easy" (158–159). They can live cheaply, change lodgings at the drop of a hat, and are not bound by debt and obligations to landlords and employers.

Matsubara's value judgment is echoed some forty years later in Kon's 1926 account of the Fukagawa-Honjo slums. By this time the two types of day laborer are living separately, though in close proximity. In the slum Kon finds doss-house areas for single men adjoining areas of working-class housing grouped around factories. The family men who lived here had somewhat higher status than the solitary males, yet as Kon toured the district after dark, he reflected that "these little households were somehow more miserable" than the solitary day laborers. The latter could at least get heartily drunk and lose themselves in dreams (Kon 1971 [1930]:122–123).

The reason why the single men strike these observers as being in a better position than the married men is stated by Matsubara and implied by Kon: neither in 1888 nor in 1926 were day laborers paid enough to support a family except in extreme poverty. The dual population described by the two Japanese scholars makes an interesting contrast with the fictionalized British day laborers of the Edwardian era described by Robert Tressell in his famous book, *The Ragged Trousered Philanthropists* (1914). The book describes the intense fear of unemployment among jobbing house painters in the fictional town of Mugsborough. The point is that *all* these men were married, and the need to feed their wives and children is described as the dominant fact of life for them. In an age when insecure labor was the norm, it carried no stigma; but its effects on family life, as described by Tressell, are disastrous.

In Japan today, if a day laborer is skilled, resourceful, careful, and lucky, he may be economically capable of supporting a family; yet family men have almost disappeared from the yoseba population. This seems to have been a fairly recent development: Nomoto (1974) describes Kotobuki with plenty of lively family life, and several informants confirmed this, in other yoseba as well as Kotobuki.[1]

During my fieldwork in Kotobuki, I came across just two day laborers who were definitely still married and maintaining family life. One was Mr. Aoyagi,* an elderly man who used Kotobuki for work contacts and maintained a house with his wife a twenty-minute walk distant. Aoyagi was intelligent—he spoke good English and read Hebrew scriptures for a hobby—and had acquired a sheaf of licenses to operate various kinds of industrial machinery. He was also well informed about all kinds of social security and insurance benefits, and ruthlessly abused the various systems. Even so he grumbled constantly about the difficulty of making ends meet, and his wife was working too. He had two grown-up children, and was struggling to finance his daughter's wedding when I knew him.

Four other men also claimed to be married and living with their wives outside Kotobuki, giving just two definite cases of sustained married life and four probables out of 158 Kotobuki informants (table 29).

Mizuno[2] ascribes the decline in family life in another doya-gai, Kamagasaki, to a pair of contrasting factors:

1. The authorities responded to the first Kamagasaki riot (1961) by trying to reduce the size of the place. One tactic was to speed up offers of municipal housing to day laborers with families, tearing down the barracks in Kamagasaki in which they had previously lived.

2. At the same time, a growing tendency for Kamagasaki to dominate the Osaka region's casual labor market at the expense of
   smaller yoseba elsewhere, brought more men into Kamagasaki.
   Doya operators responded by designing ever smaller rooms.

As in most aspects of doya-gai life, government policy plays a part
alongside broader social and economic factors. To me, the gradual
disappearance of the family man from the yoseba is one illustration of
the degree to which poverty is a social, as much as an economic,
phenomenon. Even now that Japan's "economic miracle" has given
way to prolonged recession, competent day laborers can still make
better money than at any time before the war. The difference is that
day labor used to be viewed by many women as a reasonable occupation for a husband, whereas today it seems that hardly any women
take that view. After the high-growth decades, they have come to
expect better. The economic problems of day laboring have been softened, but the stigma has strengthened. Perhaps it is true that it is
worse to be poor in a rich country than to be poor in a poor country.
    Many day laborers told me that they could not go home to their
parental families because they had been disowned. I often wondered
whether this was necessarily true in every case, or whether some day
laborers were wrongly assuming that they would not be allowed home.
Shigehirō (pp. 188–190) was pleasantly surprised to find that his parents were glad to hear from him after ten years' silence. Several owners and managers of doya told me that they were often visited by
people looking for missing menfolk, who would show them an old
photograph and ask for information. Similarly, welfare centers in doya-
gai usually have a noticeboard carrying messages from relatives, usually mothers, looking for missing men. It is impossible to put any kind
of number on this, but my intuitive feeling is that for every family that
has expelled a man for unacceptable behavior, there is one that longs
for the return of a man whose behavior—did he but know it—has in
fact been forgiven or understood.
    Whether from actual expulsion or irrational shame, a strong major-
ity of the mainland Japanese I encountered in the yoseba were isolated
from their parental families. However, the Okinawan minority were
different. Out of thirteen Okinawans among my Kotobuki field survey, six were definitely in touch with their natal family and none were
definitely isolated. Several Okinawans told me that however poor they
might become, somehow they would always find the money to make
a trip home to visit their parental family, and ancestral graves, once
every two or three years. Being a day laborer did not imply failure to
them as it did to some mainland Japanese. On the contrary, they were

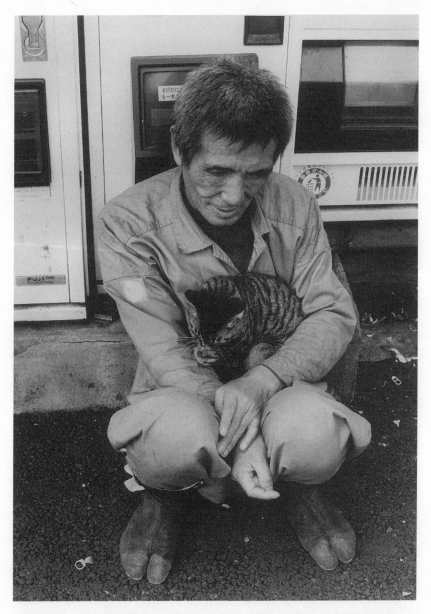

Photo 7.1 The Marginal Condition: Isolation. This man with his tabby and his *tabi* (worker's split-toe boots) was photographed in front of some vending machines at Namidabashi in San'ya by Morita Ichiroh, September 1991. Reprinted by permission.

engaging in migrant labor, something with a long and honorable tradition in the Ryukyus. Their attitudes and social situation were much closer to those of the foreign workers in Kotobuki than to those of the mainland Japanese.

Isolation from Workplace Relationships

Many writers have commented on the great importance of workplace relationships to the Japanese male (e.g., Nakane 1970; Rohlen 1974; Hendry 1987:136–140). Since most day laborers work for many different companies for short periods of time, they are naturally outside these relationships. Regular men who work side by side with day laborers show a range of attitudes toward them: some will ignore them, others enjoy their company and feel a sense of pity or admiration for their different way of life. But they certainly view them differently from their fellow regulars, who will usually fall into one of three categories: *senpai, kōhai or dōki.* These categories refer respectively to people who joined the company before, after, or at the same time as oneself. Years of service usually count for more than simple age in determining relative categories, and will deeply affect attitudes and forms of address. It follows that an awareness of rank is built into most workplace relationships, even where rank happens to coincide.

Since day laborers are outside the company, they are also outside the system of hierarchical relationships. Indeed, some specifically mention inability to get on with this system as one of their reasons for quitting or being fired from companies they once worked for. Whether they are ideologically egalitarian or not, all day laborers are outside the dominant institution enforcing hierarchy in Japan and to that extent isolation from the company implies approximate equality within the yoseba.

Marginal Dispositions

Day, Papataxiarchis, and Stewart (1999:1–24) point out that "oppositional identity" may be observed in many and various marginal groups. Introducing an interesting collection of comparative papers on marginal people, they argue that these groups define themselves in contrast or opposition to the dominant culture of more powerful neighbours in a fairly systematic and self-conscious fashion. They consider themselves "outside" society, beyond the reach of powerful and would-be controlling neighbors. They place themselves at the center of an alternative moral universe to that which is dominant, and thereby obviate the experience of dependence and domination with an imagery of cultural difference. Day, Papataxiarchis, and Stewart suggest the following aspects of oppositional identity: Hegemonic interpretations and practices are challenged, inverted, and transformed; in particular, social hierarchies are denied in favor of relations among putatively autonomous and equal actors; and there is a radical focus on the present, since any more permanent transcendence, (e.g., religious) is compromised through its close association with the dominant order, where it is often seen explicitly as a mechanism for control (1–24).

As I argue in my own contribution to the Day, Papataxiarchis and Stewart collection (Gill 1999c), This kind of oppositional identity is clearly in evidence in the yoseba. In this "alternative moral universe," the yoseba are viewed as oases of proletarian culture amid an arid desert of bland middle-class conformity. A man from San'ya can generally expect a warm welcome in Kotobuki and Kamagasaki, provided he can prove his familiarity with the day-laboring life. As I tried to show in chapter 6, the yoseba becomes an alternative hometown for many men. The inversion of mainstream practices, especially an egalitarian rejection of mainstream hierarchy, may also be observed, as may a radical focus on the present. These phenomena, which cluster around the key concept of "freedom" and might collectively be described as "positive marginality," I will discuss in the next section (pp. 153–162). However, I also noticed a counter discourse of "negative marginality," whose motifs cluster around the key concept of "fate." This I will discuss in the final section of this chapter (pp. 163–168). It is my aim to show that both these apparently contradictory discourses stem from the material and cultural conditions of yoseba life.

Freedom

The Condition of Freedom

Day laborers' detachment from family and workplace implies a condition of freedom rarely found in modern industrialized countries. The two crucial components of this free condition are mobility (freedom to go where you want) and choice-based relationships (freedom to choose whom you associate with). Both these freedoms are of course constrained by material want and social stigma—day laborers are not generally free to stay in five-star hotels or to associate with the bourgeoisie—but they are nonetheless real.

Mobility

In a sense, all construction workers are nomadic, in their work if not in their private lives. They move from one work site to another as projects finish or contracts end; and the more and the farther one's place of work moves, the more likely one is to develop a mobile personal lifestyle. Especially if one's career starts with the big move from country to city, and involves spending long periods of time in temporary work-site dormitories, this will militate against marriage and family life, and may corrode family life if it does get established. The absence of family in turn enables the worker to move about more freely in search of work.

Out of 158 Kotobuki day laborers, I found only fourteen who had any apparent reason to hang around, such as a wife, children, permanent residence, or immovable possessions. There were forty-four who travelled frequently and another one hundred of whose movements I knew little.

Mobility is a crucial aspect of the lives of Japanese day laborers, which sharply distinguishes them from many other groups commonly labelled as being in the underclass. Thus, Jones (1971:81–84) says that nineteenth-century casual laborers in the East End of London were strikingly immobile, largely because of their dependence on the small but regular incomes often earned by their wives. Davis (1995:24) quotes the U.S. writer on underclass issues, William Julius Wilson, as saying, "Residents of inner-city neighborhoods have no option other than to remain in their neighborhoods. . . . Social mobility leads to geographic mobility." Davis comments: "The underclass he scrutinizes might as well be in chains for all the mobility they have" (24). So I contend that the freedom of movement of day laborers is by no means the banal or worthless thing that some readers might imagine it to be.

Detachment from family also distinguishes day laborers from many other occupational groups commonly defined as being in the "informal economy" (Hart 1973). In the Third World context at least, the informal economy is usually portrayed as consisting of "many small-scale enterprises whose labor input is predominantly provided by relatives of the owner" (Breman 1994:6, citing an ILO report of 1976). In Japan too, there are numerous small-scale enterprises, such as *machi-kōba* ("town factories"), that make use of kin labor. But day laborers do not work for relatives. On the contrary, their labor arrangements tend to be *more* impersonal than those of people in the formal economy.

Day laborer mobility takes many forms. Some day laborers make a positive virtue of voluntary mobility, moving around for pleasure and variety as well as economic advantage. Some, like Shigehirō (pp. 188–190), oscillate between Kotobuki and San'ya; others, like Noriyuki (pp. 111–112), tour from yoseba to yoseba over a much wider district, sometimes getting away from the big cities by doing stints on rural construction projects or seasonal farm work. Many more spend periods of several years in one yoseba before moving to another, like Kimitsu (pp. 168–170). A few even roam internationally, like Ogata (p. 97) or Manabu, a man I met in Kotobuki who had a history of day laboring in the United States.[3] Some, it is true, prefer to hunker down in one yoseba indefinitely, like Kōhei (pp. 78–79)—but this too is a matter of personal choice for them. Voluntary mobility implies the possibility of voluntary immobility.

The mobility of day laborers is in sharp contrast to that of salarymen (white-collar workers), whose companies may forcibly transfer them to distant towns, often obliging them to live apart from their families (see note 13, also Shiina 1994). Although day laborers are often separated from their families permanently, at least they have a fair degree of control over where they go in their everyday working lives.

This hobo lifestyle is much glamorized by the Japanese left, as in the following quotation from a book written by yoseba activists:

> The poverty-stricken yoseba workers drifted off in search of food and work. To drift is a good thing. Water also lives by drifting. Standing water soon goes stagnant.[4]

Activists sometimes use the word *tensen* to describe the day-laboring lifestyle. This literally means "fighting from front to front," but most roving day laborers I have met are, understandably, less romantic about it. For instance I found Noriyuki's (pp. 111–112) rambling, close-to-nature lifestyle powerfully appealing, but when I asked him which yoseba he liked best, he replied: "I hate them all. I go to them because there's no alternative. Not because I like it."[5]

Choice-Based Relationships

For better or worse, most people spend large parts of their lives in the company of people they have not chosen: their parents, siblings, children, and other relatives. The relationship between spouses is the only legally sanctioned relationship in postindustrial societies that is based on choice, and in Japan parental influence on this choice is still powerful in many cases. The sheer persistence and authority of kinship relations tends to overshadow relationships of friendship for many people. But in the yoseba kinship plays a very limited role.[6] The men nearly all live alone, and they make their own networks of friendship—or not. Some, usually the more economically successful, take the view that a friend in need is a bloody nuisance, and deliberately keep to themselves. The majority, however, as well as having an emotional need for friendship, also see friends as a safety net or insurance policy: it is better to look after them, against the day when you may need looking after yourself.

I found that yoseba friendships were very variable. I met men who claimed to have known each other for several decades, and chance encounters between old friends happened frequently. Sometimes one partner in a friendship would drift off, destination unknown, and the other partner would do no more than shrug his shoulders. Sometimes a friend would take on a role usually associated with kin, such as escorting a sick man to the doctor or helping in negotiations with social services. However, I never felt I was in the presence of a friendship that carried the sheer weight of obligation associated with kinship. It is that relative lack of obligation that makes friendship less oppressive than kinship; at the same time, of course, it makes it a decidedly shaky insurance policy in troubled times.

Libertarian Dispositions

Associated with the condition of freedom, based on mobility and choice-based relationships, are a set of libertarian dispositions. As in the Day/Papataxiarchis/Stewart thesis, these are oppositional in character. They mutually overlap, but may be loosely categorized as: present orientation, informality, and egalitarianism.

The category to which day laborers most often oppose themselves conceptually is the "salaryman," the stereotypical white-collar worker at a big company.[7] He must commute vast distances from his cramped family apartment to the same boring workplace every day, bow and scrape to a dictatorial boss all day long, work many hours of unpaid overtime to display loyalty to the company, flatter the boss at drinking sessions and golf outings he would rather avoid, and when he finally goes home he has an equally dictatorial wife and demanding children waiting for him.

Against this caricature (not without a grain of truth, but still exaggerated enough to be called a resistance strategy), some day laborers like to picture themselves as free, autonomous, transacting individuals. Their working and social lives are based on free choice: the simple freedom to decide for yourself whether or not to get out of bed and go to work each morning is often mentioned, and some men make a point of describing themselves as "free workers" (jiyū rōdōsha).

This mindset has developed in opposition to an industrial culture in which companies have tended to intrude into their employees' lives far more than in most capitalist systems. Many day laborers have experienced that culture, having lived a more conventional lifestyle in the past, with a steady job and a marriage; their departure from these two dominant institutions is variously represented as rejection of them or expulsion from them according to circumstances and the man.

Certainly day laborers have to make larger choices and decisions about their work than salarymen do. Whether to work, when to work, where to work, and what sort of work to do; these issues which rarely present themselves to the regular employee are an ever-present concern to day laborers, who view themselves, rather like Day's London sex-workers, as freelance entrepreneurs (Day 1999). The terms on which they work demand strategy—consider Kōhei's policy of dealing with as many tehaishi as possible (p. 56) for example. As I have mentioned (pp. 23, 25), this strategy of deliberately limited engagement with numerous employers has a long history.

Present Orientation

During the two years I spent doing fieldwork in Kotobuki and other yoseba (1993–1995), the most striking attitude I encountered among day laborers was a powerful orientation to the present moment.[8]

Two key day-laboring words are *genba* and *genkin*—literally, "present place" and "present money." The former signifies the workplace, typically a building site, which may be different every day. The word has proletarian machismo: it suggests that actual work, in the here and now, is being done—as opposed to meaningless, unreal, pen-pushing work. The latter means "cash in hand," as in *genkin shigoto*, a cash-in-hand job, usually meaning a single-day job for which you are paid on the day. As we know (pp. 61–63), this is not the only kind of job transacted at the yoseba, but informants' comments and the job take-up rates in table 13 indicate that most day laborers prefer single-day contracts to those covering a longer period. Any delay in the reward for work done is resented, by men who often cannot afford to wait for payment because of their nonaccumulative lifestyles.

When day laborers work by the day and are paid by the day, they come about as close as one can in an industrialized society to practicing "immediate return," as defined by Woodburn (e.g., 1982) in his analysis of some East African hunter-gatherers. Perhaps, like the Gujarati laborers described by Breman (1994:133–287), Japanese day laborers may be characterized as "wage hunters and gatherers." Although of course cash is itself a store of value and hence introduces an element of delayed return absent from traditional hunter-gatherer societies, the delay is rarely very long for a day laborer. Money is soon spent, and many day laborers have the principle of not working again until they are broke—a practice long ago observed among casual workers in other industrialized countries.[9] Several day laborers quoted to me a proverbial saying dating from the Edo period: *Yoigoshi no kane wa motanai*—"Money is not something you keep overnight."

The disadvantage of the present-oriented lifestyle is that it renders people extremely vulnerable to bad weather, bad luck, and aging. This vulnerability is characteristic of day laborers, as has been all too obvious during the Heisei recession. Without savings, they are very soon in trouble when jobs dry up. They may be forced to leave the doya for want of money to pay the rent and be reduced to sleeping rough. As another proverbial expression puts it: *"Hiyatoi korosu nya hamono wa iranu, ame no mikka mo fureba ii"* ("You don't need a knife to kill a day laborer. Three rainy days in a row is all it takes").

This powerful orientation to the present—getting the reward for one's labor immediately, and spending it immediately—recalls Orwell's observation in *Down and Out in Paris and London* that "[w]hen you are approaching poverty, you . . . discover the great redeeming feature of poverty: the fact that it annihilates the future. Within certain limits, it is actually true that the less money you have, the less you worry. . . . You think vaguely, 'I shall be starving in a day or two—shocking, isn't it?' And then the mind wanders to other topics" (Orwell 1986 [1933]:16).[10]

Yoseba naturally attract the attention of the social services and of well-intentioned volunteers. Like the relations between social workers and skid-row alcoholics described by Wiseman (1970; see note 10), those between helpers and day laborers may be characterized as a dialogue between future and present orientation. For example, in an attempt to inculcate the saving habit among day laborers, the Yokohama social services have set up a special bank in Kotobuki. It has no computers or cash machines, just old-fashioned ledgers. However, it stays open until 8 P.M. in recognition of the fact that day laborers are often away at work during usual banking hours. It is lightly patronized. The people running it told me that one of their principles was to allow any number of transactions on an account in a day. Some savers would deposit a day's wage on getting back from work and then withdraw it at intervals of hours or even minutes in the course of the evening—so uneven was the struggle between long-term security and present gratification.

Many of the volunteers are Christians,[11] for whom future-orientation takes on an existential dimension. They give out food and blankets to homeless men, and some of the groups attempt to make converts. The idea is that the men should look after their physical health in the present life and look to their spiritual well-being in the hereafter.

As with the special bank, the battle with present-orientation is a tough one for the Christian volunteers. The number of converts appears to be rather small, and when it does happen, the understanding of what conversion means may differ between the missionary and the convert. Consider the following fieldnote, recording an encounter in front of a liquor store around 5:30 A.M. on a mid-winter morning:

> There was a thin little old man drinking *shōchū*, face lined with grey dirt. Said he was diabetic and had a dicky heart. "You need to be careful," I said. "I'm already 60 so it doesn't matter if I die," he replied. "I've been a Catholic for ages so I'll go to heaven. I go to church properly, every Sunday. They give you wine and bread, you know, just like this—" and he stuck out a twitchy little tongue.[12]

Ironically, this man's avowed acceptance of the Christian concept of an afterlife had become a justification for self-destructive behavior in the here and now.

Note that the stereotypical salaryman, against whom day laborers construct their oppositional identity, has to be oriented to the future, because he has his children to think of. They must have a stable home, so he must have a long-term loan. To pay the long-term loan he must have a long-term job, and to keep the long-term job he must avoid behaving in ways that might upset his employers or fellow workers. In addition, Japanese corporations have a range of systems for delaying the return to labor. About a third of annual remuneration is held back in the form of summer and winter "bonuses." Likewise, retirement payments will build up over the years and will not necessarily be paid at their full value if the employee leaves the firm before retirement.

These factors, more than any culturally given sense of loyalty, bind workers to their employers and effectively oblige them to obey the company at the cost of sacrificing personal freedom. Samuel Butler once said that it was ridiculous to speak of a man having free will if he was in the jaws of a lion; the popular view among day laborers, and among some salarymen themselves, is that a man in the jaws of the company has just as little ability to exercise free will.[13]

Egalitarianism

Despite the sometimes highly competitive labor market, many day laborers did stress egalitarian relationships between themselves. There were of course unmissable differences, in mastery of skills, degree of workplace success, standard of accommodation etc., but these were relatively small compared with the elaborate pyramidic hierarchy

160

Help me please...
For long years I've
lived in extreme pover-
ty and I can't take any
more...

No, I can't help you.

Why not?
Help me please...
You're a gentleman,
aren't you?

No, I can't help you.

Oh, You're so unsym-
pathetic and merciless
...why?

I can't help you be-
cause...

I'm just about to die
myself from overwork
...

Oh! I'm so sorry...

What a terrible
country!

Cartoon 7.1 The Fate of Day Laborers and Salarymen. Homeless and hungry, Kamayan begs a commuting salaryman for help. The latter protests that
he's about to die of overwork *(karōshi)* himself. A passing migrant laborer
comments that Japan is a scary kind of country. Cartoon by Arimura Sen
(Arimura 1989:30). Reprinted by permission.

associated with the larger type of Japanese corporation. I mostly found that day laborers would share food and drink, even with strangers, on terms that resembled "sharing" rather than "exchange" (Woodburn 1996). Street conversation, often accompanied by the kind of free sharing of alcohol described above, helped to create something like the "imagined, egalitarian community of shared moods" described by Day, Papataxiarchis, and Stewart (1999:10) in relation to Papataxiarchis's analysis of the exclusively masculine world of Greek peasant gamblers.

In addition to this overt egalitarianism, the way that gambling (pp. 66–69) and drinking (p. 69) were practiced in the yoseba also functioned as effective unseen levelling devices. Gambling is a particularly effective way of preventing the accumulation of money and of inequalities of wealth between day laborers, since the nature of the odds means that excess wealth tends to be transferred to the coffers of the gambling establishments. The most striking characteristic of yoseba gambling is that day laborers, in sharp contrast to the Greek peasants described by Papataxiarchis (1999), seldom gamble against each other, preferring forms of gambling that pit the punter against a professional house. Solidarity is expressed by not creating debts among friends. The yakuza who run most of the gambling establishments effectively skim off any surplus cash, ensuring that the community remains a net loser.[14]

A lot of money is also spent on alcohol in the yoseba, though there are sturdy minorities who neither drink nor gamble. Drinking practices also express solidarity and present orientation. The copious American sociological literature on skid row includes numerous references to "bottle gangs," semiformal groups of drinkers who contribute to the costs of buying a bottle and among whom some kind of record is kept to ensure that participants get a fair deal.[15] I found no such institution in the yoseba; rather, people would share alcohol with more or less anyone who rolled up. Some people were always giving while others always took, with no apparent assumption that debts were to be repaid in the future.

Most day laborers have very few possessions other than some basic clothes and occasionally a few tools. Indeed, possessions are widely viewed as an annoying encumbrance, since they hamper mobility. The few men I knew who *had* acquired a roomful of possessions complained that they had to carry on paying the rent on their doya room even when they were away working on period contracts or at other yoseba.

Informality

One theme that often cropped up in conversations with day laborers was that the doya-gai is a place where the formal social codes of

Photo 7.2   The Marginal Condition: Freedom. Photo of the late Nagai Tokujirō, taken in Yamashita Park, Yokohama by Tokuda Masahiro, 1983. Nagai's comment on being given a cigarette by Tokuda: "I haven't smoked one this long for years." Reprinted by permission.

mainstream society do not apply. People could make friends rapidly, being all in the same boat. There was no *uchi/soto* (insider/outsider)[16] problem because everyone in the doya-gai was an outsider anyway. People would talk straight, rather than using *tatemae* (saying things for form) for outsiders and reserving *honne* (true feelings) for insiders. In other words they presented the doya-gai as a place for "uncrafted selves," to modify Kondo (1990)—unpolished nuggets of selfhood.

One strain of Kondo's argument about how Japanese people craft their selves derives from sociolinguistics. Drawing on Harada 1975 and Bachnik 1982, she discusses the wide range of pronouns (*watakushi, watashi, boku, ore,* etc.) and other labels (kin descriptors, job titles, etc.) available to refer to oneself in Japanese as evidence for a multiple construction of selfhood in Japan (1990:29). However, a computer search of my fieldnotes threw up just three uses of *boku,* two of *watashi* (one from a very effeminate man), and one of *watakushi,* against twenty-seven uses of *ore,* the plainest pronoun, distinctively masculine and sometimes macho.[17] It may well be that the men would speak differently outside the yoseba, but inside you could, up to a point, be your simple self. This too, is an aspect of freedom—freedom from social convention.

Fate

The Fated Condition

If the marginal status of the yoseba and its inhabitants implies a large degree of autonomy in day-to-day life, it also implies *loss* of autonomy over the longer term. Nearly all day laborers, even the minority who are skilled artisans, rely on physical strength for their ability to get work. Long years of hard labor accelerate the aging process, and in many cases hard drinking and periods of rough sleeping accelerate it further still. Thus, while individual day laborers show a wide variety of character and career, the overall pattern of yoseba life is one of fairly rapid loss of physical strength.

The present-oriented lifestyle, without savings or pension entitlements, means that loss of strength implies loss of autonomy. In the hunter-gatherer groups with whom present-orientation is usually associated, the old are abandoned to their fate. This has tended to be the fate of Japanese day laborers too: a steady decline into increasingly permanent unemployment, illness, homelessness, and early death— on average, probably some fifteen to twenty years earlier than for the average Japanese man (cf p. 74).

The individual day laborer now faces his fate in the context of a profession that also appears to be in irreversible decline. Declining job opportunities (tables 1, 2, 13, 14) have made it steadily harder to maintain the old day-laboring lifestyle, and its more positive aspects have been whittled away. In Yokohama at least, the local authorities have responded by lowering the barriers preventing day laborers from going on welfare. Some 80 percent of the doya population is now on welfare (table 5), and as Stevens puts it: "This *yoseba* has changed from the macho day laborers' settlement to the 'welfare town'" (Stevens 1997:244).

Ultimately, then, the present-oriented lifestyle now has two alternative destinations: loss of autonomy as a welfare recipient, or early death. This fact of life is in the back of every day laborer's mind, and finds expression in a fatalistic outlook which is the counterpoint to the libertarian, happy-go-lucky attitudes described above. The balance between these two dispositions varies widely, but my impression was that both were present in all day laborers to a degree.

Fatalistic Dispositions

While many day laborers manage to stay well in control of their day-to-day lives, their overall view of life is often characterized by a pervasive fatalism—a combination clearly expressed by Sakashita, a skilled laborer specializing in high-level work. I remarked that his work was pretty dangerous. He responded thus:

> I'm not afraid of death. I'm aware of the possibility. If you fall, that's it. It's all over in a flash. But I'm ready for death. I can go any time. I've designed my life that way: I've no wife, no kids, and no regrets that I have no wife or kids. If I'd started a family, I'd have to take more care of my own life, I would have to think of the others. I'm better off on my own. I can die any time and it won't bother anyone. That is real freedom. I'm that sort of guy and I can't change.[18]

Sakashita shows an acute awareness of uncertainty and attempts to deal with it in this narrative by reasoning that every eventuality has been planned for—only to undermine his theme of willed living by admitting that the exercise of his own free will is itself predetermined by his own immutable character. Earlier in this conversation he blamed his wayward career on being a last child (suekko) and consequently spoiled (p. 119)—a form of sociological determinism to match the ontological variety in the passage quoted.

Sakashita twice remarked that he "just drifted" into Kotobuki in this same conversation. The verb *nagareru*, to drift, elegantly combines the concepts of mobility and passivity and is frequently used by day laborers, who are themselves sometimes referred to disparagingly as *nagare-mono* (drifters). Look again at the activists' comment quoted above, this time with emphasis added:

> The poverty-stricken yoseba workers *drifted* off in search of food and work. To *drift* is a good thing. Water also lives by *drifting*. Standing water soon goes stagnant.[19]

The imagery surrounding these drifting day laborers is liquid and piscine. They are called "angler-fish" (*ankō*) as they wait on the seabed of society for a job to come along, and go fishing (*asaru*) in rubbish bins. They are caught in labor camps called "octopus traps" (*tako-beya*); when a man is mugged while sleeping in the street they call the incident a "tuna" (*maguro*), because the victim is as helpless as a tuna on a chopping board; getting fired midway through a job is "getting the chop" (*butakiri*), a term that also derives from chopping up fish. When day laborers fail to get a job they say they have "overflowed" from the market (*abureru*); if depressed they may "drown themselves" (*oboreru*) in drink or other vices; in anger they call a man "scum" (*kasu*), and when it is time to leave town, they may simply "evaporate" (*jōhatsu suru*).[20]

Thus do day laborers present themselves as protean but passive beings. The yoseba vocabulary at once suggests the cunning and slippery
fish (mobile agent); the same fish on the chopping board (passive victim); and the liquid around it (helplessly spilled and poured substance).

In all sorts of ways, day laborers seem to deny their responsibility for
their own actions. Those who had once been married would rarely admit
to having walked out on their wives; they would prefer to say that they
had been "booted out" (*oidasareta*). One doubts whether marriage break-
ups are really as one sided as that, and one man even told me he'd been
booted out when we first discussed the topic and then said he'd got fed
up and walked out when we discussed it again at a later date.

During my many hours spent drinking and gambling in Kotobuki,
it occurred to me that these popular yoseba activities might also be
read as tools for denying self-agency. After all, when you drink, you
delegate agency to the drink. When drunk, you are "not in your right
mind," hence not responsible for actions, not an agent. *Yopparateta
kara....* ("Because I was drunk...") is used to excuse a lot of poor
behavior, not only in Japan and not only by day laborers.

The case of gambling is even more striking. The key variants in
forms of gambling are:

1. the chance of winning;
2. the scale of money that may be won (which varies in inverse
    proportion to the previous item;
3. whether the opponent is a professional house or a fellow punter;
    and
4. the degree to which the wager entails skill and luck.

Roughly speaking, one end of the gambling spectrum is represented
by poker or mah-jongg (good chance of winning, small-scale payout,
usually played against a fellow amateur, large skill element); and the
other end by the *takarakuji* (public lotteries; very poor chance of winning, potentially huge payout, professional opponent—the government,
no less—and no skill involved, just luck). Now the most popular form
of gambling among day laborers is race betting (pp. 66–67), an intermediate form of gambling in which luck and skill are subtly mingled,
and where the odds are far better than on the lottery but the payout
will not be enough to change one's life. It is a form of gambling likely
to appeal to the conflicting elements of autonomy and fatalism that
seem to be part of so many day laborers.[21]

In race betting you delegate agency to the horse or cyclist or boat
pilot. Once the money is on, you cannot influence what happens to it.

At the track, you can admittedly hope to encourage your man by cheering; but off-track betting is even more alienated. You can do nothing but stand around waiting for the result. If the horse, cyclist, or motorboat pilot loses, that is their fault, usually, and you curse them for lack of skill or effort. Occasionally you may blame their vanquishers for unfair tactics. It certainly isn't your own fault, anyway. If your selection wins, on the other hand, you suddenly remember that it was *your* brilliant idea to back it.

A related aspect of the Kotobuki concern with fate and human agency is the popularity of divination. Several Kotobuki men practiced fortune telling, one of them professionally.[22] The favored method was palmistry. I had my palm read several times, once by a yakuza who correctly diagnosed that I was an eldest son. Again, several day laborers told me that they believed in the predictions of Nostradamus. When you are flat broke, the idea that everyone is going to die on a specified date in the near future is kind of comforting. One day laborer I knew used to get drunk and stagger around shouting "We're all gonna die!" *(Minna shinjau!)*. Others believed in telling character from blood groups, a popular modern variant on the idea that one's fate is in one's blood. Remember too that several men ascribed their character and career to their birth order position (pp. 118–120).

These are of course deeply determinist modes of thought. The fate of mankind is already decided; one's personal destiny is written in one's own hands or blood or one's sibling position; and one has no control over these things. Sometimes determinism bordered on paranoia: one was *damned* by circumstance of birth. Sakae bordered on this extreme view (p. 12).

One day laborer, Ōta Naosuke, had a modified apocalyptic view: he said Nostradamus predicted that 3 percent of the human race would survive the cataclysm of 1999, and that the pure of heart would be among them. So the individual has a chance. Still laughing, he added that Nostradamus's predictions were "98 percent accurate."

He also had a theory that all horse races had their results fixed in advance by some shadowy syndicate. He believed the results were disseminated in advance, through a secret code buried in the welter of data in the fine print of the racing press; he reckoned he was on the verge of cracking the code. In all his theories, a pervasive paranoia was modified by the possibility that the individual had a slight chance of beating the great tides of fate: the 2 percent chance of Nostradamus being wrong; the possibility of escaping doom by having a pure heart; the chance of cracking the horse race code. He saw himself as fate's whipping boy; yet with some small room for maneuver.[23]

In the end I came to think that this small space was the true meaning of the "freedom" espoused by many day laborers; that there was really no insurmountable contradiction between Sakashita's expressions of autonomous willed action and of passive drifting. Both are part of the day-laboring life. On an everyday basis, one chooses whether to try for a job or stay in bed, whether to stay in Kotobuki or go to San'ya or Kamagasaki, whether to go for a one-day contract or a period contract, etc. But these decisions are made within a broad framework over which one has no control. Your coal mine closes down. The bubble economy bursts. Social mores dictate that you cannot join a respectable company if your previous employment was doing casual labor out of a yoseba. On these matters, one can but shrug one's shoulders.

Of course this kind of attitude to life makes it very difficult to organize day laborers in support of their civil and employment rights. The day laborer unions sense this fact and their propaganda often reads like a desperate attempt to haul day laborers away from fatalism: *Yararetara yarikaese*, "If they get you, get 'em back," is the most famous slogan of the movement and has become the title of a book (Kama-Kyōtō 1974) and a film. Another important one, also used as a book title (Funamoto 1985), is *Damatte Notarejinu-na*, "Do not be silent and die in the gutter." Couched in the imperative, union slogans are demands from an activist minority, for a passivist majority to get its act together.

At the same time, activists frequently indict employers for practicing *tsukai-sute* ("using, then throwing away") on day laborers. To activists, the commoditization of labor, as something handy and disposable, is an affront to human rights. Day laborers themselves, however, have a sober awareness that whether they like it or not, disposability is their key selling point in a competitive labor market.

When day laborers get too weak to sustain the present-oriented lifestyle, the absence of any noncontributory pension, and their own refusal to save money, means that they will end up on the street or on welfare. This prospect provokes widely varying reactions. To some, applying for welfare is the ultimate disgrace: a de facto admission that all the talk of freedom and rejection of conventional lifestyles was just so much drunken bragging. These men would sooner die on the street than take money from the state—and it is convenient for local officials to exaggerate their numbers. To others, welfare is just part of the "natural abundance"[24] of Yokohama's relatively liberal postindustrial environment; there is no contradiction in going on welfare, since unlike the despised salarymen, they do not predicate their identity on work. Yet others take the pragmatic view that they will work while they can and apply for welfare when necessary.

Junichirō, the Kotobuki union, is attempting to change the perception that claiming welfare is an unmasculine, helpless form of behavior by encouraging day laborers to demand welfare as a right, guaranteed by the Japanese constitution[25] and earned by long years of hard labor. They lead day laborers in negotiations with local authorities, sometimes staging protest marches and sit-ins. Hence, "receiving welfare" (passive) is rewritten as "getting welfare" (active).

Kimitsu

I first met Nishikawa Kimitsu in October 1993 and saw him throughout fieldwork thereafter. I was immediately captivated by his genial manner, his mastery of English, and his encyclopedic knowledge—of British politics, world history, existential philosophy, jazz, photography, cinema, postmodernism etc., etc. His tiny room in the Daimaru doya was stacked to the ceiling with heavyweight intellectual books and he also played the guitar. In a conversation at the Apollo Cafe, he introduced me to Heisenberg's uncertainty principle, sketching erratically mobile subatomic particles on the back of a serviette and comparing them to his own uncertain life. From that incident came the title of this book.

Kimitsu hails from Kyushu. He was born in Kumamoto prefecture, near Mount Aso, around 1941. The oldest son of a prosperous banker, he had one older sister and two younger brothers. His father was a movie buff, and used to stage private showings of films at the Nishikawa homestead. He had a proper screen. All the local kids would come and watch.

The war spoiled everything. The *Kenpeitai* (secret police) forced Kimitsu's father to quit his excellent job with Yasuda Bank (today's Fuji Bank), and he started working for a public agency distributing emergency supplies of rice, for a quarter of his previous salary. Family fortunes never recovered after the war, and the result was that Kimitsu couldn't go to high school.

After that there is a gap in the story. At some point Kimitsu did a couple of years as a truck driver in the Ground Self-Defense Force, but even then he was a heavy drinker and he left after several near-accidents. Later he had a regular job with a small construction company, and then there were a couple of decades of

(continues)

(continued)

day laboring. He worked out of Harappa, the Kawasaki yoseba, for some ten years before shifting to Kotobuki. He also spent a couple of years in San'ya a few years back.

During the footloose years, he was disowned by his family. There has been no contact for more than twenty years. The last time he saw his folks was when he went back to Kumamoto for his father's funeral. "My brothers and cousins beat on me. Say 'bastard! Go back to Yokohama.' Only my mum defend me." Today, he doesn't even know if his mother is still alive. His sister is a kindergarten teacher and has stayed at the parental home in Kumamoto. One of his brothers is in Osaka, another "somewhere in Kansai." "They are scattered. Like civil war! Family civil war!" (Loud, long, almost hysterical laughter). "But here (Kotobuki) is good place for me. This is my right place." (Quotations in original English).

Kimitsu prefers longshore work to construction because of the romance of the sea. He loves any taste of foreign culture, though he has never been abroad. Dock work has helped him to pick up a lot of English and a smattering of various other languages. During the high-growth years the port of Yokohama was exceedingly busy, and Kimitsu recalls working back-to-back shifts, day and night for two or three days at a stretch. Now those days are long gone and he takes whatever work he can get, from the labor exchanges or the tehaishi.

By 1995 he was still making it as a day laborer, but only just. He was averaging about two days' work a week, and was usually broke and a few days behind with the rent on his doya room. Luckily he had been staying in the same room for many years, which made his Korean landlady less inclined to throw him out. But it seemed to me that Kimitsu was on a downward trajectory and would probably be out on the street in another two or three years. He said he expected to die at sixty. This did not seem to bother him. He argued that wealth of experience, not length of years, made a good life.

He reckoned to average ¥12,000 per day worked. The doya cost ¥1,500, and his liquor habit about the same. He didn't eat much—mostly rice and pickled vegetables bought from market stalls and eaten at the doya—and daily outlay was about ¥1,500 again. He gambled only occasionally. With total outgoings of about ¥5,000, he should have had a surplus of about ¥7,000 from an average day with work. And yet he usually woke up the next day with just one or two thousand-yen notes left in his pocket. "I have never been able to understand this mystery," he ruefully remarked.

(continues)

170

(continued)

It seemed to me that two characteristics defined Kimitsu. One was tolerance. Shoved out of the way in the rush to bag a job at the exchange, he would laugh it off, saying that all day laborers were in the same boat. When his landlady got angry and threatened to chuck him out, he would put it down to the long history of Japanese imperialism in Korea. Again, and unlike many day laborers, he never condemned the tehaishi—he was grateful to them for finding work for him. Even the yakuza were only doing their job. He was a free-wheeling liberal and showed no interest in the union. His concept of solidarity was broad enough to embrace most of the day laborers' class enemies as well as themselves.

The other key characteristic was paranoia. Though he hardly ever thought ill of known individuals, Kimitsu was deeply suspicious of authorities, governments, and abstract social forces. I once found him waving his arms around and shouting "espionage!" outside the labor center. A run of failures to get work had convinced him that some traitor had blacklisted him. Like the subatomic particles analyzed by Heisenberg, human beings were unpredictable, yet subject to laws over which they had no control. He had an obsessive interest in the Holocaust, and drew large cartoons of Nazi officers on walls around Kotobuki. We went to see the film *Schindler's List* together and he never stopped talking about it. His point was always the same: that the yoseba was itself a prison camp, with the added irony that its inmates were blissfully unaware of the fact.

This paranoid element fed into a bleak personal philosophy. He once described the gruelling work he had to do as "hard labor . . . punishment for existing." But this was said with a great roar of drunken laughter, which convinced me that here was a genuine existentialist hero.

8

The Role of the Yoseba in Contemporary Japanese Society

Zoned Tolerance

ACCOUNTS OF JAPANESE SOCIETY, whether by Japanese or foreign observers, tend to emphasize the strictness of social controls and the relatively limited space within which individual freedom may be exercised. We are told that there is a high degree of conformity in lifestyles, and a low degree of tolerance for those who deviate from social norms. Japan is often described as a "control society" *(kanri shakai)*,[1] and the most commonly quoted Japanese proverb in the literature of Japanological clichés is "The nail that sticks out gets hammered in."[2]

In fact, the nail that sticks out is not always hammered in. Often it is left to rust in the wood. Large areas of this "control society" are not controlled; they are treated with tolerance or indifference. In many zones of Japanese life, the apposite theme is containment rather than control. These zones are often defined in terms of social geography.

Thus, prostitution, for example, is illegal in Japan, but the law is not strictly enforced within the flourishing red-light districts to be found in every Japanese city. Again, people in mainstream Japanese society rarely dare to openly identify themselves as homosexuals, yet there is a thriving gay scene, and within the artistic and theatrical professions homosexuality is generally tolerated. Effeminate and transvestite males are even more widely accepted, and may often be observed on TV, not necessarily as figures of fun but often as sought-after commentators on fashion and popular culture. Public drunkenness is generally tolerated, especially in entertainment districts after dark.

In short, the imposition of public morality in Japan includes elements of benign neglect and selective enforcement that are not properly accounted for in the simpler versions of the control society model.[3] This is a society with numerous zones, defined spatially, temporally, or socially, in which expectations, norms, and law enforcement vary greatly from the mainstream. The yoseba is a striking instance of this.

Marginal Geography

Yoseba are very clearly defined zones, with perceptible borders setting them apart from the surrounding cityscapes. Any day laborer of Yokohama could draw a rectangle around Kotobuki on a map of the city, and the borders of San'ya and Kamagasaki are no harder to identify. Yoseba tend to be located in fairly central city districts, with good rail and road access, reflecting their original raison d'être, as a convenient supply of instant disposable labor to city industries. And yet the social geography of these districts shows that they carry meanings that go far beyond a particular role in the industrial economy.

As I hope will be apparent from my accounts of arrival in San'ya (pp. 1–2) and Kotobuki (pp. 40–41), entering the yoseba is almost like arriving in a foreign country—one with a different atmosphere and different modes of behavior. Moreover, the yoseba are subject to different standards of policing from the rest of the city. I have already referred to the relatively light sentencing for yoseba murders (chapter 6 n. 26); at the other end of the criminal scale, Kotobuki is also the one part of Yokohama where you can park illegally with little risk of having your vehicle towed away by the police.

The marginal status of the yoseba is encoded in its proximity to other places inhabited by marginalized groups. As we have seen, there is a marked tendency, with a long history, for yoseba to be located adjacent to *baishungai* (red-light districts; pp. 83, 99), to execution sites and graveyards (pp. 82, 99), and to zones inhabited by discriminated minorities such as Burakumin (pp. 82, 99, 105) and ethnic Koreans (pp. 46–49, 105, 107–108). The concentration of facilities for people with mental or physical disabilities in Kotobuki (pp. 42–44) is another case of clustering stigmatized groups, though it also reflects difficulties faced by the local authorities in locating such facilities in more "respectable" districts.

Another marginal group to be found in the yoseba are the yakuza. As we have seen, there are always yakuza to be found in yoseba districts, whether because they are engaged in labor racketeering, gambling, etc. in the yoseba, or because they find it a convenient base from which to conduct operations elsewhere. Within the yoseba they are left largely undisturbed by the police and mainstream citizenry, and have a ready supply of labor for errands in the form of unemployed day laborers. Their membership overlaps to a considerable degree with the discriminated minorities in the yoseba and their presence, too, reflects a combination of relative acceptance in the yoseba and resistance elsewhere.[5] We have seen also that within the yakuza world there is a tendency for the weaker, less glamorous gangs to be involved in yoseba business, which is insufficiently lucrative to attract the bigger fish (pp. 44, 101).

It is generally possible to trace the formation of the yoseba, its concentration of despised minorities, and its proximity to other despised districts, to deliberate state policy. For hundreds of years central and local governments have dictated where casual workers will gather, through zoning regulations on where cheap houses and lodging places may be built, just as they have used licensing systems to restrict prostitution to particular districts and discriminatory legislation to confine Burakumin to specified districts, typically near rivers, where the land is not well suited to human habitation (Yoshino and Murakoshi 1977:72). In recent decades, more progressive legislation, designating certain areas with high Burakumin populations as zones for special housing programs, have had the same effect of concentrating the Burakumin population in fixed zones of the city.

I have already described how the government of Yokohama established the postwar yoseba at Kotobuki (pp. 48–49); the other side of the zoning operation is the removal of yoseba elements from other parts of town, as in the case of Nakamura-chō, a precinct just down the road from Kotobuki, which used to have a mixture of doya and private dwellings. It had been a slum district since well before the war, being located on undesirable marshy land at the foot of the Yamate bluff. The prewar kichin yado were completely destroyed in allied bombing raids, but landlords swiftly replaced them with about a dozen doya after the war. In July 1962, with one eye on the major riot in Kamagasaki the previous year, the Kanagawa prefectural government opened the Aisen Home, a settlement house for homeless people, in Nakamura-chō (Tokuji 1972:17).

There was much friction between the domestic residents and the doya landlords, on two main fronts. Firstly the doya, mostly cheaply constructed of wood and surrounded by dwellings, were a serious fire risk; on the night of 11 January 1970, two of them burned down, with four fatalities. Secondly, the domestic residents disliked the doya dwellers, who were mostly day laborers and were allegedly given to urinating in the street, throwing cigarette butts and mouldy fruit and vegetables out of windows, getting drunk and shouting, and making campfires in the children's parks (Tokuji 1972:19). The doya dwellers were also suspected of being "criminals and sexual deviants living under false names" (19).

While a vociferous citizens' movement was demanding the removal of the doya from Nakamura-chō (1970–1971), the government of Yokohama was reviewing its policy on Kotobuki. The conclusion, reached in 1971, was that "rather than dispersing the Kotobuki district, there is nothing for it but to aim at improving the standard of the district" (Tokuji 1972:19). This decision led to construction of the General Labor Welfare Center, the massive building that dominates Kotobuki to this day.

With Kotobuki's future as a yoseba/doya-gai thus assured, the pressure to "clean up" Nakamura-chō became irresistible. The doya were gradually closed down, usually by suddenly noticing illegal fire hazards that had previously been tolerated, or by refusing planning permission for enlargements and improvements. The net result is that today the doya of Yokohama are concentrated in Kotobuki, while Nakamura-chō is a nondescript district of working-class family dwellings. I quote this case at some length to show how a blend of tolerance (toward the special zone) and intolerance (toward people associated with it but living outside) can find expression in gradually altering the urban landscape into zones with clearly defined boundaries.

So we see that the yoseba may be despised by the mainstream, but it also has its value, both economic (supply of cheap, flexible labor) and social (dumping ground for misfits). A senior Yokohama police officer told me that despite Kotobuki's high rate of crime, he and his colleagues had no intention of trying to clean the place up or shut it down: "Given that human nature, and therefore cities, are not perfect, it's not a bad idea to concentrate the problems in one place. The relatively high rate of crime in Kotobuki must be seen in the light of the lower rates in other parts of Yokohama. The two are surely connected."[6] He went on to compare Kotobuki to the medieval *kakekomi-dera* or temples of sanctuary. These were Buddhist nunneries, to which married women would escape if they wanted a divorce. Three years of religious observances would dissolve the tie. I was reminded of an occasion when Mr. Kagoshima of Junichirō, the Kotobuki day laborer union, compared Kotobuki to an *ubasute-yama*—in Japanese folklore, a mountain where old women would be left to die when they had outlived their economic usefulness.

It is striking that both these similes refer to institutions designed for women. Perhaps this is another instance of different categories of social discrimination being lumped together, a conceptual equivalent to the spatial concentration of discriminated identities in and around the yoseba. Be that as it may, the distinction between mountain of abandonment and temple of sanctuary is that between involuntary victimhood (stressing the yoseba's value to the mainstream) and deliberate escape (stressing its usefulness to the margin). I found a similar ambivalence among day laborers themselves, reflecting the tension between active and passive philosophies discussed in the previous chapter. Some would curse the day they entered the yoseba; others, perhaps a majority, were glad it was there. It was, after all, a kind of community, a kind of refuge. Thus, the yoseba seemed to share the ambiguity of the medieval European ghetto, as described by Roth: "It is significant that the gates were furnished in many cases with bolts on the inner side for use in emergency . . . with an insight rare in the oppressed, the Jew realized that segregation, however humiliating it might be, tended to be a powerful preservative of solidarity and culture" (Roth 1969:297–298).

Clark's account of the black ghetto in the United States is even more assertively ambiguous: "The ghetto is hope, it is despair, it is churches and bars. It is aspiration for change, and it is apathy. . . . It is the surge toward assimilation, and it is alienation and withdrawal within the protective walls of the ghetto" (Clark 1965:11–12). That same paradox is clearly observable in the yoseba. Day laborers sometimes referred to it negatively as a ghetto or dumping ground, yet it was also the site of a constructed alternative identity in which it became a stronghold of nonmainstream living.

The View from the Mainstream

In my conversations with non-day laborers who knew Kotobuki, I was struck by a tone they adopted of sympathy, or even envy. Day laborers would be viewed as *yosutebito*—people who have thrown away the cares of the world. Several regularly employed building workers told me they admired Kotobuki men for maintaining their independence, while others said that they felt day laborers would regret abandoning family life when they reached old age.

Consider also the case of Ōtsuka Yōsuke. A successful commercial cameraman, he abandoned his career to become a day laborer after coming across Kotobuki in the course of an assignment. His superb collection of black and white photos of day laborers in Kotobuki is entitled *Rakantachi* (1983).[7] A *rakan* is a Buddhist monk who has achieved enlightenment—an *arhat, arahat,* or *arahant* in English.[8]

Here Ōtsuka is tapping into the tradition of the noble outcast, which is very strong in Japan.[9] He thinks the Kotobuki men have something. He does not feel sorry for them. Perhaps one reason why most Japanese do not feel any great urge to help homeless doya-gai dwellers may be this view that they are pursuing a different path through life which is not necessarily inferior to their own. By contrast, the small minority of Christians in Japan see the poor as a focus for pity and charity, hence the numerous doya-gai missions.

At the other extreme, some Japanese react to the doya-gai and their inhabitants with disgust expressed in physical violence. There have been countless incidents of day laborers being beaten up, especially when they are sleeping rough, and even murders are not uncommon. In the mid-1980s at San'ya there were several murders of men in the street committed by youths, and in 1992 there was a spate of attacks in which fireworks were let off in the direction of men sleeping rough near Yokohama baseball stadium. In 1994 there was a horrific assault upon a fifty-seven-year-old man in Fukuoka. Some young people, probably school children, attacked him with an industrial-size stapler and left him with five one-centimeter staples in his head. He was drunk and asleep in a shrubbery adjoining the approach to a Shinto shrine at the time, so this was a very literal violation of sanctuary.[10] Similarly Matsushige (1988:208–210) describes a 1986 airgun attack by school-age boys against a group of men from Kamagasaki who were sleeping in the grounds of a Buddhist temple. In November 1995 the Tokyo metropolitan police announced that they had arrested three teenage boys for beating and kicking to death a sixty-nine-year-old unemployed man in the Jūjō district of northern Tokyo.[11] A few weeks before that, a sixty-three-year-old homeless laborer drowned after he was tipped into the Sumida river by two young men who found him sleeping on the wheelbarrow he used to collect cardboard for recycling.[12]

The above are just a tiny selection of incidents that have become commonplace. The most notorious case of this kind happened in 1983, when a gang of schoolboys assaulted sixteen homeless men in Yokohama, killing three.[13] This famous case, described by Kan (1986:18) as "a prominent expression of the discriminatory nature of our civic society," is documented in great detail by Sae (1983) and Aoki (1984), from whose works I now summarize the most important points.

Although this case is sometimes referred to in Japan as the "Kotobuki Incident,"[14] few of the assaults actually happened in Kotobuki. There is safety in numbers within the zone, but as I mentioned (p. 129), homeless men tend to sleep in a more dispersed area around Kotobuki. Most of the assaults were committed by a gang of ten boys, all of them aged around fifteen and attending the same junior high school in Yokohama. Seven of the ten had divorced parents, and most of them were not doing well at school. They called their gang the *Kyōmai Rengō* (which translates roughly as "Terrifying Dance Alliance"), but lived in fear of a stronger gang called the *Chūka Rengō* (Chinese Alliance, though its members were also Japanese boys). On 31 January 1983, a showdown was set between the two gangs for 6 February a week later.

The Kyōmai boys had attacked homeless men before, but the assaults escalated as the showdown approached. On 4 February a fifty-year-old man called Okada was found dead in front of a bank in Chōjamachi (near Kotobuki), though the police later decided there was insufficient evidence to prosecute the boys for this murder. At 8:20 P.M. the following evening, the boys attacked eight different men in the lee of Yokohama Stadium, one of their victims suffering a broken arm. They then proceeded to Yamashita Park, where they came upon Sudō Taizō, aged sixty, who was living in the park. They "attacked him truly like wild animals, repeatedly kicking and beating him, and then they threw the unconscious Mr. Sudō into a rubbish bin. They span the bin round and round" (Aoki 1983:33). Sudō was discovered at 10:30 P.M. by a passing tourist, who heard his moans coming from a shrubbery where the boys had abandoned him. He had hideous wounds to his head and chest, numerous broken ribs, and was drenched in blood. He was taken to hospital but died two days later.

Like most of the other assaults perpetrated by the boys, this one happened in a well-frequented part of Yokohama, quite early in the evening. There must have been witnesses, yet neither Sae nor Aoki could find anybody who would admit to having seen any of the assaults. Nor was the Kyōmai gang inventing a new sport: the police investigation found evidence that similar attacks had been going on for years.

One lingering image of the affair is of the studied indifference of the authorities. The police did not set up an investigation headquarters until several days after the murders (Aoki:32–34) and the boys were not heavily punished. Nine of them were sent to a reformatory *(shōnen-in)* and one to a somewhat tougher kind of reform school *(kyōgō-in)*. To add insult to injury, the city government of Yokohama sent "condolence money" of ¥30,000 to relatives of each man killed, and ¥10,000 to each man hospitalized (37)—roughly $300 and $100 respectively.

According to Aoki, several of the boys were genuinely surprised when they were arrested. They told reporters that the men were "dirty and smelly," and that they thought they were doing the city of Yokohama a service by "cleaning rubbish off the streets." They added that they did it "half for fun," and that "it was fun to watch their pathetic attempts to escape." One boy commented: "When I put the boot in, the bones broke with a kind of crisp, popping sound that made me feel refreshed."[15]

The newspapers made great play of the fact that the boys' victims did not resist—they were kicking a poor defenseless man. In fact, as Aoki points out (1983:67–68), any attempt by a Kotobuki man to fight back at his assailants would be far more likely to bring the police to the scene than the original assault. Ōnishi (1994:10) describes a case in Nagoya where a homeless worker hit back at some youths who were tormenting him. The police arrested him and charged him with attempted murder. The youths were not arrested or charged.

The day laborers of Kotobuki did not ignore the 1983 incident. A protest rally was held, and bands of day laborers were still handing out leaflets outside junior high schools around Yokohama two months later. They were headed simply WE ARE ANGRY, and appealed to all school students not to forget the murders.[16]

The View from Inside

It is impossible to generalize about how day laborers view their own status, since their views often conflict. For example: I was asked to write an article about Kotobuki for a Japanese magazine, and a young photographer had came along to take some pictures in front of the Labor Welfare Center. It was a rather desolate scene, with three or four yankara sitting round a bonfire, black all over their faces, and a couple of dozen men waiting for the labor exchange to open.

One of them objected to being photographed. *"Hottoite kure, omē to kankei nē daro"* (Leave us in peace, it's got nothing to do with

Photo 8.1 Portrait of Sudō Taizō. This famous picture taken on Christmas Eve 1982 by Tokuda Masahiro depicts Sudō Taizō, one of the men murdered by schoolboys in Yokohama in 1983. Note the swollen hands, a sure sign of alcoholism, and the Christmas party hat. Reprinted by permission.

you!), he shouted. A second man argued back: *"Don-don toreba ii'n dayo. Zehi kono sanjō no koto o sekai ni oshiete moraitai!"* (He should take as many pictures as he likes. We want the truth of this tragic scene told to the world!).

A different objection came from Nishikawa Kimitsu, who was also standing in front of the shutters. He didn't like the second man's use of the word *sanjō* (tragic scene): *"Iie, sanjō ja nai. Futsū na hito dake dayo"* (No, this isn't a tragic scene. We're just ordinary guys).[17]

Here are three quite different views of doya-gai life from three men who know it from the inside. The first man views the doya-gai as a shameful place, or at least a private place, and resents outsiders poking their noses in. The second man shares the negative view of the doya-gai, but blames it on failings in Japanese society rather than on

the men themselves, and wants the outside world to be made aware
of what's going on. The third man rejects outright the whole idea that
the yoseba is a special, problematic zone.[18]

Yoseba versus Skid Row

The absence of family life and structured social relations in the yoseba
distinguishes it from most slum and ghetto areas, but aligns it rather
closely with the American skid row, a resemblance explicitly discussed
by several Japanese and American scholars.[19]

I have already drawn attention to some differences in behavior
between day laborers and skid row inhabitants (p. 161 and chapter
7 n.15). There are striking similarities too, however, especially with
the *prewar* skid row. *The Hobo*, Anderson's classic account of
Hobohemia, a skid row district of Chicago in the early 1920s (Anderson 1965 [1923]), is the only non-Japanese book included in the list of
"100 yoseba literary contributions" published by the Japan Association for the Study of Yoseba (Matsuzawa 1990),[20] and 1920s Hobohemia does indeed show many suggestive similarities to the 1990s
yoseba:[21]

1. Both have cheap hotels with tiny rooms, housing a mix of
permanent residents, seasonal regulars, and passing trade. There
are also flophouses in Hobohemia resembling the "bedhouses"
in San'ya and Kamagasaki. (Anderson 1965[1923]: 31)
2. Anderson divides Hobohemians into "at least five" types: the
"seasonal worker"; the "hobo" (a transient or occasional
worker); the "tramp" (who "dreams and wanders"); the "bum"
(who seldom wanders and seldom works); and the "home-
guard" (who lives in Hobohemia permanently and seeks work
close to home) (89). There is a slightly discriminatory ring to
Anderson's typology; still, each type does sound familiar from
my yoseba encounters.
3. As in the yoseba, there is a bipartite labor market, with public
labor exchanges fighting an unequal battle against private,
tehaishi-type agencies, albeit the latter usually seem to operate
out of offices rather than on the street. (110–117)
4. Some Hobohemians are single-day specialists (117–120), though
the proportion may be smaller than in the yoseba.[22]
5. There is much heavy drinking in Hobohemia, especially of the
binge ("spree") type, with many alcoholics (134–135), but fewer
drug abusers. (67–69)
6. Hobos benefit, or come into their own, when disaster strikes.
"After a flood, a fire, or an earthquake, there is a great de-

mand for labor. The migratory worker is always ready to respond" (109). As the 1995 Kobe earthquake demonstrated, the same is true for day laborers in modern Japan. Men from Kamagasaki did much of the dirty work at Kobe, pulling bodies out of the rubble, etc.

7. "The majority of homeless men are unmarried. Those who are married are separated, at least temporarily, from their families. . . . Of the 1,000 men studied by Mrs. Solenberger, 74 per cent gave their marital status as single. Of the 400 interviewed by the writer 86 per cent stated that they were unmarried. Only 8 per cent of the former and 5 per cent of the latter survey claimed they were married. The others claimed to be widowed, divorced or separated from their wives." (137)

8. Like San'ya and Kamagasaki, Hobohemia is next door to a prostitution district. "These women . . . do not live in the 'main stem,' but adjacent to it." (142–143)

9. Hobohemia's amenities resemble those of a doya-gai. One street on the "main stem" had eight cheap hotels, ten private employment agencies, seven cheap restaurants, six bars, five cheap clothing stores, two gambling dens, two fortune-telling shops, one cigar store, one drug store, and one Christian mission (15). All of these facilities may be found in Kotobuki.

10. As the presence of fortune-telling shops suggests, the Chicago hobos shared the day laborer's interest in fate and fortune. In his discussion of hobo reading material, Anderson says: "Works on phrenology, palmistry, Christian Science, hypnotism, and the secrets of the stars, etc., are of perennial interest." (15)

11. Both Kotobuki and Hobohemia have an area of improvised housing on wasteland close to the zone, containing men living in "improvised shacks" (11) who inhabit even more marginal territory than the zone itself.

12. Hobohemia attracts Christian charity (171, etc.). Many skid row studies include accounts of missionary work,[23] and it may well be that skid row was the model for the Christian missions active in the doya-gai around Japan. Just as men have to "sing for their supper" at the skid row missions (Miller 1982:5), so in the doya-gai the rule is *"amen de ramen"* (getting noodles by saying "amen").

13. The hobos had a penchant for poetry (Anderson 194–214). Many Japanese day laborers also write poetry, and examples may be found in the periodical *Yoseba Shijin* (Yoseba Poets). The bittersweet theme of lonely freedom runs through the hobo and day laborer poetry alike.

14. Anderson describes various political movements to unionize hobos and raise their political consciousness (230–249). These

groups show some similarity to the yoseba movement, notably a tendency to schisms and infighting. (247–249)

15. The reasons given by Chicago hobos for leaving home cover many areas also mentioned by my own informants: Seasonal work and unemployment; "industrial inadequacy" (e.g., mental or physical handicap, alcohol or drug addiction, old age); defects of personality; crises in the life of the person; racial or national discrimination; and wanderlust. (61–86)

I also observed the following *dissimilarities* between Hobohemia and the yoseba: Hobohemia had a greater range of employing industries, including agriculture; clothes and food in Hobohemia were cheap (Anderson 15), whereas in Kotobuki they could be surprisingly expensive, with shopkeepers taking advantage of day laborers coming home from work carrying ready cash and too tired to shop elsewhere; and there is relatively little begging in the yoseba, whereas all accounts of Hobohemia/skid row mention begging.

Finally, there is one more important difference between the yoseba and skid row: the major yoseba still survive today, while skid rows have disappeared from many American cities.[24] Symbolically, the last bar on the Bowery—Al's Bar—closed on Christmas Day, 1993.[25] On 8 May 1995, the Bowery was featured in the *Style* section of Britain's *Sunday Times* as the latest fashionable place for rich young kids to party at bars with trendy decor. Presumably these bars were unlike Al's Bar.

The American skid rows have fallen prey to urban renewal and gentrification (Miller 1982). Owners of cheap hotels and other property in skid row areas have been made unrefusable offers for the land, while establishments such as Al's Bar that rented their premises have been forced out by sharp rent increases. Thus, the cheap hotels and bars have gradually given way to office buildings and penthouses. Ironically, this is more or less what Donald Bogue, one of the best-known 1960s writers on skid row, recommended should be done to it (Rossi 1989:32–33).

Tsuchida (1966) and Aoki (1989) have compared the yoseba with the postwar skid row. By the time Tsuchida was writing, skid row had lost much of its prewar function as a source of casual labor and was rapidly becoming a home for drunks and social misfits, which he sharply contrasts with the proud working men of the yoseba. Aoki maintains the argument, though the tone is softened to reflect a certain shift in the status of the yoseba, which he describes as *sukiddorō-ka* (skid rowization).

Still, Aoki in 1989 is able to claim that:

1. yoseba people are younger than skid row people;
2. the skid row has more people incapable of working than the yoseba;
3. personal relations are more casual and disorderly in the skid row, whereas there is a degree of order and solidarity in the yoseba;
4. drinking culture is far more dominant in the skid row, whereas yoseba culture is based on the lifestyle of the day laborer, of which drink is only one part; and
5. the skid row resembles a "slum of dissolution" *(kaitai-gata suramu)*, whereas the yoseba resembles a "slum of integration" *(tōgō-gata suramu)*. (Aoki 1989:56–57)

I believe these differences were smaller than Aoki suggests in 1989 and have been further eroded since then. Rapid aging, which was already apparent enough to warrant a footnote in Aoki's book, has gone much farther; there are plenty of people incapable of working; relations often seem casual and disorderly; and the cultures of drinking and gambling now rival the culture of work as the dominant feature of yoseba life.

In short, viewed from the start of the twenty-first century, the yoseba and skid row look like very similar institutions indeed: rather than being divided by culture, as Tsuchida and Aoki seem to suggest, perhaps they have been divided mostly by a difference in chronology. Despite its flamboyant name, Hobohemia was a place to get work. Famously, the hobo was "a man who works and wanders" (Anderson 1923:87). In postwar American writing, however, "Hobohemia" seems to be used more or less as a synonym for skid row.[26] That term, too, was originally associated with work rather than social failure: it is a corruption of "Skid Road," deriving from "the skidways on which lumberjacks in the Northwest transported logs" (Bahr 1973:32).[27]

Only with the Depression of the 1930s, "when great numbers of disconsolate unemployed men invaded skid row and changed its character" (Rooney 1970:18), did the skid row start to lose its work associations, and take on its present image, as a place for people who are themselves "on the skids" (the term is a back formation). In 1923 there were ten employment agencies on West Madison Street, Hobohemia's "main stem"; by 1964 there was just one (Hoch and Slayton 1989:93). The district's population fell from roughly 60,000 in 1907 to 30,000 in 1923 and 12,000 in 1958 (92).

By 1965, Wallace was able to sum up the history of skid row by saying that its function had shifted "from employment pool to old age rest home" (Wallace 1965:25). Two years later Bahr published "The Gradual Disappearance of Skid Row" (Bahr 1967), and by 1970, Rooney was saying that the aged, ill, and disabled seemed to be locating elsewhere, leaving skid row "to serve as an open asylum for alcoholics and the psychically disabled" (Rooney 1970:34). In 1982, Miller published *The Demolition of Skid Row*.

The yoseba now seems to be undergoing a similar transformation and decline. The place retained its working identity for longer than skid row, but is now shedding it more quickly. In Kotobuki the proportion of welfare recipients in the doya rose from 36 percent in 1990 to 81 percent in 1998.[28] In other yoseba, harsher welfare policies have put more ex-day laborers on the street.

Why has the yoseba retained its working character for longer than comparable American institutions? Partly because urbanization came later and faster to Japan, providing numerous jobs in construction, an industry that was also relatively slow to mechanize. Many day laborers refer to the 1964 Tokyo Olympics as the high water mark for day laboring in construction, and in those days bucket gangs were still used on building sites in Japan. Again, postwar Japan has famously seen a massive increase in international trade, supporting employment in longshore work, the other classic day laborer occupation.

Change is now rapidly overtaking both sectors, with prefabricated building units and containerization eating into employment. Also, the yoseba have become overly reliant on these two industries, particularly construction,[29] and now the prolonged recession of the 1990s has administered another severe blow to casual employment.

Tsuchida happened to compare the skid row and yoseba at a time when the transformation from work zone to outcast zone was already well advanced in the former and had yet to begin in the latter; Aoki when it was complete in the former and only halfway progressed in the latter. They mistook differences in location on similar developmental curves for cultural differences. Aoki, and most other left-wing observers of the yoseba, stress the identity of its inhabitants as "workers." He even coins his own word, *hatarakido* (a working-person), to describe them. Yet the fact is that a growing number of yoseba inhabitants cannot or do not work.

The differences in transformational timing between doya-gai and skid row have to do with historical and macroeconomic factors. Japan's defeat in World War II slowed her down in midcentury and created rootless workers and demand for their labor. Later, Japan overtook the United States in economic growth and automation, ultimately speeding the decline of the yoseba.

Overall, the similarities between these two institutions are far more striking than the differences; the Oriental/Occidental divide seems very narrow. However, despite their locations, often on prime urban land, the yoseba have yet to be demolished like so many of the American skid rows. It may be that the sudden collapse of Japanese urban land prices at the start of the 1990s saved the yoseba from being demolished to make way for middle-class housing, but in this case I do also sense a cultural factor at work.

Containment versus Dispersal

Both the yoseba and the skid row started off as pools of workers providing a flexible response to the needs of capital; both subsequently changed their character as the surrounding society became more prosperous and the demand for casual manual labor waned, becoming associated with social failure and exclusion. But the response of the American and Japanese authorities to this transition has varied. Both see the yoseba/skid row in sociopathological terms, but they think in different metaphors. Many American cities have employed a *cancerous growth* metaphor, seeking to *break up* the skid row and *disperse* its inhabitants, seeing the threat to society lessened when spread more thinly. The result has often been to scatter homeless men all over the city, not necessarily to anybody's benefit. Japanese cities, by contrast, have tended to employ a *germ infection* metaphor, seeking to *seal up* the source of the potential social infection by *concentrating* or *containing* supposedly deviant elements inside the yoseba. For better or worse, this means that the yoseba, and the lifestyle and culture associated with it, is likely to outlive the loss of its employment function.

Containment policy is a subtle mix of tolerance and oppression, designed to enable day laborers to maintain their traditional lifestyle within set geographical and chronological limits. Geographically, they are contained as far as possible within the yoseba districts; chronologically, they are supported for as long as they remain useful to the employing industries.

The key legal measures supporting this containment approach are:

1. provision and location of casual labor exchanges in yoseba districts;
2. day laborer insurance, which may only be claimed at certain specified exchanges;

Photo 8.2 Skid-row-ization? Queuing for a Food Handout in Triangle Park. After the bursting of the bubble economy at the start of the 1990s, long lines of men waiting for volunteer food handouts became a common sight in Kamagasaki's Sankaku Kōen (Triangle Park). Photo by Nakajima Satoshi, 1993. Reprinted by permission.

3. street-corner employment regulations, which outlaw informal recruitment outside the yoseba;
4. regulations on the building of cheap hotels, designed to restrict them to doya-gai districts;
5. social welfare policy, which places single-parent families and other welfare claimants in yoseba districts; and
6. "extra-legal assistance" in the form of food and lodging coupons that may only be redeemed in the yoseba district.[30]

These formal measures are supported by ad-hoc, ground-level implementation of the law. As we saw in the case of the sudden decision to ignore legal requirements for employers to enroll in various insurance programs (p. 72), bureaucratic morality is decidedly situational. Public officials charged with administering legally established systems will make calculated decisions to break the law when they view it as being in the interests of employers and/or day laborers. The ad-hoc scrapping of the insurance requirements made day laborers easier to use and abuse for employers; while for the laborers it may have meant a slight reduction in unemployment.

At street level, the difference between the American and Japanese approaches has a huge impact on individual lives. Spradley's classic account of American tramps (1999[1970]) describes a lifestyle punctuated by endless arrests for vagrancy and public drunkenness. One of his informants was arrested 114 times for public drunkenness in Seattle between November 1957 and June 1968, receiving fifty-eight jail sentences totalling just over eight years (1999[1970]:195)—a "life sentence on the installment plan" as Spradley describes it (252). By contrast, vagrancy and public drunkenness are not criminal offenses in Japan (Parker 1984:107). The Japanese equivalents of Spradley's tramps are often to be found in the yoseba, but during two years of fieldwork only one of my informants was arrested to my knowledge, and that was for a violent assault on a woman.

Spradley argues that the police in Seattle deliberately target skid row areas and are more likely to arrest tramps there than elsewhere. In Yokohama, the reverse seems to apply: except for their occasional swoops on the gambling dens, or when serious crimes occur, the police tend to stay out of Kotobuki. In nearly two years I never saw a policeman patrolling there; I only saw them when incidents had occurred. Admittedly their presence is considerably more obtrusive in San'ya and Kamagasaki,[31] and doubtless less obtrusive in some states than others in the United States, but still it seems probable that yoseba are generally less heavily policed than skid rows.[32]

The difference between official attitudes to skid row in the United States, and to the yoseba in Japan, will largely determine the long-term fate of these institutions. The controversial effects of the US dispersal policy are now well documented,[33] and at least one prominent scholar (Jencks 1994) has gone so far as to argue for areas of cheap lodging houses to be deliberately reinstated in American cities: an argument seen by some as advocating the return of skid row. At present, however, there is no sign of a dispersal policy being applied to the yoseba. Even if the day finally comes when there is no longer any demand for the supply of casual labor from the yoseba, the containment policy I have described makes it more likely that they will become giant, shabby welfare facilities for the aged poor and homeless, something that is already starting to happen in Kotobuki (Stevens 1997:178).

Perhaps the most important tool in this policy of containment is the blind eye. There is no simple dichotomy between legitimacy and illegitimacy in the yoseba: a third category, "illegitimate but tolerated" covers a vast band of yoseba activity: the bookmakers; some practices of the labor recruiters; the employment of foreign workers with expired or inappropriate visas; the use of public places as sites for homeless people to live in; all the way down to unenforced parking regulations. The selective blind eye is the ideal tool of containment, for it allows the authorities to tolerate or crack down at their convenience. The blind eye can suddenly regain its vision, for example to deport foreign migrants when demand for their labor falls, to turf out homeless people when complaints from local residents reach a certain pitch; or to round up some yakuza bookmakers and their clients when arrests are required to embellish a police officer's record.

Thus, the yoseba and its inhabitants live always on the sufferance of the authorities, never knowing when tolerance may be withdrawn and legal principles suddenly remembered and enforced. When that happens, the victims are rudely reminded of the limits to what individual ingenuity can achieve. That moment is well described by Rey Ventura, a Filipino who lived in Kotobuki as an illegal migrant worker in the late 1980s, before being arrested and deported during one of the immigration authorities' periodical purges. His arrest prompted the following observation:

> All our efforts to live invisibly were nothing more than a charade in which the workers, the recruiters, the Mig-mig (immigration officials) and the police all played their part. We lived in hiding. They pretended not to see us. When public opinion demanded, they made a token raid. For the rest of the time, we were a necessary evil. We thought we were so clever. We thought we knew the ropes. *Whom did we think we were kidding?* (Ventura 1992:171)

Shigehirō

With his thin, pale face, high cheekbones, prominent adam's apple, slightly effete curly perm, and gold-rimmed glasses, Shigehirō exuded insecurity and nerves. But he loved to talk, and was the most eloquent social theorist among the day laborers I knew.

Shigehirō was thirty-nine when I first met him in January 1994. He was born in a small fishing village in Miyagi prefecture, the oldest of three sons. One of his younger brothers is now looking after the family home; the other is in the Air Self-Defense Force. Shigehirō himself used to be a barman: his finest hour came in 1977 or 1978, when he was runner-up in the Saitama prefecture area finals of the All-Japan Cocktail Contest.

(continues)

(continued)

His ambition was to serve drinks at one of the big international hotels, but he failed for want of good handwriting and foreign language ability. At twenty-nine, he was still working in a revolving restaurant at the top of a love hotel, making ¥200,000 a month with no bonus and having to pay his own taxi fare home at 3 A.M. every night.

At this point his wife left, taking their son with her. The boy was eighteen in 1994; Shigehirō hadn't seen him for ten years. He and his mother were living near the mother's family at a village in Ibaraki prefecture, and his ex-wife would ask his parents for help with money sometimes. He himself never sent his ex-wife any money—he spent what he earned and worked once he was broke.

Shigehirō hadn't been back to his parental home in a decade; he said the village was a conservative place, and the neighbors would think badly of his folks if they allowed him to come back. On the other hand, he was fairly confident that his family would arrange for his body to be interred in the family grave after his death: once he was dead, the neighbors would think badly of his family if they did *not* take him back. His family has belonged to the Sōdōshū Buddhist sect for fifteen generations and has its grave in the grounds of the local Sōdōshū temple.

When his family life collapsed, he abandoned bartending and went to San'ya, where he retrained himself as a *tekkin-kō*—the man who builds the framework of steel rods used in making reinforced concrete. In San'ya he could make around ¥18,000 a day with this semiskilled work. If he could find twenty days work in a month, that made ¥360,000—nearly double his old bartending wage.

Shigehirō preferred period contracts of ten or fifteen days, rather than single-day jobs: if you worked by the day, he said, you ended up spending all the money the same day. But he had no wish to become a regular employee of one of the construction companies he worked for. "That way they can boss you around—and besides, the money's worse." He reckoned regular tekkin-kō only averaged about ¥16–17,000 per working day. They also suffered tax and insurance deductions (which the casual laborer could usually avoid) and were paid their wages a whole month in arrears, far longer than Shigehirō had to wait. Also, he said, when there was a big project at a work camp, the regulars had about ¥1,500 a day deducted for accommodation in a prefab dormitory, whereas the casuals got it free.

(continues)

190

(continued)

The downside, of course, was that when the work ran out, the regulars still had an income and the casuals did not. Shigehirō was struggling to find fifteen days work a month when I met him. He admitted that casual laboring didn't look so attractive in a recession, but as he remarked, "The trouble with the casual laboring life is that you get used to it—and then you can't change."

He had thought deeply about the day laborer's life, and was knowledgeable about how to make a go of it. He was always on the lookout for a good thing, and liked to read books on how to succeed in business. Politically he was well to the right, respecting the emperor and interested in racial theories about the origins of the unique people of Japan.

Shigehirō mostly worked out of San'ya, where the money was somewhat better, and came to Kotobuki mainly to drink, gamble and visit prostitutes; activities that he called "immoral but necessary." In the case of prostitutes he said, "If the girls are forced into it, that's quite wrong; but if they are doing it willingly, I can but be grateful to them." I met him at the winter and summer festival seasons in Kotobuki, but the last time I saw him was in March 1995, when he had decided to work out of Kotobuki for a while.

He told me then that he had resumed contact with his parental family. He had just collected ¥150,000 for a period contract. On an impulse he rang up his mother, who invited him to his cousin's wedding. He spent all his money on a suit, presents, and a train ticket, and went home for the first time in more than a decade. It was a strange but moving experience, and he was surprised to find that his parents were keen to re-establish relations with him. This brought new problems: now they wanted to know his address and phone number, and he had neither. He'd been lying about his circumstances (claiming to be a regular construction worker), and keeping in touch only through telephone calls from his end. His parents seemed to suspect that he was involved in some kind of criminal activity.

I suggested that maybe he should tell them the truth. Better to be known as a day laborer than taken for a criminal, surely? He shook his head. "I know what you mean, but I just can't . . . I mean, well, maybe I will one day."

Another sign of change in Shigehirō's wandering life was his purchase of three pet goldfish, which he kept in his doya room. Previously he had not owned anything that could not be packed into one fairly small bag. Would he just flush the fish down the toilet next time he made a move, or were they the first step toward settling down?

9

Epilogue
The Rise of Uncertainty, the Fall of Solidarity

A S I HAVE MENTIONED (p. 95), the Osaka yoseba of Kamagasaki is dominated by an enormous grey concrete employment/ welfare center. It is of striking appearance:

Gustav Dore would have loved to draw the Airin Labor Center. It has great gloomy recesses where the sunlight barely penetrates, where old men lie on rush mats, half undressed with their tongues hanging out. It even has a round hole cut in the ceiling of the ground floor through which people on the top floor love to look down upon their fellow workers. Below the hole is a fountain, with bronze cherubs. It doesn't seem to work. Rush mats spread out from the fountain, making it look like an ornate clock face when viewed from above.

Hundreds of men were milling round the gloomy concrete expanses. The effect was somewhat softened by some 20 assorted shops—newspaper sellers and coffee shops downstairs, cheap restaurants upstairs. Mr. Fukada (a Kamanichirō activist) told me that these establishments had been doing business on the land where the Center was built, and were granted concessions within the Center as part of the deal under which their previous premises were demolished.

On the ground floor, the sound which kept booming out was the call of "KOH . . ." "KOH . . ."—all that is left of the word *tekkin-kō* after thousands of repetitions. These men, who make steel frames for reinforced concrete, were in demand. I stayed until 8 A.M., and there were still minibuses with men calling for "KOH . . ." "KOH . . ." When the recruiters—generally stout, businesslike men dressed slightly smarter than the workers—spotted a known tekkin-kō, they descended on him and tried to argue him onto their minibus, sometimes tugging at their sleeves. If the man showed the slightest willingness, they would frogmarch him to the minibus and bundle him in.[1]

I asked Fukada Kazuo of Kamanichirō, the Kamagasaki Day Labor Union, for his views on the institution of this massive central building. He said it was convenient for the union, because everyone gathered there in the morning, making it the natural setting for meetings and demonstrations; convenient for employers, because it was a one-stop shop for recruitment; and convenient for the workers because it offered a single, unified job market with a lot of peripheral services.[2]

To me, this remark was revealing, not just about this one building but about the yoseba in general. Despite all the conflict, there is perceived to be a shared interest among workers, employers, and activists in getting people together in a "gathering place"—the literal meaning of *yoseba*. Whether you go there to shop for disposable labor, to earn a crust, or to instill political awareness, there is a shared interest in the simple act of coming together that may help to account for the historical continuity of the institution. From the workers' point of view, it is both exploitative and functional. Being there is stigmatized; not being there would arguably be worse. The yoseba gives day laborers a place to exchange information on employment conditions and a web of personal connections that help to dispel anomie and can be a valuable safety net in times of trouble.

The data presented in this book suggest that the traditional day-laboring lifestyle is on the wane, and I believe that this is indeed the case. However, what is disappearing is not the phenomenon of insecure, low-commitment labor, but the communal aspect of the day-laboring lifestyle.

Far from disappearing, the phenomenon of insecure labor is getting steadily more prevalent in the Japanese economy.[3] The practice of "lifetime employment," which day laborers conceptually oppose to their own ultra-short-term working arrangements, never applied to more than a minority of the work force anyway: those employed by large, elite corporations. Statistics must be treated with caution, since job descriptions at Japanese companies can be slippery: "part-time workers" who work full time; "temporary workers" who work permanently; "irregular workers" who work regularly. There is an inner periphery of insecure workers within the company as well as the outer periphery employed as casuals or through subcontractors (Chalmers 1989). As I write, a decade of recession has eaten away at employment security across the board, and all too many workers have discovered that industrial relations based on mutual trust last only as long as it suits the management side.

At the same time, it would be wrong to say that all Japanese workers necessarily regard long-term workplace relationships as an unmixed blessing. It is not only day laborers who find something oppressive about working for the same boss in perpetuity: there are many others who can see the appeal of a more distant relationship with the employer. A cover story in a Japanese employment magazine[4] encourages its readers to "declare free agency," a term borrowed from the labor relations of professional baseball. The independent, freelancing craftsman is the magazine's ideal type, and the argument is that you can do better auctioning your skills to a plurality of companies than by devoting yourself to just one. Day laboring may not have much appeal to youngsters, but change the word to *furii arubaitaa* ("free arbeiter") and the same basic concept is altogether more appealing. It's all in the cultural wrapping.[5]

There is even some suggestive evidence that some Japanese people do, in certain circumstances, positively choose to be day laborers. If day labor were purely residual labor, one would expect the day laborer population to fall during a boom and rise during a recession—in a boom more people ought to be able to quit day laboring and get steady jobs, while in a recession, more people would lose steady jobs and become day laborers. No such pattern is discernible in the Japanese statistics.[6]

One reason why this is not the case is that day laboring wages are much more sensitive to shifts in supply and demand than regular salaries are. Employers will pay what they need to secure the number of casuals they need, and wages can shift from day to day and week to week. The day laborer unions campaign with limited effectiveness to keep them above a certain minimum, but otherwise terms of employment are decided on broadly free market principles. So when

In a top-ranking company like this, the workers don't mind doing overtime.
(This man's a cleaner, sub-contracted from a cleaning company)

They must have very stable positions...
(Actually, this is a temporary employee of a computor software company...)

They must get really good salaries...
(These girls are part-time employees of a worker-supply company)
(This girls was sent by a man-power employment agency)

Hey boss! You must be looking forward to promotion soon...

(The truth is this man's prospects in the company aren't very bright and he's been temporarily transferred from another company!)

Kamayan has no idea how hard it is in a big company...

Cartoon 9.1 The Spread of Insecure Labor. Kamayan the cartoon day laborer gets a cleaning job at an office through a temp agency. He envies the staff their job security and good incomes. Unknown to him, however, they are all temporary workers just like himself. Even the boss has been found surplus to requirements and dumped on this company by a bigger firm with which it has a clientelistic relationship. Cartoon by Arimura Sen (Arimura 1989:158). Reprinted by permission.

there is a labor shortage—as was the case for most of the mid–1980s—day-laboring wages will rise sharply (table 16).[7] At the same time, the risk of not being able to find work when one wants it is diminished. Put these factors together and you have quite a strong incentive to quit a regular job, which may itself be very badly paid and not particularly secure, and become a day laborer.

As for the recessionary phase of the business cycle, Mr. Sekine, the man in charge of Kotobuki affairs at the Yokohama city government, offered this explanation: "In hard times, companies tend to draft the more reliable day laborers into the regular workforce as employees of their subsidiaries. They take advantage of the workers' weak position to gain stronger control over them. The control society strengthens [kanri shakai ga tsuyomaru]."[8] Again this is more or less the opposite to what one might expect: in hard times one would expect construction companies to be firing, not hiring. I cannot assess the validity of Mr. Sekine's opinion, but at least the fact that a man in his position can hold it suggests that irregular working arrangements are not perceived unproblematically as favoring management at the expense of workers.[9]

This may have something to do with the historical supply of and demand for labor. Jones (1971:67), describing the situation in Victorian London, asserts (without seeing any need to defend the statement) that "[i]t was a basic precondition of the casual labor market that supply should be permanently and chronically in excess of demand." This does not appear to apply to Japan either historically or in modern times. As I mentioned (pp. 19, 23–24), there have been severe labor shortages at critical junctures in the development of Japanese capitalism. Shortages occurred again during the bubble economy of the late 1980s, and day laborers still talk fondly of the high wages and desperate struggles by employers to secure their services in those heady times.

I also heard, from a bureaucrat at the Ministry of Labor, that large numbers of carpenters (daiku) and spidermen (tobi) had quit regular jobs in order to work as day laborers in the massive operation to restore the city of Kobe after the 1995 earthquake there.[10] The disaster had caused a regional construction boom and these people evidently felt they could make better money as day laborers in Kobe than as regulars in some other town.

Natural disasters such as the Kobe earthquake remind us of one of the reasons why certainty is so highly valued in Japanese culture: Japan's natural environment is unpredictable. At the same time, such disasters bring the men of uncertainty into their own. The quake brought a temporary boom to Kamagasaki. For many months there was plenty of work. It was tough, sometimes harrowing work, but it helped to restore the men's pride.[11] Likewise, one day laborer recalled being paid a bounty for each body retrieved after the great typhoon that devastated Ise Bay back in the 1960s. Another, in Fukuoka, told me he was hoping for a typhoon that would rip a lot of tiles off the houses and enable him and his mates to eat hot noodles again.[12] It is indeed an ill wind that blows no one any good. Even in normal times, an important category of work for day laborers is demolition—like undertakers for humans, they are called in when a building has ended its life.

The Kobe earthquake, the collapse of the bubble economy, and the end of the Liberal Democratic Party's monopoly of political power are signs that forces of uncertainty are once more on the rise in Japan. The 1995 nerve gas attack on the Tokyo subway by the Aum Shinrikyō cult was followed in the late 1990s by a confidence-shattering series of bankruptcies among banks, stock brokerages, and even insurance companies. Then, in September 1999, the serious radiation leak at the Tōkaimura uranium-processing plant brought a terrifying reminder of the fallibility of the "authorities" who run Japan's infrastructure.

The LDP's success was always built on people's desire for certainty. No one ever loved the LDP, but it was the devil they knew. I remember during Nakasone Yasuhiro's double election campaign of 1985, seeing an LDP poster that had a picture of a smiling housewife washing the dishes, and the slogan *Anzen, Antei, Anshin*—"Safety, Stability, Peace of Mind." Even Britain's Conservative Party has never struck such a ruthlessly conservative note in its appeals to the public. But now the economy is mired in recession, the government and bureaucracy are intensely unpopular, and the affective business and workplace relationships that used to be cited as keys to economic success are widely denounced as corrupt and ultimately destructive of efficiency and long-term prosperity. Sassen (1991:244) says that in Tokyo "the majority of new jobs in the 1980s were part-time jobs and temporary employment agencies constituted one of the fastest growing industry branches." This trend appeared to strengthen during the 1990s, and was accompanied by a steady rise in unemployment, which rose above U.S. levels and reached a postwar record high of 4.9 percent in the summer of 1999.

The Japanese government made two policy moves near the end of the 1990s that showed a degree of commitment to defending the declining system of institutionalized day labor and a long-delayed recognition of the related problem of rising homelessness. One was the institution of a temporary program, the Emergency Day Labor Supplementary Employment Subsidy (*Kinkyū Hiyatoi Tasu Koyō*

Shōreikin). This program had a budget of ¥1 billion and applied to the major yoseba regions in Tokyo, Osaka, Yokohama, and Nagoya, for a fifteen-month period from 1 January 1999 to 31 March 2000. It was designed to pay companies ¥5,000 per worker per day for employing extra registered day laborers, up to a maximum of ¥1.25 million per company per month. Since the national average day wage is around ¥10,000, this represents a hefty 50 percent subsidy. However, the total budget represented only 200,000 person-days of subsidized labor, or about five days per registered day laborer, so it was little more than a gesture. Moreover, according to Endō Hideo of the Kotobuki Labor Office,[13] employers were not obliged to use the casual labor exchanges to employ men under the program. Hence, the subsidies were often claimed by companies employing elite day laborers on a semiregular basis. In the case of Yokohama, these men would often be working as truck or forklift drivers at the docks, so that there was little advantage to men who lacked the relevant licenses.

The second policy decision was one to allocate a budget of ¥1.1 billion to do something about homelessness in FY2000, and to conduct the first-ever national survey of the homeless population. This represents long-overdue recognition of a problem that was for many years ignored by central government.

Various measures have also been taken at the local level to defend day labor. In the case of Yokohama, in September 1999 the mayor sent out a directive to all construction companies engaged in tendering for public works contracts in the city, strongly requesting them to employ more day laborers whenever they succeeded in winning contracts. This is another measure unlikely to have much concrete effect, since the companies that win the contracts very seldom employ day laborers directly. The message has to filter down several levels of subcontractors before reaching the small companies that patronize Kotobuki, and in the fall of 1999 the staff of the Labor Center were busily ringing up contractors to encourage them to pass on the message.

Measures such as these will not reverse the long-term decline of the yoseba, as reflected in dwindling numbers of workers and jobs, and the tendency for doya to be either half-empty or full of welfare recipients. However, these trends do not signify a decline in casual labor as such. I believe they stem from three other factors:

1. The steady loss of jobs in traditional yoseba industries: containerization at the ports, prefabricated units on the building sites.
2. The steady shift from Japanese labor to migrant labor where those jobs still exist. With the one exception of Kotobuki, where

the historical Korean connection and blind-eye policing have
allowed illegal Korean migrants to form their own community,
these foreigners avoid the yoseba. As Komai points out
(1995:112), the "gathering place" is an easy target for immigration officials, so migrants tend to use other, less visible routes
to the workplace.
3. This is more speculative, but it may be that with more and
more people working on a casual basis, the fact of lacking
corporate affiliation may be losing some of its negative conno-
tations. At the same time, with Japanese people tending to marry
later in life, more of them staying single, and the divorce rate
rising, detachment from family life may also be losing some of
its stigma. Consequently, the connection between irregular labor and residence in a stigmatized zone may be gradually
weakening.

To sum up, what we are seeing in Japan is a transformation in the
pattern of casual labor: from heavy industry to the service sector, from
the middle aged and elderly to the young, from men to women. A
new vocabulary accompanies the transition: in place of the *hiyatoi
rōdōsha,* or the more derogatory *ankō* or *pū-tarō,* we have the eminently
respectable *rinji saiyōsha* (temporary employee), the pleasantly exotic
pāto (a contraction of "part-timer"), or even the appealingly libertar-
ian-sounding *furiitaa* (a contraction of "free arbeiter"; see p. 193). Recruitment is handled by large, legal companies which nevertheless
take just as large a cut of the casual wage as the tehaishi standing on
the street corner (cf p. 60). The people who do these jobs do not gather
anywhere: they get employment through the rapidly proliferating
employment magazines, from the pages of sports newspapers, and
even in some cases through the Internet. The pool of labor is no longer
a physical entity: the visible casual work force, with its potential for
solidarity or even rebellion, and its susceptibility to stigma, is evapo-
rating. In its place are scattered solitary casuals, driven by metaphors
of freelance entrepreneurship. Insecure labor itself will never disappear from the capitalist industrial economy, while the places known
as "yoseba" may well survive as great conglomerations of the homeless and the poor. But the yoseba combination of freelance labor and
alternative community is becoming steadily harder to sustain.

Appendix: Statistical Tables

Table 1 Registered Day Laborers and Monthly Employment/
Unemployment Averages, 1970–1998

Year	Registered laborers [A]	Laborers finding one or more days work per month [B]	B/A(%)	Person-days of labor arranged per month	Person-days of unemployment benefit claims/month
1970	256,000	229,000	89	4,342,000	698,000
1975	171,000	136,000	80	2,524,000	531,000
1980	163,000	114,000	70	2,047,000	501,000
1985	129,000	75,000	58	1,209,000	652,000
1986	119,000	56,000	47	905,000	528,000
1987	106,000	41,000	39	653,000	413,000
1988	91,000	34,000	37	539,000	372,000
1989	78,000	28,000	36	418,000	316,000
1990	68,000	23,000	34	327,000	266,000
1991	61,000	19,000	31	249,000	239,000
1992	55,000	16,000	29	197,000	189,000
1993	47,000	13,000	28	143,000	153,000
1994	45,000	11,000	24	115,000	151,000
1995	45,000	9,000	20	93,000	142,000
1996	44,000	8,000	18	63,000	140,000
1997	44,000	7,000	16	60,000	—
1998	42,000	6,000	14	51,000	—

(continues)

199

Table 1 continued

NOTE: Five year intervals to 1985, annual data thereafter. These statistics are compiled from returns at Ministry of Labor casual employment exchanges and do not include jobs negotiated at non-MoL labor exchanges or with unregistered employers on the informal street labor market. Figures have been rounded to the nearest thousand, and percentage of minimally active workers (B/A) calculated, by the author.

SOURCE: Ministry of Labor, Employment Security Bureau. Figures up to 1996 in Japan Statistical Handbook (Management and Coordination Agency 1975–1999).

Table 2   Average Days per Month Spent Working or Claiming Unemployment Benefit by Registered Day Laborers, 1970–1998

Year	Working days/month [A]	Claiming days/month [B]	[A/B]
1970	17.0 [19.0]	2.7 [3.1]	6.2 [6.2]
1975	14.8 [18.6]	3.1 [3.9]	4.8 [4.8]
1980	12.6 [18.0]	3.1 [4.4]	4.1 [4.1]
1985	9.4 [16.1]	5.1 [8.7]	1.8 [1.9]
1990	4.8 [14.2]	3.9 [11.6]	1.2 [1.2]
1991	4.1 [13.1]	3.9 [12.6]	1.1 [1.0]
1992	3.6 [12.3]	3.4 [11.8]	1.1 [1.0]
1993	3.0 [11.0]	3.3 [11.8]	0.9 [0.9]
1994	2.6 [10.5]	3.4 [13.7]	0.8 [0.8]
1995	2.1 [10.2]	3.2 [15.6]	0.7 [0.7]
1996	1.4 [8.2]	3.2 [18.2]	0.4 [0.5]
1997	1.4 [8.6]	—	—
1998	1.2 [8.5]	—	—

NOTE: Five year intervals to 1990, annual data thereafter.

SOURCE: Derived from table 1. Main figures derived using figures for all registered day laborers; bracketed figures using figure for minimally active registered day laborers, i.e., those getting at least one day's work per month at Ministry of Labor employment exchanges.

Table 3   Day Laborers (Broad Definition) by Gender, in Millions, 1953–1998

	1953	1955	1957	1960	1965	1970	1975	1980	1985	1990	1995	1998
Men	0.90	0.92	1.09	0.77	0.79	0.66	0.69	0.67	0.61	0.58	0.52	0.55
Women	0.49	0.60	0.70	0.45	0.48	0.52	0.54	0.63	0.65	0.68	0.68	0.70
Total	1.39	1.52	1.78	1.21	1.27	1.18	1.23	1.30	1.26	1.26	1.20	1.26

(continues)

Table 3 continued

NOTE: Five-yearly intervals, plus 1953 (first year for which statistics exist) and 1957 (peak year for both men and women).
SOURCE: Management and Coordination Agency 1960–1999; Japan Statistical Association, 1987:390–394.

Table 4 Number of Day Laborers (Broad Definition) and Other Nonregular Workers in the Japanese Working Population, in Millions of People

Year	Total	Self-employed	Family workers	Casual employees	Day laborers	Irreg % of total
1955	40.90	9.50	12.84	–	1.52	58.34+α
1960	44.36	9.48	10.61	1.30	1.21	45.35
1965	47.30	8.48	9.15	1.52	1.27	43.17
1970	50.94	8.10	8.05	1.65	1.18	37.26
1975	52.23	7.70	6.28	1.77	1.23	32.51
1980	55.36	7.65	6.03	2.56	1.30	31.68
1985	58.07	7.25	5.59	3.21	1.26	29.81
1990	62.49	6.85	5.17	3.93	1.26	27.54
1995	66.66	5.91	3.97	4.33	1.20	23.12
1998	67.93	5.72	3.67	4.93	1.26	22.93

NOTE: The figure for "self-employed" people excludes those who have employees working for them. The irregular percentage I derived myself from "self-employed without employees" + "family workers" + "casual employees," divided by "total work force." The category "casual employees" was only introduced in 1959 and is thus missing from the 1955 calculation.
SOURCE: Management and Coordination Agency Annual Labor Force Surveys.

Table 5 Population of the Kotobuki Doya, 1984–1998

Year	Total Doya Pop. [No. of Doya]	Men	Women	Children[c]	Aged 60+	Welfare Cases[a]	Handi-capped[b]	Foreigners
1984	5,653 [91]	5,434	185	33	504	2,675	123	–
1985	5,694 [94]	5,474	185	35	588	2,424	133	–
1986	5,718 [91]	5,456	225	37	628	2,238	170	–
1987	6,004 [90]	5,769	196	39	711	2,250	166	–
1988	5,967 [88]	5,764	174	39	744	2,270	168	–
1989	6,151 [88]	5,918	211	22	780	2,341	182	533
1990	6,362 [90]	6,050	282	30	817	2,199	181	814

(continues)

Table 5 continued

Year	Total Doya Pop. [No. of Doya]	Men	Women	Children[c]	Aged 60+	Welfare Cases[a]	Handi- capped[b]	Foreigners
1991	6,334 [90]	5,928	368	38	920	2,291	192	1,146
1992	6,476 [90]	6,008	434	34	1,056	2,590	203	1,059
1993	6,205 [92]	5,711	449	45	1,382	3,188	199	932
1994	6,331 [91]	5,935	359	37	1,650	4,129	204	1,083
1995	6,340 [92]	5,991	320	29	2,036	4,672	237	651
1996	6,243 [94]	5,983	238	22	2,042	4,835	270	465
1997	6,401 [97]	6,108	268	25	2,219	4,950	274	424
1998	6,495 [99]	6,200	275	20	2,500	5,274	–	377

[a] The unit for welfare recipients is households. The huge majority of Kotobuki "households" consist of a single man living in a doya room (see table 6). The rapid increase in the number of welfare recipients from 1993 followed a decision by the Yokohama city welfare authorities to increase the rent component of welfare payments from ¥1,500 a day to ¥2,000 a day, thereby greatly increasing the number of doya rooms that could be afforded.

[b] These are figures for people with handicaps officially recognized by the government. Handicaps are categorized in order of severity, grade 1 being the most severe. Thus, in 1997 there were 42 people in Kotobuki with grade 1 handicaps, 74 with grade 2, 60 with grade 3 and 98 with grades 4 to 6.

[c] These figures are for children under 15 living in doya rooms. The Kotobuki Seikatsukan conducts a separate annual survey of all children living in the Kotobuki area, and in recent years this has generated figures roughly double those shown here, reflecting the fact that a number of children live in the municipal apartments located above the Labor Center. The Seikatsukan survey shows 505 children under 15 living in Kotobuki in 1969; 211 in 1980; 121 in 1985; 72 in 1990; 54 in 1995; and 47 in 1997. In 1997 there were also 6 children aged 15 to 17, for a total of 53. 31 were living in municipal apartments, 15 in doya rooms, and 7 in private apartments etc.

SOURCE: Mostly from annual reports of the Kotobuki Welfare Center, compiled in December of each year. Handicapped figures from the annual "Report on the Activities of the Kotobuki Livelihood Building" (Kotobuki Seikatsukan Jigyō Hōkoku-shū).

Table 6 Household Composition of Kotobuki Doya Population, 1990–1998

	1990	1993	1995	1998
Total population	6,362 [814]	6,205 [932]	6,340 [651]	6,495 [377]
Men	6,050 [710]	5,711 [633]	5,991 [467]	6,200 [274]
Women	282 [96]	449 [264]	320 [161]	275 [93]

(continues)

Table 6 continued

	1990	1993	1995	1998
Children	30 [8]	45 [35]	29 [23]	20 [10]
Households	6,091 [722]	5,893 [735]	6,109 [530]	6,343 [321]
Single man	5,808 [626]	5,443 [471]	5,789 [369]	6,066 [228]
Single woman	54 [12]	179 [99]	115 [62]	137 [44]
Childless couple	205 [78]	237 [138]	180 [79]	122 [40]
Couple and child[ren]	20 [6]	31 [27]	21 [20]	10 [6]
Mother and child[ren]	3 [0]	3 [0]	3 [0]	6 [3]
Father and child[ren]	1 [0]	0 [0]	1 [0]	2 [0]

NOTE: Bracketed figures: foreigners.
SOURCE: Kotobuki Welfare Center surveys, conducted 30 December each year.

Table 7 Population of Kotobuki by Class (1994) and Ethnicity (1994, 1995, 1998)

	1994	1995	1998
Total pop. of Kotobuki zone, including homeless: approx.	8,000	–	–
A. Regularly working day laborers *[gen'eki-sō]*	1,500	–	–
B. Occasionally working DLs *[fuantei shūrō-sō]*	800	–	–
C. Welfare recipients *[seikatsu hogosha]*	4,000	–	–
D. People living in poverty *[hinkon-sō]*	700	–	–
E. Foreigners *[gaikoku-jin]*	1,083	651	377
The foreigners are further divided thus:			
E.1. Foreign men	816	467	274
E.2. Foreign women	242	161	93
E.3. Foreign children	25	23	10
And thus:			
E.4. Korean	824	533	264
E.5. Philippine	170	91	77
E.6. Thai	89	24	30
E.7. Others	0	3	6

NOTES: In 1998 the 264 Koreans consisted of 197 men, 60 women, and 7 children. The 77 Filipinos consisted of 63 men, 14 women, and no children. The 30 Thais consisted of 9 men, 19 women and 2 children. "Others" consisted of 5 men and 1 child. The income of the various groups is roughly estimated thus:
A. ¥250,000 +   B. ¥80,000 to ¥180,000   C. ¥120,000   D. Under ¥50,000
E. Upper class: ¥400,000+. Lower class: On the streets.

SOURCE: Figures for foreigners come from the Kotobuki Welfare Center survey, conducted every year on 30 December. The social class figures are rough estimates by researchers affiliated with Junichirō.

Table 8 Age Range of Workers Registered at Kotobuki Labor
Center, 1975–1998

Year	Age 0–29	30–39	40–49	50–59	60+	TOTAL	Mean age
1975	14%	40%	39%	7%	0%	–	c.38.6
1980	7%	29%	39%	25%	2%	–	c.43.1
1985	62	601	1,155	506	54	2,375	44.6
	(3%)	(25%)	(49%)	(21%)	(2%)		
1988	45	399	1,172	816	93	2,525	47.0
	(2%)	(16%)	(46%)	(32%)	(4%)		
1991	22	242	999	1,029	199	2,490	49.8
	(1%)	(10%)	(40%)	(41%)	(8%)		
1994	3	103	1,246	1,555	216	3,123	51.1
	(0%)	(3%)	(40%)	(50%)	(7%)		
1997	8	88	822	1,548	194	2,660	52.1
	(0%)	(3%)	(31%)	(58%)	(7%)		
1998	83	146	917	1,438	186	2,770	51.4
	(3%)	(5%)	(33%)	(52%)	(7%)		

NOTE: Five-year intervals to 1985, three-year intervals thereafter. Percentages only to 1980, numbers and percentages thereafter.

SOURCE: Kotobuki Labor Center annual reports, 1985–1998.

Table 9 Age Range of Welfare Recipients in Kotobuki District, as of April 1, 1996

Age	0–29	30–40	41–54	55–59	60–64	65+	TOTAL
Recipients	15	98	1,116	874	833	1,052	3,988

According to Naka Ward Office, by 1 January 2000, the overall number of welfare recipients in the Kotobuki district had risen to 5,462 people. They lived in 5,419 households, meaning that nearly all recipients were living alone. As of that date, 78% of Naka ward's welfare population—equivalent to 18% of the welfare population of the entire city of Yokohama—was concentrated in the Kotobuki district. Gender and age breakdowns were not available.

SOURCE: Naka Ward Welfare Bureau.

Table 10 Age of My Informants in Kotobuki as of 1 January 1995, as Told to Me

35–39	40–44	45–49	50–54	55–59	60–64	65–69	70–74
3	6	5	10	11	6	2	2

NOTE: Total sample: 45; Modal class: 55–59; Median class: 50–54; Mean: 53.2.
SOURCE: Fieldnotes.

Table 11 Population Trends in the Three Precincts Containing
Parts of the Kotobuki District, 1950–1999

Year	Kotobuki-chō	Ogi-chō	Matsukage-chō	TOTAL
1950	0	0	0	0
1955	8	5	0	13
1960	1,309	542	280	2,131
1965	3,843	977	3,148	7,968
1970	2,230	900	2,518	5,648
1975	2,577	934	2,325	5,836
1980	2,254	904	2,288	5,446
1985	2,215 [83%]	910 [79%]	2,281 [86%]	5,406
1990	2,451 [85%]	971 [85%]	2,572 [88%]	5,994
1995	2,118 [80%]	739 [79%]	1,924 [82%]	4,781
1999	2,600 [84%]	1,025 [77%]	2,316 [86%]	5,941

NOTE: Figures in brackets indicate male residents as a percentage of the
total population.
SOURCE: For figures to 1980, *Naka-ku Kushi* (The History of Naka Ward).
Yokohama City Government, 1986. For figures after 1980, Naka Ward
Bureau of Electoral Statistics. Population figures are as of 1 January of each
year, except 1995 (30 September) and 1999 (31 July).

Table 12 Household Composition in the Three Precincts
Containing Parts of the Kotobuki District, 1980–1999

Year	Kotobuki-chō	Ōgi-chō	Matsukage-chō	Total
1980				
Population	2,254	904	2,288	5,446
Households	1,744	674	1,927	4,345
Pop/household	1.29	1.34	1.19	1.25
1990				
Population	2,451	971	2,572	5,994
Households	2,113	821	2,312	5,246
Pop/household	1.16	1.18	1.11	1.14
1999				
Population	2,600	1,025	2,316	5,941
Households	2,302	828	2,092	5,222
Pop/Household	1.13	1.24	1.11	1.14

NOTE: For comparison, figures for the total population of Naka-ku are as follows:
1980: 121,474 (46,711 households). Pop/household: 2.60
1999: 126,040 (64,487 households). Pop/household: 1.95
SOURCE: For 1980: *Naka-ku Kushi* (The History of Naka Ward). Yokohama City
Government, 1986. Thereafter: Naka-ku Bureau of Statistics. Population/house-
hold ratios calculated by the author.

Table 13 Person-Days of Employment Transacted at the Kotobuki Labor Center, 1975–1999

	1-Day Contracts	Period Contracts [Person-Days]	Total Person-Days	Change
1975	5,848 [97%]	29,217 [75%]	31,347	–
1976	21,541 [98%]	41,236 [70%]	62,777	+100.3%
1977	46,008 [98%]	55,222 [74%]	101,230	+61.3%
1978	51,692 [97%]	88,617 [77%]	140,309	+38.6%
1979	59,613 [96%]	99,260 [80%]	158,873	+13.2%
1980	64,431 [98%]	98,626 [80%]	163,057	+ 2.6%
1981	43,816 [99%]	118,874 [92%]	162,690	–0.2%
1982	42,492 [99%]	109,077 [91%]	151,569	–6.8%
1983	52,009 [98%]	102,417 [89%]	154,426	+ 1.9%
1984	49,762 [98%]	97,988 [87%]	147,750	–4.3%
1985	40,312 [97%]	104,848 [85%]	145,160	–1.8%
1986	39,403 [96%]	115,171 [82%]	154,574	+ 6.5%
1987	45,983 [93%]	101,342 [67%]	147,325	–4.7%
1988	46,923 [89%]	89,180 [64%]	136,103	–7.6%
1989	43,740 [91%]	65,843 [62%]	109,583	–19.5%
1990	55,848 [88%]	48,252 [61%]	104,100	–5.0%
1991	53,120 [97%]	50,650 [79%]	103,770	–0.3%
1992	35,556 [99%]	46,427 [93%]	81,983	–21.0%
1993	22,014 [100%]	28,792 [95%]	50,806	–38.0%
1994	23,903 [99%]	29,593 [89%]	53,496	+ 5.3%
1995	25,662 [99%]	27,076 [76%]	52,738	–1.4%
1996	31,173 [98%]	28,172 [77%]	59,345	+12.5%
1997	26,694 [99%]	24,366 [89%]	51,060	–14.0%
1998	19,698 [100%]	17,622 [95%]	37,320	–26.9%
1999	17,295 [99%]	16,201 [88%]	33,496	–10.2%

Take-up rates shown in brackets.

NOTE: The Kotobuki Labor Center opened for business in October 1974. The following figures are for April-March financial years, starting FY1975.

Change from peak bubble year (1986) to first trough year (1993):–67.1%.

One-day contracts:–44.1%. Period contracts:–75.0%.

Change from peak bubble year (1986) to second trough year (1998):–75.9%.

One-day contracts:–50.0%. Period contracts:–84.7%.

Bracketed percentages show take-up rate. E.g., In 1995 employers requested 26,012 person-days of work on one-day contracts, and got 25,662, leaving 350 contracts not taken up, for a take-up rate of 99%; whereas employers only

(continues)

Table 13 continued

secured 27,076 person-days of period contract labor out of 35,564 requested, leaving 8,488 person-days' worth unfilled, for a take-up rate of 76%.

SOURCE: Kotobuki Labor Center statistical reports, 1976–2000. Take-up rates calculated by the author.

Table 14   Day Labor Contracts[a] and Unemployment Payments at the Kotobuki Labor Office, 1992–1998

Year	Labor contracts		Unemployment claimants[b]	
1992	5,791	(483)	29,816	(2,485)
1993	3,280	(273)	25,689	(2,140)
1994	3,368	(281)	25,644	(2,137)
1995	2,611	(218)	25,254	(2,105)
1996	2,162	(180)	25,035	(2,086)
1997	1,324	(110)	24,321	(2,027)
1998	636	(53)	21,978	(1,832)
1999	836	(70)	20,893	(1,741)

[a] The Labor Office only deals in single-day contracts.

[b] The unit here is "one person claiming the day laborer dole at least once per month." Hence the annual figure may include the same person counted up to 12 times. The monthly figure is more significant, being a reliable indicator of the number of active registered day laborers in Kotobuki.

NOTE: April to March financial years; monthly averages in brackets.

SOURCE: Labor Office statistical reports, 1993–2000.

Table 15   Where Do Kotobuki Day Laborers Go When They Need a Job?

1. The Kotobuki Labor Center	97	(92)
2. Personal arrangement with employer *(kao-zuke)*	37	(45)
3. Street market recruiters *(tehaishi)*	36	(49)
4. Introductions from friends	35	(32)
5. The Kotobuki Labor Office	33	(58)
6. The San'ya Labor Center	25	(-)
7. Newspaper advertisements etc.	7	(15)
8. Other	0	(1)
Total answers	270	(292)

SOURCE: Kotobuki Labor Center, 1998:8. Bracketed figures show results of previous survey, 1994:8. Survey of 100 men using the Labor Center; multiple answers permitted. This questionnaire was administered at the Labor Center, and so inevitably exaggerates the role of the Center.

Table 16 Average Kotobuki Day-Wage Levels, 1985–1998 (One-Day Contracts)

Job Description	1985	1987	1989	1991	1993	1995	1997	1998
Laborer (Dokō)	8,589	9,579	11,526	13,007 [+51%]	13,549	13,595	13,445 [+3%]	13,418
Odd-job man (Zakkō)	8,331	9,127	10,733	12,379 [+49%]	12,626	12,397	12,331 [No change]	12,322
Driver/ laborer (Untenshu/ dokō)	9,214	10,671	12,180	13,742 [+49%]	14,290	14,278	12,661 [–8%]	13,566
Carpenter (Katawaku daiku)	12,688	12,080	16,507	15,963 [+26%]	16,650	16,600	17,068 [+7%]	15,527
Spiderman (Tobi)	12,393	13,037	16,764	18,621 [+54%]	20,178	20,015	20,175 [+8%]	19,279
Tobi:Zakkō ratio	1.49	1.43	1.56	1.50	1.60	1.61	1.64	1.56

NOTE: Pay per day, in yen. Bracketed figures show percentage change, 1985–1991 (six bubble years) and 1991–1997 (six recession years). Tobi/zakkō ratio shows the advantage of the best-paid over the worst-paid type of worker.
SOURCE: Kotobuki Labor Center annual reports.

Table 17 Companies Registered at the Kotobuki Labor Center, by Industrial Sector, 1985–1998

Industrial Sector	1985	1987	1989	1991	1993	1995	1997	1998
Construction	626	672	712	642	589	537	562	581
Transportation*	34	37	34	30	28	26	24	24
Manufacturing	23	23	18	13	13	9	8	9
Services, etc.	27	14	14	11	10	9	7	7
Total	710	746	778	696	640	581	601	621

*Includes longshoring and warehousing
Change: 1985–1989: +10%; 1989–1995: -25%; 1995-1998: + 7%
Construction as percentage of whole: 92% (1985, 1989, 1995 alike).
SOURCE: Kotobuki Labor Center 1991–1996 Vol. 17 (1990:6) and Vol. 22 (1995:4).

Table 18   Job Descriptions Used in "Help Wanted" Ads at
Kotobuki Labor Center, 1990–1998

Job	Laborer	Odd-job	Driver[a]	Carpenter[b]	Spiderman	Stevedore	Other	Total
			One-Day Contracts					
Year								
1990	35.5%	46.5%	4.0%	0.1%	3.4%	10.3%	0.3%	63,287
1994	47.3%	21.6%	4.7%	1.7%	4.0%	18.2%	2.5%	24,106
1998	52.2%	7.3%	6.7%	0.7%	2.6%	27.2%	3.3%	19,752
			Period Contracts					
1990	73.3%	3.6%	16.5%	1.6%	3.0%	–	2.2%	79,601
1994	76.8%	1.0%	17.7%	1.0%	2.5%	–	1.0%	33,242
1998	70.7%	3.4%	23.5%	0.9%	0.1%	–	1.4%	18,596

[a] The great majority of these jobs are for "driver-cum-laborer."
[b] Nearly all these jobs are for "molding carpenter" (*katawaku daiku*), meaning the person who builds the wooden frames into which concrete is poured to make foundations.
SOURCE: Kotobuki Labor Center 1991–1998.

Table 19   Do Employers Think the Day Laborers of Kotobuki
Do a Good Job?

Responses of employers to the questionnaire item: "Please assess the quality of the workers and the work done by them."

Year	1994	1998
Good	26%	29%
Ordinary	46%	48%
Bad	28%	23%

These figures were generated by asking employers to say what percentage of day laborers employed by them fell into each category, then dividing total by the number of employers responding—110 in 1994, 164 in 1999.

Why are good day laborers good?

	1994	1998
1. They work diligently	41%	50%
2. They know the job well	27%	26%
3. We use the same guys regularly so they know our ways	26%	21%

(continues)

Table 19 continued

Year	1994	1998
4. They have useful skills and qualifications	6%	3%
5. Other	1%	0%
Why are bad day laborers bad?		
1. Bad attitude; don't want to work	28%	29%
2. Lacking in physical strength	28%	29%
3. Always complaining about things	15%	13%
4. Unprofessional appearance	14%	14%
5. Troublemakers	7%	5%
6. Don't obey instructions	7%	8%
7. Other	1%	3%

SOURCE: Kotobuki Labor Center Survey of Employers, 1994, 1998.

Table 20   How Often Does It Happen That You Hire a Worker on a Period Contract but He Quits before Completing the Contract?

	1994	1998
Never	25%	30%
About 10% of cases	29%	29%
About 20 to 30% of cases	29%	27%
About 40 to 50% of cases	6%	11%
About 60 to 70% of cases	8%	3%
80% or more of cases	3%	1%

Responses from 145 employing companies (1994), 121 employing companies (1998).
SOURCE: Kotobuki Labor Center Survey of Employers, 1994, 1998.

Table 21   When You Hire a Worker on a Single-Day Contract, How Often Does It Happen That He Works for You the Next Day as Well?

Year	1994	1998
Never	14%	11%
About 10% of cases	20%	27%
About 20 to 30% of cases	23%	25%
About 40 to 50% of cases	17%	14%
About 60 to 70% of cases	10%	4%
80% or more of cases	16%	18%

Responses from 17 employing companies (1994), 141 employing companies (1998).
SOURCE: Kotobuki Labor Center Survey of Employers, 1994, 1998.

Table 22 How Do Day Laborers Pay for Medical Treatment When
They Get Ill or Injured?

	1994	1998
1. Use the day laborer health insurance	26	49
2. Use the national health insurance	11	7
3. Pay for it myself	27	16
4. Ask for help at the welfare office	33	–
5. Other / No answer	4	28

SOURCE: Kotobuki Labor Center surveys of 100 men, 1994: 8, 1998:8. In the 1998
survey, "asking for help at the welfare office" was subsumed in the "Other"
category.

Table 23 Distribution of Lodging-House Vouchers (Doya-ken) and
Food Vouchers (Pan-ken) by the Yokohama City Welfare Office to
People Living in the Kotobuki District, 1990–1999

	Doya-ken issued	Pan-ken issued
FY 1990	10,478	12,781
FY 1991	11,858 [+13%]	18,844 [+47%]
FY 1992	33,039 [+179%]	65,823 [+249%]
FY 1993	79,817 [+142%]	198,303 [+201%]
FY 1994	73,583 [–8%]	225,646 [+14%]
FY 1995	84,341 [+15%]	207,242 [–8%]
FY 1996	108,911 [+29%]	215,531 [+4%]
FY 1997	130,413 [+20%]	240,806 [+12%]
FY 1998	170,464 [+31%]	325,053 [+35%]
FY 1999	198,954 [+17%]	346,138 [+6%]

April to March fiscal years.   In brackets: year-on-year change.
SOURCE: Yokohama City Welfare Bureau.

Table 24 Symptoms Most Commonly Reported by Visitors to the
Kotobuki Clinic, FY1992, FY1997

	FY 1992	FY 1997		FY 1992	FY 1997
1. Back trouble	141	60	8. Numbness in		
2. Stomach complaints	80	53	hands or feet	36	–
3. Abnormal blood pressure	79	74	9. Bowel complaints	35	–
4. Colds	64	86	10. Coughs/phlegm	31	–
5. Lethargy/fatigue	50	20	11. Wounds/injuries	30	59
6. Hand or arm pains	48	–	12. Pulmonary		
7. Diabetes	37	–	tuberculosis	28	–

SOURCE: Kotobuki-chō Kinrōsha Fukushi Kyōkai annual reports, 1993:13, 1998:15.
Inconsistent use of categories makes the comparison of only limited value.

Table 25 Payment for Treatment at the Kotobuki Clinic, FY 1993–1999

Mode of payment	FY 1993	FY 1995	FY 1997	FY 1999
"Special treatment"	58.2%	41.0%	22.8%	16.6%
Private insurance	2.5%	4.1%	3.0%	1.0%
National insurance*	11.8%	14.0%	9.4%	5.1%
Day laborer health insurance	16.1%	16.0%	8.8%	2.7%
Welfare cases (free)	4.3%	10.8%	50.2%	69.4%
Pay full cost/other	7.1%	11.8%	5.8%	5.2%

*Includes old people's insurance.
SOURCE: Kotobuki-chō Kinrōsha Fukushi Kyōkai annual reports, 1998:14, 2000:27.

Table 26 Day Laborer Placement by Prefecture: The Top 10 in FY1996 (Bracketed Data: 1990)

Prefecture	No. of registered day laborers [A]	Person days of work arranged through exchanges [B]	B/A*
1. [1] Osaka	18,011 [19,330]	858 [18,490]	0.0 [1.0]
2. [2] Tokyo	7,522 [13,643]	162,003 [606,797]	21.5 [44.5]
3. [7] Aichi	3,952 [2,139]	151,597 [129,393]	38.4 [60.5]
4. [5] Kyoto	2,849 [3,859]	0 [171,574]	0.0 [44.5]
5. [6] Kanagawa	2,593 [3,515]	18,134 [96,380]	7.0 [27.4]
6. [4] Fukuoka	2,163 [5,328]	116,624 [908,367]	53.9 [170.5]
7. [3] Hyogo	1,698 [5,919]	6,413 [165,319]	3.8 [27.9]
8. [8] Hiroshima	754 [1,447]	58,970 [148,202]	78.2 [102.4]
9. [10] Kumamoto	683 [999]	03,191 [170,733]	151.1 [170.9]
10. [11] Kagoshima	405 [946]	12,033 [141,201]	29.7 [149.3]
JAPAN TOTAL	42,867 [66,357]	754,856 [3,923,320]	17.6 [59.1]
% change, 1990–1996	–35.4%	–80.8%	–70.2%

* This ratio represents the number of days' work arranged for the average registered day laborer during the year. The very low figure for Osaka is an anomaly, caused by the use of the *aitai hōshiki* system of job introductions (see pp. 96–97). The very high figure for Fukuoka in 1990 reflects special public works projects in a depressed former coal-mining region. Kyoto's zero figure for day laborer employment in 1996 reflects the fact that there are no casual labor exchanges in Kyoto. Prior to that year, day laborer employment consisted entirely of jobs under the unemployment countermeasures (*shittai*; P.E.S.O.), which were wound up at the end of FY1995.

SOURCE: Ministry of Labor statistics, available in Management and Coordination Agency Japan Statistical Yearbook, 1993–1999.

Table 27   Geographical Origin of Workers in Kotobuki, by
Prefecture/Region

1. Northern Japan			4. Kansai region			7. Chūgoku region		
Hokkaido	[14%]	5.2%	Osaka	–	2.1%	Okayama	–	0.8%
Aomori	[2%]	2.9%	Shiga	–	0.2%	Hiroshima	[2%]	1.0%
Iwate	[6%]	1.9%	Kyoto	–	0.7%	Yamaguchi	–	0.9%
Akita	[2%]	2.3%	Wakayama	[2%]	0.4%	Tottori	–	0.3%
Miyagi	[6%]	3.4%	Nara	–	0.1%	Shimane	–	0.6%
Fukushima	–	3.4%	Hyōgō	–	1.5%			
Yamagata	–	2.9%						
Subtotal	[30%]	22.0%	Subtotal	[2%]	5.0%	Subtotal	[2%]	5.6%

2. Kantō region			5. Chūbu region			8. Kyushu region		
Gunma	[2%]	2.7%	Yamanashi	–	1.3%	Fukuoka	[2%]	3.2%
Tochigi	[2%]	2.5%	Nagano	[2%]	1.7%	Saga	–	1.0%
Ibaraki	[2%]	3.0%	Shizuoka	[8%]	2.7%	Ōita	–	1.7%
Saitama	–	2.5%	Aichi	–	1.5%	Nagasaki	–	1.5%
Chiba	[6%]	3.9%	Gifu	[4%]	0.5%	Miyazaki	[4%]	1.5%
Tokyo	[3%]	8.3%	Mie	–	0.3%	Kagoshima	[2%]	1.9%
Kanagawa	[14%]	13.1%				Kumamoto	[2%]	1.6%
Subtotal	[29%]	36.0%	Subtotal	[14%]	8.0%	Subtotal	[10%]	12.4%

3. Hokuriku region			6. Shikoku region			9. Okinawa, etc.		
Niigata	[4%]	2.4%	Kōchi	[1%]	0.5%	Okinawa	[22%]	0.8%
Ishikawa	[4%]	0.6%	Kagawa	–	0.2%	"Other"	–	5.3%
Toyama	–	0.7%	Ehime	–	0.9%			
Fukui	–	0.3%	Tokushima	–	1.3%			
Subtotal	[8%]	4.0%	Subtotal	[1%]	2.9%	Subtotal	[22%]	6.1%

SOURCE: Materials published by Junichirō, the Kotobuki Day Laborer Union,
in conjunction with the nineteenth Annual Winter Survival Campaign (Ettō),
27 December 1992. Figures in brackets are percentages of my own personal
sample (50 cases of day laborers who told me their place of origin, 1993–
1995). One man was born in Kōchi but moved to Tokyo in infancy.

Table 28 Occupational Background Reported by My Informants before Arriving in Kotobuki

Occupation	Self	Father's
Longshoreman	6	–
Seaman	5.5	1
Catering [cook/barman]	5.5	–
Military	4	–
Engineer	4	–
Career day laborer	4	–
Yakuza	3.5	–
Spiderman [tobi]	3	–
Fisherman	3	2
"Salaryman"	3	–
Farmer	2	6
Boxer	2	–
Miner	1.5	2
Carpenter	1.5	–
Massage parlor barker	1.5	–
Pilot	1	–
Auto worker	1	–
Tourist information	1	–
Dairy worker	1	–
Warehouseman	1	–
Boss of small company	1	–
Guerilla	1	–
Computer engineer	1	–
Street artist	1	–
Civil servant	–	3
Greengrocer	–	1
Sample total	56	15

NOTE: Where informants mentioned two or more previous occupations, I counted 0.5 to each of the two that were mentioned in most detail.
SOURCE: Fieldnotes.

Table 29 Apparent Marital Status of My Kotobuki Informants

Married, living with wife	6
Widower	2
Divorced/separated	8
Bachelor	12

(continues)

Table 29 continued

Single, status unclear	48
Unknown	82
Total	158

SOURCE: Fieldnotes.

Table 30 Sibling Order of Day Laborers in Kotobuki and Other Yoseba

	Kotobuki	San'ya	Chikkō	Kamagasaki	Sasashima	Total
Chōnan (oldest son)	20	10	2	5	0	37
Hitorikko (only child)	2	2	0	0	1	5
*Chōnan/suekko**	4	2	0	1	0	7
Suekko (last child)	22	6	2	6	0	36
Jinan (2nd son)	3	1	1	3	0	8
San'nan (3rd son)	5	3	0	0	0	8
"Naka" ("middle")	2	1	0	0	1	4
Total	58	25	5	15	2	105

*See chapter 5 (pp. 116-117) for explanation of terms.
SOURCE: Fieldnotes.

Table 31 Simplified Sibling Order Figures

	Kotobuki	San'ya	Chikkō	Kamagasaki	Sasashima	Total
Chōnan	23	12	2	5.5	0.5	43
Suekko	25	8	2	6.5	0.5	42
"Middle"	10	5	1	3	1	20
Total	58	25	5	15	2	105

SOURCE: Derived from table 30.

Table 32 Degree of Success in Day Laboring by Simplified Birth Order Class

Chōnan		Suekko		"Middle"	
*****	2	*****	3	*****	1
****	1	****	5	****	3
***	2	***	4	***	4
**	7	**	5	**	3
*	3	*	1	*	0
Sample: 15		Sample: 18		Sample: 11	
Star av. 2.47		Star av. 3.22		Star av. 3.18	
Making it [3*+]: 33%		Making it [3*+]: 67%		Making it [3*+] 73%	

NOTE: Well-known Kotobuki informants only: sample size 44
***** Works regularly, skilled, saves money, has regular apartment.
**** Often works, keeps doya room long term, controls drinking behavior.
*** Sometimes works, rarely sleeps rough, keeps out of hospital.
** Rarely works, often sleeps rough, drinking problem, spirit unbroken.
* Never works, sleeps rough, depressed, in and out of hospital for alcoholism, accidents, mental problems etc.
SOURCE: Fieldnotes.

Table 33 Average Number of Homeless People Found by Volunteer Patrols in Kanagawa Prefecture, 1991–2000

	Location					
Year	Kannai area	Yokohama station[a]	Outer Yokohama[b]	Kawasaki	Outlying cities[c]	TOTAL
1991	93	–	–	–	–	–
1992	97	–	–	–	–	–
1993	129	–	–	–	–	–
1994	129 [23]	–	–	–	–	–
1995	108 [26]	62	47	317	13	547
1996	97 [27]	66	56	299	13	531
1997	115 [34]	63	55	327	16	576
1998	200 [28]	99 [30]	70 [11]	478 [33]	71	918
1999	231 [32]	108 [32]	91 [13]	572 [35]	81	1,083
2000	182 [22]	141 [21]	75 [12]	524 [23]	85	1,007

NOTES: Bracketed figures: Number of patrols made in the year. Figures for 2000 are up to September 15.

Note that increasing figures can reflect greater reach of patrols as well as more homeless people.

a. From about 1998, patrols to Yokohama station started to include Sakuragichō as well.

(continues)

Table 33 continued

b. "Outer Yokohama" mainly covers the districts of Mitsuzawa and Totsuka.
c. To 1997, "outlying cities" means Fujisawa. From 1998, regular patrols started reporting from several other cities. In that year the following homeless averages were reported: Fujisawa 13 (23 patrols); Sagamihara 13 (17); Kamakura 7 (24); Yokōsuka 23 (24); Odawara 15 (31). Averages for 2000 to September 15 were Fujisawa 29 (18 patrols); Sagamihara 11 (8); Kamakura 9 (15); Yokōsuka 20 (15); Odawara 16 (11).

Figures exclude patrols made during the special conditions of the Ettō period.
SOURCE: To 1994, *Sukabura*, journal of the Kotobuki Thursday Patrol. Thereafter, handwritten records kept at the Seikatsukan.

Table 34 Food Handouts *(Takidashi)* by Volunteers in the Kotobuki District, 1994–1999

Year	A No. of handouts	B Meals served	A/B	Av. No. of volunteers
1993–1994	20	10,130	507	–
1994–1995	20	10,911	546	29
1995–1996	20	11,536	577	30
1996–1997	18	12,057	670	36
1997–1998	33	24,249	735	36
1998–1999	33	27,312	828	37

NOTE: Figures exclude special daily handouts during the Ettō period over New Year.
SOURCE: Kotobuki Takidashi no Kai.

Table 35 Homelessness and Hunger in Central Yokohama during the Winter Survival Campaign (Ettō)

These tables show (1) number of people living in temporary prefabricated accommodations supplied by the Yokohama city government; (2) number of people found sleeping rough by patrols of volunteers, mainly in the Kannai area (including Kotobuki) and the area around Yokohama station; and (3) number of meals served each day by Ettō volunteers.

1992–1993: Nineteenth Ettō

Date:	28/12	29/12	30/12	31/12	01/01	02/01	03/01	Mean
1. Prefabs:	–	163	213	243	265	284	341	252
2. Homeless:	168	129	125	95	108	45	108	111
3. Meals served:	460	1,000	494	800	1,211	926	1,011	843

(continues)

Table 35 continued

	1993–1994: Twentieth Ettō							
Date:	28/12	29/12	30/12	31/12	01/01	02/01	03/01	Mean
1. Prefabs:	–	402	487	502	512	529	535	495
2. Homeless:	111	160	253	152	251	176	274	197
3. Meals served:	–	1,100	910	1,210	1,405	1,343	1,348	1,219

	1998–1999: Twenty-fifth Ettō							
Date:	28/12	29/12	30/12	31/12	01/01	02/01	03/01	Mean
1. Prefabs:	–	199	252	291	296	301	301	274
2. Homeless:	–	302	291	267	328	338	309	306
3. Meals served:	–	1,500	1,081	1,200	1,695	1,204	1,417	1,350

	1999–2000: Twenty-sixth Ettō							
Date:	28/12	29/12	30/12	31/12	01/01	02/01	03/01	Mean
1. Prefabs:	–	160	189	204	220	236	236	207
2. Homeless:	–	299	286	258	287	324	316	295
3. Meals served:	–	1,200	824	1,200	1,473	1,121	1,275	1,182

The prefabs usually open on 29 December and stay open for roughly three more days after 3 January. The sharp rise in prefab population in 1993–1994 reflected increased capacity: more dormitories were built that year. In 1994–1995 (21st Ettō), mean prefab population dropped back to 254, partly because this was the year of the first ever Ettō at Kawasaki. It ran 29 December to 3 January, with up to 418 people sleeping at the Kawasaki Municipal Gymnasium. Many of these people had traveled to Kotobuki in previous years. In subsequent years the prefab population was further reduced by the opening and expansion of a permanent shelter at Matsukage-chō, adjoining Kotobuki-chō. The city authorities also house homeless men in doya, as at other times of year. Thus in 1998–99, as well as housing 301 people in prefabs, the authorities also placed 130 in the Matsukage shelter and 525 in doya rooms; in 1999–2000 there were 236 in the prefabs, 116 in the Matsukage shelter and 647 in doya rooms.

Table 36 Donations to 1994 Kotobuki Summer Festival

Type of donor	*No.*	*Total given*	*Mean*
Doya	52	¥351,000	¥6,750
Doya associations	2	¥30,000	¥15,000
Other local businesses	32	¥455,000	¥14,219
Support groups [13]; unions [3]	16	¥121,000	¥7,563
Individuals	10	¥74,000	¥7,400
Total	112	¥1,031,000	¥9,205

NOTE: These figures do not include donations collected by passing the hat at the rock concert.
SOURCE: Noticeboard at festival.

Notes

Chapter 1: Introduction

1. This murder is discussed on p. 87.

2. E.g., "In media reports they use the term 'vagrant' *(furōsha)* or 'laborer' *(rōmusha)*, a discriminatory term used to distinguish them from 'workers,' although they work just the same" (Ōnishi, 1994:11).

3. For instance, Nakamura Mitsuo, veteran day laborer and activist of San'ya (Fieldnotes, 28 January 1995) used "rōmusha" to describe himself; note also that a Kamagasaki workers' newsletter of the 1970s was entitled *Rōmusha Tosei* (The Laborer's Profession); see Terashima 1976.

4. These terms literally translate as "day-earning navvie," "day-pay worker," and "daily-use earner."

5. The five slang terms are explained in the glossary.

6. The Japan Association for the Study of Yoseba (JASY; *Yoseba Gakkai*).

7. Steven (1988:103), using different definitions and terminology, calculates a "floating reserve army" of more than 13.2 million people in the Japanese working class, with another 9.2 million economically inactive people classified as "latent" and "stagnant" reserve.

8. Kōriyama (1983) is the autobiography of a female radical activist who worked as a day laborer in Tokyo during the 1950s.

9. Police figures, cited by Ministry of Labor official, 7 March 1995. Yoseba activists gave slightly higher estimates at the time.

10. This recession takes its name from the Heisei era, which officially started in 1989 with the accession of Emperor Akihito to the imperial throne. Official government records state that Japan was in recession for thirty months from 1991 to 1994, falling back into recession in 1998. In the yoseba the recession is generally thought to have started around 1991 and still to be in progress at the time of writing (mid-2000).

11. Fowler got to the yoseba two years before me and was more successful in finding work. The diary of his 1991 work experience is in Fowler
1996:175–224.

12. Fieldnotes, 28 June 1993.

Chapter 2: General Historical Background

1. Fieldnotes, 2 August 1994.

2. De Vos and Wetherall assert, without citing any authority, that it was
the other way round: "The highest in status of these lower groups were the
Hinin . . . Beneath the Hinin were hereditary outcasts called Eta . . . " (1983:4).

3. I was heavily dependent on Gary Leupp's excellent book (Leupp 1992)
in writing this section. The two chapters on Tokugawa period day laborers
were a truly invaluable source. I thank him.

4. These figures have to be treated with some caution, since the various
words for "day laborer" seem to have varied in significance from "vagrant"
to "any wage-worker." "Wage-work *(chinpu)* is, by the current custom, referred to as day labor *(hiyō)* . . . "(Dazai Shundai, c.1730, quoted in Leupp
1992:17).

5. Takayanagi Shinzō and Ishii Ryōsuke, *Ofuregaki Kanpō Shisei* (Tokyo:
Iwanami Shoten, 1976) No.2343, cited in Leupp 1992:160.

6. Yoshida Nobuyuki, *Toshi Minshū no Seikatsu to Henkaku Ishiki*, in
Rekishigaku Kenkyū #534, October 1984, cited in Leupp 1992:163–164.

7. "The aim was that of preventive detention and intimidation of the rest
of the population" (Matsuzawa 1988b:152).

8. Takikawa 1994 is a biography of Hasegawa.

9. I met day laborers who mentioned working on river-dredging projects;
while many older yoseba men turn to collecting cardboard for recycling as a
modest source of income. They are called *bataya*.

10. From an article in *Rōdō Sekai*, 1 April 1898, p. 6, translated in Gordon
1985:36.

11. The emergence of the tako-beya has been dated to the 1890s, when
work began on opening up Hokkaido for commercial exploitation. "Tako-
beya" literally means "octopus room." There are many theories as to the origin
of the word, the most popular being that it comes from the idea of an octopus
pot: you can get in but you can't get out (Furukawa in Takada 1977:219–220).

12. Nimura (1997) has a detailed English-language account of the Ashio
riot. He suspects it of having been secretly provoked by the oyakata, who
mediated employment at the mine and had an ambiguous role somewhere
between being workers' representatives and employers' cronies. Their influence was under threat from the growing strength of unionism among the
work force.

13. Marx, *Capital*, quoted in Matsuzawa 1988b:147.

14. Nimura (1997) mentions day laborers being used as a supplementary
labor force at Ashio. I have not found cases of day laborers being used as scab
labor to break up Japanese strikes, though it has happened in the United
States (Anderson 1965 [1923]:120–121).

15. See Louis C. Fraina, in Katayama 1918:25.

16. Many day laborers insist that tako-beya still exist today, and for example that entrapment in them is the fate awaiting many illegal foreign workers. Lesser hells are called *han-tako* ("semi-octopuses").

17. Kusama's monumental study of the urban underclass (Kusama 1936) made him Japan's best-known writer on poverty during the interwar period. He cites government statistics that mention 1,678,460 day laborers in a working population of 6,901,576 in 1931 for an unspecified district, probably the greater Tokyo region (Kusama 1932:293).

18. The government unemployment figures cited by Kusama divide workers into three categories: "salaried men" (roughly 25 percent), "day laborers" (ditto), and "other laborers" (roughly 50 percent). These categories are not defined, nor is unemployment. The rather low figure of 11.5 percent for day laborers may stem from the exclusion of anyone getting a day of work in the month. Such anomalies plague day labor statistics.

19. A similar divide-and-rule tactic was used in the prewar Liverpool docks, where casual dock hands were divided between "low numbers"—workers with good reputations who could generally be sure of work—and "high numbers" who had to make do with whatever labor demand was left over (Williams, 1912:6, 18).

20. In this book I refer to members of Japan's permanent Korean minority as "Japan-resident Koreans," as opposed to recent, usually temporary migrants, who are usually referred to as "newcomers." Fukuoka (1993, 2000) gives a vivid picture of the Japan-resident Korean minority. See also Lee and De Vos (1981).

21. Figures from Eguchi 1980 Vol.1:156.

22. Ministry of Labor statistics, March 1995.

23. See p. 103.

24. "The blue ones were much better, they carried superior dole entitlements and pension entitlements too. When the government scrapped the system they bought back the blue handbooks from their holders, paying off the pension rights in a single, large, lump sum. A lot of guys went on massive drinking and gambling sprees and threw away prospects of a secure old age in a few weeks or months"—Nagoya day laborer. Fieldnotes, 15 December 1994.

25. During fieldwork, I received a first-hand account of a major public construction project in Yokohama. The contract went to a consortium of four companies, one of which was a front for a yakuza gang and did no work despite getting 10 percent of the ¥5 billion contract. Most of the actual work was done by several small subcontractors that were not even members of the consortium and were housed in separate, inferior offices on the work site. For more detail see Gill 2000c: 125–126.

26. The even more literal *oyaji* (dad) is also used.

27. Fieldnotes, 29 December 1993.

Chapter 3: Ethnography of Kotobuki

1. The bureaucratic organization of this welfare facility is as follows. The first floor is run by Kanagawa prefecture, the second floor by Yokohama city,

and the third and fourth floors by the Kotobuki-chō Kinrōsha Fukushi Kyōkai, (Kotobuki-chō Workers Welfare Association), an organization jointly funded by the city and prefecture. Japanese welfare systems often show this kind of organizational complexity.

2. Fieldnotes, 22 February 1994.

3. Agency for Cultural Affairs, Yearbook of Religious Affairs (*Shūkyō Nenkan*), 1992.

4. Police interview (Fieldnotes, 1 February 1994).

5. In the four years after I left, many of the younger foreign workers left Kotobuki (see table 6). By 1999, Mr. Kagoshima of Junichirō estimated that the average Filipino in Kotobuki was in his late thirties and the average Korean in his late forties.

6. Koh 1996 is an impressively thorough Japanese-language account of the lives of migrants from Cheju island in Japan. Kotobuki is featured.

7. "They had gone there [i.e., to Kotobuki] not to make money but to make *more* money, not for their daily bread but for the finer things in life" (Ventura 1992:125).

8. My principle historical sources are Kawase 1991 and Murata 1992.

9. All events described in this paragraph are from Matsunobu 1989.

10. Selling blood was a source of emergency income for day laborers for many years.

11. Interview with Nomura Yoshiaki, 10 September 1999. He added that he knew for a fact that similar considerations led to the double-exchange system in San'ya.

12. These were issued by the Labor Center, even to men who lacked the white handbook used by the Labor Office.

13. Cf. the practice in early-twentieth-century Salford of propping spades up against a wall and giving jobs to the first men to reach them from 100 yards away, described in Roberts 1971:66.

14. Assuming very roughly five thousand men interested in getting work. The Labor Center's estimate is about six thousand (Kotobuki Labor Center 1996:3).

15. A Labor Center official said that the market for period contracts in 1993 was the worst since the Center was founded in 1974, during the oil shock recession (Fieldnotes, 31 January 1994).

16. There are no statistics for the street labor market. However, a Labor Center official admitted that the two employment exchanges could not account for more than 10 percent, at the very most, of Kotobuki job contracts (interview, 31 January 1994).

17. Some day laborer unionists think the Nakasone government's 1985 Labor Dispatch Act effectively legalized pin-hane. See p. 30.

18. Saito (1994:129) says that some two hundred tehaishi operate in Kotobuki. Half of them are "semi-pros," laborers who do some recruiting on the side. The other one hundred are "pros," often connected to yakuza. Their numbers must have greatly dwindled in the last few years.

19. Fieldnotes, 30 June 1993.

20. These imports were necessitated by the failure of the Japanese rice harvest in 1992.

21. Fieldnotes, 11 June 1994.

22. Fieldnotes, 7 July 1993.

23. Fieldnotes, 4 January 1994.

24. Fieldnotes, 24 June 1994.

25. The employment and health insurance programs are described below. Industrial accident insurance is another system run by the Ministry of Labor, whereby employers pay premiums to insure their companies against the cost of compensating for workplace accidents.

26. In the month of August 1993, for instance, the Labor Office supplied a grand total of 1,573 person-days of work, yet paid out 16,231 person-days of dole money. The Labor Center supplied 3,753 person-days of work that month, and since the system requires at least one day's work per claiming day, that leaves roughly 11,000 person-days' worth of stamps emanating from a combination of street-market jobs with stamps, men staying on for extra days (table 21), plus fraudulent claims.

27. Fieldnotes, 21 October 1993.

28. Cf. Shigehirō, pp. 188–190. For a U.S. comparison: "There seems to be an understanding among this class of men not to work for less than 50c an hour, and they are loath to accept steady employment at 35c to 37.5c [an] hour when they can do temporary work, and work at a different job every day, or any day one pleases, at 45c to 50c an hour" (Anderson, 1923:120).

29. Ventura and a dozen Filipino friends got work coiling cables for KDD, Japan's international telephone company (Ventura 1992:46).

30. There is nothing in the rules of the Labor Office to prevent it from dealing in period contracts, but in practice employers always advertise such jobs at the Labor Center. According to Endō Hideo of the Labor Office, some employers are under the mistaken impression that the Office and Center are two branches of the same institution, with the former handling one-day contracts and the latter period contracts. This is quite untrue, of course. Interview with Endō Hideo, 10 September 1999.

31. For instance, eight men died in a nocturnal fire on 6 July 1994, at a very dangerously designed construction workers' dormitory at Ebina, twenty miles from Yokohama. Most of the fifty-three men staying there were migrant workers from Hokkaido and Tōhoku. Press reports said the dormitory belonged to a small construction company called Komuro-gumi (e.g., *Asahi Shinbun*, 6 July 1994, evening edition, p. 17). In fact it belonged to Tōkyū Construction, a massive company using Komuro-gumi as a subcontractor. Tōkyū escaped publicity.

32. A survey by the Seikatsu-kan found that in FY1997, there were 6,719 doya rooms in Kotobuki.

33. Fieldnotes, 17 October 1993.

34. By the end of 1998 there were some 6,700 doya rooms in Kotobuki. 5,274 were occupied by welfare recipients, some 350 by migrant workers, some with their families, and another 350 or so by people with accommodation vouchers. Simple arithmatic suggests that only about 700 to 750 rooms

were left for independent Japanese day laborers (and anyone else). Cf. tables 5, 6, 23.

35. Source: Yokohama City Welfare Bureau surveys, 1990–1998. Available in annual reports of the Kotobuki Seikatsu-kan.

36. The Seikatsu-kan survey quoted above found that 62.8 percent of doya rooms were 3 mats (5 square meters) in area. 18.0 percent were 2 to 2.5 mats (3.3 to 4.1 square meters), 12.7 percent were 3.5 to 4.5 mats (5.8 to 7.4 square meters), and only 2.6 percent were bigger than that. "Unclear" accounted for the remaining 3.9 percent. Mean floor-space was 3.07 mats (5.1 square meters).

37. *Keiba, keirin, kyōtei,* the "three Ks" of yoseba leisure. The three Ks of work are three Ds in English: *kitsui, kitanai, kiken* (demanding, dirty, dangerous).

38. I was told that police raids on the nomiya were more frequent in the month or two preceding the annual round of promotions, being a simple way for officers to improve their records. Men caught in the nomiya would be arrested only if found in possession of a betting slip . . . another little gamble.

39. Fieldnotes, 3 August 1993.

40. See *Tokyo Insideline* #21 p. 8 (29 October 1993) and #28 p. 6 (31 May 1994).

41. Interview with Murata Yoshio, 19 November 1994.

42. Fieldnotes, 7 July 1993.

43. For example, there were no murders and two manslaughters in Kotobuki in 1993 (Police interview, 1 February 1994).

44. The yakuza sometimes sell fraudulent sets of stamps *(yami inshi).* The service includes franking the stamps with the seal of a company registered at the Labor Office.

45. Labor Center interview, 31 January 1994. This situation stemmed from bureaucratic backbiting. Health insurance for day laborers was thought up by the Ministry of Health and Welfare, but the Labor Office is run by the Ministry of Labor, which has never liked the system.

46. Sometimes literally translated as "livelihood protection."

47. Interview with Kagoshima Masa'aki, 11 September 1999. Life expectancy for Japanese males was recorded as 76.36 years in 1995 (Ministry of Health and Welfare).

48. Interview with Dr. Saiki, 31 January 1994.

49. Reported in *Kotobuki Iryō-han Tsūshin,* the Iryō-han's monthly newsletter, #67, May 1996.

50. It takes its name from the Tagalog word for a water buffalo, a representative beast of burden.

51. Interview with Kagoshima Masa'aki, 11 September 1999.

Chapter 4: Ethnography of Other Doya-Gai and Yoseba

1. I have written a journalistic account of San'ya (Gill 1994); see also de Barry 1985; Fallows 1988; Fowler 1992, 1996.

2. Usually written with characters meaning "Field of Small Tumuli," sometimes "Field of Bones."

3. It was used as a tennis court when observed a few years earlier by Kogawa (1987:170), who saw this as a demonstration of the authorities' determination to encourage middle-class incursion into San'ya.

4. I have more on Kon's street observations in Gill 1996.

5. This had risen to 197 by 1994.

6. Source: Doya owners' union membership list, 1991.

7. See Tokyo City Government 1969; also Funamoto 1985 *passim*, Kaji 1977 Vol.1 42–54.

8. The Kanamachi gang is affiliated to the Great Japan Pure Country League *(Dai-Nippon Kokusuikai)*, an ultra-nationalist organization.

9. Fieldnotes, 15 January 1995. Satō was stabbed to death near the Sōgidan headquarters on 22 December 1984. He had been trying to make a film about San'ya. Yamaoka took over the project, only to be shot dead on 13 January 1986, in another part of Tokyo. A junior Kanamachi Yakuza was arrested for the murder. The film, *Yama: Yararetara Yarikaese* (San'ya: If they get you, get 'em back), was completed but is rather rarely shown due to factional disputes over the content. Yamaoka's work survives him (e.g., Yamaoka 1984).

10. *Asahi Shinbun,* 15 June 1994, evening edition, p. 12.

11. A 1999 quantitative survey counted just 378 men apparently leaving San'ya for work one weekday morning in December (Marr et al. 2000:5).

12. Japanese officialdom has a long history of razing the homes of the poor for the sake of prestige events, meticulously documented in Enami et al. 1989.

13. Fieldnotes, 4 August 1994.

14. In Britain the riot made the BBC television news. Hester (1991) has a full account of it.

15. *Asahi Shinbun,* 10 October 1990.

16. *Japan Times* and *Mainichi Daily News* (both 3 October 1992) and interviews.

17. *Asahi Shinbun,* 27 April 1994, evening edition.

18. Sumida Ichirō of the Airin Labor Center estimates that day laborer dole payments pump ¥7–8 billion a year into the Kamagasaki economy—roughly $70 million.

19. Kamayan stars in Arimura 1987a, 1987b, 1989, 1992. Arimura discusses his creation in English in Arimura 1991.

20. As of summer 1994; interview with Sumida Ichirō, 9 August 1994.

21. Fieldnotes, 12 August 1994.

22. A small temporary job program was granted in the winter of 1994–1995. There is still no government program to assist those ineligible for welfare, but large-scale food handouts in Triangle Park are conducted by several volunteer groups.

23. Interview, 10 August 1994; cf pp. 17–18.

24. Police interview, 16 December 1994.

25. Interview with exchange officials, 16 December 1994.

26. Police interview, 16 December 1994.

27. Interview, 28 September 1999.

28. "Lazybones," pp. 130–131, is a case in point.

29. It was written with the same characters but pronounced in the indigenous Japanese style, "Mizuguruma," rather than the Chinese-derived "Suisha." Perhaps "Suisha" was itself a euphemism.

30. Source: Monthly bulletin of Fukuoka Central Labor Exchange, April 1994. In that month day laborers in Fukuoka got 29,496 person-days of work, of which 26,124 (88.6 percent) came from the P.E.S.O. program.

31. Source: Fukuoka Prefecture Central Employment Exchange.

32. These places are also sometimes described as *hanba* in western Japan, though "hanba" usually means a work site with its own dormitory in eastern Japan.

33. There have been reports of similar institutions in the United States, where men are arrested for vagrancy and delivered to labor contractors in the Louisiana oil exploration business or agribusiness. "The labor contractor houses and feeds the men and in exchange receives and keeps most of their wages, having charged them for numerous services whether rendered or not" (Peterson and Wiegand 1985:227).

34. Interview with Ōtō Katsu, 22 July 1994.

35. "Riverside people" *(kawaramono)* is one of the many old euphemisms for Eta (Price 1972:13).

36. Fieldnotes, 22 July 1994.

37. Interview, 24 July 1994. Nimura (1997) has a detailed account of the naya system at the Ashio copper mine before the 1907 riot, though the term *hanba* was preferred.

38. Part of the disused land is now covered by Space World, a theme park built by Nippon Steel to employ some of its cast-off workers.

39. Fieldnotes, 30 July 1994.

40. A feud between rival ninpu-dashi owners over control of the Yahata work force culminated in the summer of 1959, when the chairman of the Association of Workers' Boarding Houses *(Rōdō Shukuhakujo Kyōdō Kumiai)* was shot dead in the street at Harunomachi by two men (Kamata 1970:69).

41. Fieldnotes, 28–30 July 1994.

42. Fieldnotes, 7 and 10 August 1994.

43. Fieldnotes, 7 August 1994.

44. Fieldnotes, 10 December 1994.

45. Personal communication, in Fieldnotes, 1 January 1995.

46. Interview, 24 July 1994.

47. Some Japanese saunas are in big buildings, with restaurants, cinemas, etc. Many are open twenty-four hours a day and you can sleep in the cinema, which has no seats—you lie down to watch. The basic cost of living in a sauna is about double the average doya but with free bath facilities.

Chapter 5: Who Are These Men?

1. Throughout this chapter the data refers only to Japanese day laborers and not to international migrants.

2. Caldarola (1968:515) states that only 25.5 percent of his 1964 doya-gai sample come from rural backgrounds—a figure I find surprisingly low. I can

only guess that (1) with the Japanese economy still maturing, the yoseba remained an option for a greater number of urbanites and (2) many of them subsequently left the yoseba during the decade of high growth that followed Caldarola's survey. Again, Caldarola does not state how he defines "urban" and "rural," and may have been using different criteria from mine.

3. This is just a rough rule of thumb. Of course there are large cities in "rural" prefectures, and large rural areas in "urban" prefectures.

4. This pattern, of losing work in declining heavy industry and drifting to the yoseba, is chiefly associated with Hokkaido and Kyushu. There may well be more such people at the larger yoseba in Tokyo and Osaka.

5. Junichirō references in this paragraph are from p. 7 of the materials for the 1994–1995 *Ettō*.

6. For a populist view of birth order as a determinist system to rival blood groups and horoscopes, see Hatada 1994.

7. Ministry of Health and Welfare population trend survey, 1993.

8. The 102 men who told me how many siblings they had reported a total of 483 siblings including themselves. Since most of them came from rural families, it is not surprising that sibling group size is slightly larger than the national average for this period.

9. Of the 483 siblings mentioned, 102 were the informants themselves and in 170 cases gender was not specified (e.g., "I was the oldest of a family of four"). That left 211 gender-specified siblings, of whom 126 were boys and eighty-five girls.

$$\text{Boys} = 126/211 = 59.7\%$$

$$\text{Girls} = 85/211 = 40.3\%$$

The preponderance of males may have some meaning, e.g. unusually high levels of male competition in the family, but the sample is too small to say for sure.

10. Fieldnotes, 19 October 1993.

11. Fieldnotes, 24 February 1994; conversation in English.

12. Bahr (1971) studied 203 Bowery men, 199 inmates of Camp La Guardia, a hospice for infirm men located on the Bowery, and a control sample of 125 men living in a low-income Brooklyn neighborhood. He found 10 percent only children on the Bowery and 12 percent in La Guardia, against 5 percent in the control. Last-born men were somewhat overrepresented in Camp La Guardia but not in the Bowery population. Oddly, 56 percent of last-born men in Camp La Guardia were heavy drinkers, against 34 percent of first-born men, but identical proportions of 33 percent were heavy drinkers among first- and last-born Bowery men.

13. *Sōryō*, another word signifying an eldest son, literally means something like "general steward." This is a reference to the traditional idea that the eldest son inherits the household as a manager on behalf of the family rather than as an individual owner.

14. Fieldnotes, 3 January 1994.

15. Fieldnotes, 26 March 1994.

16. Fieldnotes, 3 June 1994.

17. Sending money home is a feature sometimes mentioned in day laborer narratives. Kamagasaki activist Fukada Kazuo says that he also knows instances of the reverse case: doya-gai remittance men who rely on money sent by relatives (Fukada, personal communication, 3 May 1999).

18. Caldarola (1968:512) quotes Yokoyama (1899) as reporting that the original inhabitants of Kamagasaki and San'ya were "generally tramps, migratory workers, and vagrants who came in from the countryside in order to gain some experience in urban living but intended to return to their villages after having earned some cash." This would suggest that the pattern of "temporary" migrants getting stuck in the yoseba may have a long pedigree.

19. Fieldnotes, 14 July 1993.

20. Fieldnotes, 25 February 1994.

21. Fieldnotes, 26 July 1994.

22. Belief in levels of hell is strong in Japanese Jōdo (Pure-Land) Buddhism, as it is in some strands of Christian tradition and European mythology.

Chapter 6: The Meaning of Home

1. However, in the late 1990s the practice of living in a car became more widespread. A wave of youth unemployment left some young people living in cars, finding casual work, and maintaining their social networks via the ubiquitous mobile telephone—a revolutionary device that has called into question the traditional association between stable residence and social affiliation. The more successful yoseba workers also use mobile telephones.

2. In September 1999 the Yokohama city government announced that a survey the previous month had found 534 people homeless in Naka ward, where Kotobuki is located, out of 794 in the whole of Yokohama. The figures had roughly doubled in one year. The city's two shelters, with one hundred beds between them, were permanently full (*Asahi Shinbun* Yokohama edition, 15 September 1999, p. 27). In August 2000, the capacity of the shelter at Matsuleage-chō, next-door to Kotobuki, was raised from 70 beds to 170 beds.

3. Fieldnotes, 15 December 1994. I recalled this conversation when it emerged in 1999 that the Osaka police were ordering supermarkets and convenience stores in the Kamagasaki area to mix sand with food that had passed its sell-by date before throwing it out, specifically to prevent homeless people from eating it. The move was prompted by the revelation that some people were making a business of collecting the thrown-out food and selling it in the Kamagasaki street market for a fraction of its ticketed price. Police cited legal and health considerations in defending what was seen by many as a very callous move.

4. Fieldnotes, 1 January 1995.

5. One writer who defies political orthodoxy in a spirit of quirky postmodernism is Kogawa Tetsuo. He defines homeless people as "people who cut across space" (*supēsu no ōdansha*), and controversially suggests that they have—perhaps unconsciously—chosen a different lifestyle. He calls Japanese homeless people "post-homeless," and obscurely contrasts them with U.S. homeless, many of whom are simply unable to feed and house themselves, he believes (Kogawa 1987:173–175).

6. People do sometimes die of starvation in contemporary Japan. Mizushima (1993) describes how his mother starved to death in Hokkaido after being turned down for social security. There was a similar case in the papers in spring 1996, when a mother and son starved to death in Shizuoka prefecture. These deaths were caused by relative cultural want rather than absolute material want. Some people simply cannot scramble for discarded food from convenience stores.

7. Fieldnotes, 8 July 1993.

8. Source: *Sukabura,* publication of the Thursday Patrol.

9. Article by Mary Jordan, *International Herald Tribune,* 23 January 1996:1, 6.

10. "If I went to the shelter at night, my things would be stolen." (Homeless man in Kotobuki, quoted in article by Steven R. Weisman: "Japan's Homeless—Seen Yet Ignored," *New York Times,* 19 January 1991:4.)

11. Stevens (1997) has comparative accounts of both these Kotobuki events.

12. This figure is disputed, because at various times rival left-wing factions have sponsored rival festivals in San'ya.

13. Some children also take part in the Kamagasaki summer festival.

14. Fieldnotes, 15 August 1993.

15. Fieldnotes, 13 August 1993.

16. For some people, of course, Kotobuki is their literal hometown. The highlight of the 1993 festival was a performance by an all-female song-and-dance troupe led by Kikutsuru Sen, a well-known singer of *enka* (sentimental ballads). She was raised in Kotobuki, and often performs at the festival in homage to her hometown.

17. Fieldnotes, 2 August 1994.

18. Fieldnotes, 7 January 1994; cf. Stevens 1995a:176–177.

19. As with the summer festival, rival factions have held Ettō-type events in San'ya. I attended the San'ya Ettō on New Year's Eve, 1989–1990. Rival factions took it in turns—quite amicably—to provide entertainment. See Aoki (1988, 1989 in Japanese, undated in English), for a metaphysical interpretation of the Kamagasaki Ettō.

20. The *Asahi Shinbun* described the Tokyo Ettō prefabs in its evening edition of Saturday January 8, 1994. Whereas in Yokohama shelters are set up in the heart of Kotobuki, in Tokyo they are set up at Heiwajima, many miles from San'ya. Users are bused in under strict security. The shelters closely resemble prison camps. Riot police maintain a permanent presence; there is a barbed wire fence; inmates wishing to leave the shelters, permanently or temporarily, must sign out and explain why they want to go out; outsiders are not allowed in. The *Asahi* quoted one man as saying he was going back to San'ya, because sleeping rough was preferable to sleeping in a concentration camp.

21. Hoch and Slayton (1989:130) surveyed rooms in Chicago single-room occupancy hotels (SROs) in 1984 and rated them thus: three points for a bath, two for a toilet, and one each for a sink, heater, window, stove, phone, and television. Except for two cubicle hotels that averaged 0.85, the Chicago SROs averaged 9.60. Doya rooms usually have windows and the pricier ones have TVs; still, Hoch and Slayton would not award more than two points to most

doya rooms. Most doya will not even let residents use their own stoves or heaters, for fear of fire and electricity bills.

22. In some of the San'ya and Kamagasaki doya, as in traditional Japanese inns, there is a tertiary division of space. One swaps outdoor shoes for plastic slippers on entering the doya, then takes off the slippers on entering a room. In Kotobuki, the Korean landlords are less fussy and one wears outdoor shoes in the corridor and on the stairs.

23. Fieldnotes, 14 December 1994, Nagoya.

24. Fieldnotes, 29 May 1994.

25. A drunk man fell into the bonfire and had suffered very serious burns by the time we managed to extinguish his burning clothes. He was rushed to hospital and his life saved. I met him again a year later. Once more he was drinking by the bonfire. (Fieldnotes, 26 November 1993 and 30 December 1994).

26. Despite a strenuous campaign to prove his innocence by the union and other sympathizers, an appeal to the Supreme Court was rejected on 24 October 1995. Nobuta is currently serving an eight-year prison sentence. To day laborers there is a double affront here: Nobuta was convicted without witnesses, solely on the strength of a forced confession which he later retracted. At the same time, the eight-year sentence is unusually light for murder, reflecting a tendency among judges to undervalue the lives of day laborers. Thus, the affair is seen as an insult both to Nobuta and to the dead man, a day laborer named Yamada Takao (Nomura 1992, Nobuta 1996).

27. Fieldnotes, 31 January 1994.

28. Fieldnotes, 25 March 1994.

29. A reference to Dore 1978:138.

30. Dore 1978:133.

31. Fieldnotes, 25 March 1994.

32. Dore 1978:138, 140–142.

33. Fieldnotes, 31 January 1994.

Chapter 7: Marginal Identity in the Yoseba

1. In the case of Kamagasaki, there are gender-based population figures that show that as recently as 1955 there were more females (17,959) than males (16,110) living there. By 1980, however, there were 21,984 males and 9,892 females, and the gender imbalance has doubtless widened since (Kamagasaki Resource Center 1993:229).

2. Personal communication. Mizuno Ashira of Kamagasaki is a radical day laborer and a distinctive voice in Japan's budding "men's lib" movement. His book (Mizuno 1997) is a firsthand account of how one, very exceptional, man has succeeded in combining the freewheeling life of a day laborer with marriage and family life.

3. Manabu said that casual labor tended to be tougher in Japan than in the United States. The American agency he used to work for divided work into four types, according to how physically demanding it was. Manabu had only signed up for the less demanding "C" and "D" categories, but he said all the work available in Kotobuki was "Class A"—the toughest—by U.S. stan-

dards. He had also worked as an untrained sushi chef in Kentucky. I thought of this as a highly skilled trade, but he scornfully insisted that anyone could do it, though it impressed employers if you happened to look Japanese.

4. *"Kuitsumeta yoseba no rōdōsha wa shoku* [= food/work, both characters in text] *o motomete nagarete itta. Nagareru koto wa yoi koto da. Mizu mo nagarete koso ikite iru. Tamari-mizu wa jiki ni kusaru mono da"* (Kama-Kyōtō 1974:190).

5. Fieldnotes, 19 October 1993.

6. I found just one pair of brothers during fieldwork, in Kamagasaki. Otherwise, kin were virtually absent from the daily lives of my informants.

7. In reality, only about 30 percent of employed Japanese males conform to any degree to the "salaryman" stereotype. Nevertheless, this has become a dominant image of Japan at home and abroad.

8. This characteristic of "present orientation" is far more easily expressed in Japanese, with the single word *setsunashugi*—"the principle of living only for (the pleasure of) the moment" (Masuda 1974:1503).

9. In his classic prewar study of American casual laborers, Parker notes that most of the ones he knew would stop working as soon as they had enough to live on (1920:78–79). Williams makes the same observation about British casual dockworkers (1912:31–32).

10. A number of American sociologists have also discussed present-orientation in association with lower social class, juvenile delinquency, and mental illness. As Murray puts it (1984:155): "Deviant behavior is related to deviant time orientation." He also quotes Wiseman (1970), who suggests that skid-row alcoholism programs often fail because the counsellors are oriented to the future and the alcoholics to the present; and Liebow (1967:68–69), who argues that the present orientation of his street-corner informants is in fact a realistic orientation toward a future that is "loaded with trouble."

Murray himself trumps everybody by arguing that time in skid row is cyclical, rather than linear. He gives two reasons: "One's primary goal is survival, a goal which must be re-achieved every day"; and "The cyclic schedules of the institutions which affect the homeless" (Murray 1984:157). In the yoseba, point 1 applies to some of the older, weaker inhabitants; point 2 does not apply in terms of the one-day cycle, since the vast majority are not in the kind of regimented shelters common in U.S. skid rows, which chuck the men out every morning and let them back in the evening. Homeless shelters are still rare in Japan, and they tend to limit residence by specifying a maximum number of weeks rather than by limiting hours of residence in the day.

In my own view, all sorts of conflicting conceptualizations of time coexist in the yoseba, as they do anywhere. The cycle of the seasons is very important to day laborers, some of whom abandon their spendthrift ways as winter approaches and attempt to save money to tide them over this most difficult time of the year (e.g., Noriyuki, pp. 111–112). A few others were saving money toward their retirement. They were, however, a very small minority.

11. Cf p. 44; also Stevens (1997) on Christian yoseba volunteers.

12. Fieldnotes, Wednesday 5 January 1994.

13. In recent years, the terms *karōshi* (death by overwork) and *tanshin funin* (forced relocation by the company, leading to separation from one's family) have become widely recognized as serious social problems. There have been several legal actions attacking companies for inflicting these evils on their permanent employees. A survey unveiled in October 1999 found 350,000 cases of tanshin funin, up 60,000 from the year before. See Shiina 1994.

14. Day laborers certainly feel an affinity for romantic losers, as evidenced in the widespread support within the yoseba for the Hanshin Tigers—a very popular but notoriously unsuccessful baseball team, comparable to the Chicago Cubs in the United States, or perhaps to Manchester City in English soccer.

15. The bottle-gang debate of the 1950s and 1960s is summarized by Bahr (1973:157). Some observers stress flexibility, others formality. The most formalized account is by Rooney, who compares the West Coast bottle gang to a business corporation: "The management of the capital is handled by a leader who acts as general chairman. Each member is a stockholder and maintains rights to consumption of the communally purchased bottle of wine..." (Rooney 1961:449). Giamo (1989:182–183), visiting the New York Bowery at the end of the 1970s, finds a similar institution with the same name, twenty years and the width of America away from Rooney's study. See also Rubington (1968), Mars (1987).

16. *Uchi/soto* (inside/outside) is one of the most venerable dyads in the Japanalogical literature. The idea, that there are totally different codes of behavior depending on whether you are dealing with someone inside or outside a certain social circle, is invariably mentioned in accounts of Japanese culture and society. Doi (1971) discusses the theme at length, and more recently Bachnik and Quinn (1994) have devoted an entire book to it.

17. The sample is rather small because I usually write fieldnotes in English, recording the original Japanese only for especially striking statements.

18. Fieldnotes, 26 March 1994.

19. Kama-Kyōtō 1974:190. See note 4, this chapter, for Japanese original.

20. All these terms are in the glossary, some with longer explanations. Note, incidentally, the similarity between this liquid imagery and that of the celebrated "floating world" (*ukiyo*) of geisha and courtesans.

21. Gambling is just as much a part of Japanese popular culture as saving is. The average Japanese household was recently saving about 15 percent of its disposable income (Bank of Japan, 1993)—a high figure by Euro-American standards, but lower than it used to be and far behind South Korea and Taiwan. A 1999 survey by the American Express Corporation found that Japanese households were saving $291 a month, well below the U.S. figure of $361 (*Japan Times*, 5 October 1999). Meanwhile Japan is thought to spend some 5.7 percent of its GNP on gambling. This latter figure is probably the highest in the world, at least for industrialized countries. Per capita sales of betting slips are 2.3 times higher than in the United States and four times higher than in Britain (AERA magazine, Vol.7 No.30, July 25 1994:32–39). Japan also has pachinko, a multi-trillion yen gambling enterprise which dwarfs race betting and lotteries and is not shared by any other country to any significant degree.

22. Mr. Furukawa. His stage name was "Billy" (English version) or "Bi Li" (Chinese version, written with the characters "Beautiful Logic"). A dockworker and occasional sailor, he said he filled in the time between jobs by telling fortunes. He charged ¥1,000 to read a palm, and used to work an excellent pitch in front of Ishikawa-chō station, very near Kotobuki. Later he moved to a hypermarket in Kamioka, another district of Yokohama, after the Kotobuki yakuza started demanding protection money from him (Fieldnotes, 15 April 1994).

23. Fieldnotes, 30 July and 13 August 1993.

24. This concept is borrowed from the Introduction to Day, Papataxiarchis and Stewart (1999:1–26).

25. The official translation of article 25 of the Japanese constitution states: "All people shall have the right to maintain the minimum standards of wholesome and cultured living. In all spheres of life, the State shall use its endeavors for the promotion and extension of social welfare and security, and of public health."

Chapter 8: The Role of the Yoseba in Contemporary Japanese Society

1. This is a term associated with a liberal-to-left critique of Japanese society. Japanese works on the control society include Arakawa (1970), Kurihara (1982), and Shōji (1989). In English the approach can be seen in the works of Sugimoto Yoshio, such as "Friendly Authoritarianism," chapter 10 of Sugimoto 1997.

2. *Deru kugi wa utareru*. This proverb is also the title of a book by a French priest, describing, among other things, his encounters with day laborers in Kawasaki (L'Henoret 1993, 1994).

3. Some versions of the control society model seek to account for evidence of tolerance or neglect as "safety valves," exceptional social sites that enable most people to be better controlled most of the time. My feeling is that exceptions to the control model are too numerous to be accounted for in this way. I discuss the issue briefly in English (Gill 2000b), and at greater length in a Japanese-language paper (Gill forthcoming).

4. Nowadays at least, day laborers cannot afford to patronize prostitutes on anything like the scale that would justify this proximity. Rather, the patrons of Yoshiwara and Tobita are mostly mainstream males. My impression is that the proximity of yoseba and prostitution districts is more to do with shared outcast status than with a patron-client relationship between the two.

5. See Raz for a vivid account of fieldwork with a yakuza gang, briefly in English (1992) or at length in Japanese (1996).

6. Police interview, 1 February 1994.

7. Ōtsuka subsequently abandoned his camera altogether, married a teacher from the Kotobuki kindergarten, and is now raising a family in an abandoned hamlet in the mountains of Nagano prefecture, growing his own organic vegetables and laboring for cash in a nearby town. Sadly, the negatives of the *Rakantachi* pictures were lost long ago and this has prevented me from reprinting them in this book.

8. Boddhisattvas are enlightened beings who forego nirvana in order to try and save others. Arhats, by contrast, make no attempt to share their enlightenment. Some Tokugawa texts depict them as selfish.

9. The Chinese character *sei*, meaning 'sacred,' also has a purely Japanese reading *hijiri*, meaning a wandering mendicant monk.

10. Asahi Shinbun, 8 October 1994.

11. Ibid., 14 November 1995.

12. Ibid., 18 October 1995.

13. The number of victims varies from one account to another. Sixteen were documented by police, but there may well have been more. One of the three murder victims was killed by a different group of boys to the main group implicated in the incident (Aoki 1984:37).

14. E.g., in Kan, 1986:18, and Matsuzawa 1988b:148.

15. *"Ashigeri o ireru to hone ga bokki-to ore, kibun ga sukatto shita."* (Sae 1984:140).

16. Compare the attitudes of the Kyōmai boys with this: " [T]he tramp is consciously and enthusiastically imitated. Around the camp fire watching the coffee pot boil or the 'mulligan' cook, the boys are often found mingling with the tramps and listening in on their stories of adventure.

"To boys the tramp is not a problem, but a human being, and an interesting one at that. He has no cares nor burdens to hold him down. All he is concerned with is to live and seek adventure, and in this he personifies the heroes in the stories the boys have read. Tramp life is an invitation to a career of varied experiences and adventures" (Anderson 1965 [1923]:85).

17. Fieldnotes, 4 February 1994.

18. This despite the fact that on other occasions (p. 170) Kimitsu compared Kotobuki to a Nazi concentration camp.

19. The ones known to me are Tsuchida (1966), Caldarola (1968), Aoki (1989), Giamo (1994), Yoshida (1995), and Marr (1997). I review the debate in Japanese in Gill 1999a.

20. In mid-2000, JASY was approaching completion of a new bibliography of three hundred yoseba studies. In addition, I myself contributed a bibliography of about forty English-language materials. One of them is Paul Groth's *Living Downtown* (1994). In this fascinating study of the American tradition of living in residential hotels, Groth greatly complicates the skid row picture by describing several other kinds of residential zone showing degrees of similarity to the doya-gai: the "workers' cottage district," the "mid-priced transient hotel neighborhood," the "rooming house district," and the "cheap lodging house district." The latter roughly corresponds to skid row but has a far more overwhelmingly male population (Groth 1994:131–167). Groth's account of San Francisco's Chinatown (156–159) is much more reminiscent of Kotobuki than of Yokohama's present-day Chinatown.

21. Yoshida (1995) makes the explicit link between prewar Hobohemia and the contemporary yoseba, noting particularly the similarities in geographical patterning and workers' lifestyles.

22. Anderson gives the example of John M., who seems to have done twenty-six single-day jobs in three months from 4 May to 26 July 1922: "John M. is a casual laborer. He is one of a type that works by the day, is paid by the day, and lives by the day" (Anderson 1965 [1923]:118–119).

23. E.g., Anderson 1965(1923); Allsop 1967; Bahr 1973; Giamo 1989; Rossi 1989.

24. Notwithstanding all the talk about the destruction of skid row, there are still some recognizable skid row districts in the United States, notably in Seattle and Los Angeles. The political battle over what to about the L.A. skid row is described in Goetz 1992.

25. "Last Call for Bowery's Last Gin Mill," *New York Times,* 25 December 1993, p. 16. Quoted in Giamo 1994:1, 15.

26. For example: "Every metropolis has its Hobohemia populated by homeless and often jobless males who live in barren rooms and eke out a drab existence" (Gist and Fava, 1964:368).

27. Bahr says that the original Skid Road was a cluster of "lodging houses, saloons and establishments . . . contiguous to the 'skid road' running from the top of the ridge down to Henry Yesler's mill" in Seattle (Bahr 1973:32).

28. Derived from the figures in table 5.

29. Bogue's classic study of the postwar skid row in twenty-four American cities found that 20.4 percent of inhabitants worked in restaurants, 16.4 percent on railways, and 15.7 percent in manufacturing. Construction ranked only seventh, with 5.7 percent, and longshore work did not feature at all (Bogue 1963:177).

30. Point 6 applies only to Yokohama. But in the case of Tokyo, food handouts are made from the Jōhoku Welfare Center, located in San'ya. This similarly gives poor people a reason to gather in the yoseba district.

31. Both San'ya and Kamagasaki have large police stations in central locations (pp. 85, 95), and Kamagasaki has outdoor surveillance cameras (p. 95). By contrast, Kotobuki has just a small police box in one corner. It is supposed to have a staff of four, but I often saw it empty during my fieldwork in Kotobuki. It is fair to say that my argument about zoned tolerance is less well supported in the San'ya and Kamagasaki cases. However, the police there appear to be concerned mostly with preventing street rioting. It is my impression that on the whole there is relatively little police interference in everyday yoseba life.

32. Japan is a relatively lightly policed country. In 1990 Japan had one police officer per 556 people, against one per 384 in the United Kingdom, 379 in the United States, 311 in Germany, 288 in Italy, and 268 in France (National Police Agency white paper, 1991). Imprisonment rates are also low. In 1997, thirty-nine out of every 100,000 people in Japan were in prison. The figures for Britain and France were roughly ninety per 100,000, while the United States had no fewer than 645 prisoners per 100,000 people. The Japanese figure comes from the 1998 edition of the *Japan Statistical Yearbook* (Management and Coordination Agency 1960–1999), the others from Loic Wacquant, "Imprisoning the American Poor." In *Le Monde Diplomatique,* English ed., September 1998 pp. 8–9.

33. Various aspects of the destruction of skid row and scattering of homeless men are described in Rossi 1989, Hoch & Slayton 1989, and Giamo and Grunberg eds. 1992.

Epilogue: The Rise of Uncertainty, the Fall of Solidarity

1. Fieldnotes, 2 August 1994. The cover photo of this book was taken inside the Airin Labor Center.

2. Ibid.

3. Consider, for example, the steady increase in "casual employees" in table 4.

4. The 10 February 1994 issue of GAT'N, published by Recruit Co.

5. A turn of phrase borrowed from Hendry 1995.

6. Registered day laborers have shown falling numbers since 1970, through boom and bust alike (table 1); while numbers of broad-definition day laborers (see pp. 5–6) have hardly changed since 1960 (table 3).

7. Why was the sharp rise in Kotobuki day wages during the bubble years not followed by a corresponding fall after the bubble burst (table 16)? As well as the union, the Kotobuki Labor Center has also campaigned informally to defend the day wage. "If an employer rings up asking for men at a wage that seems on the low side, we say 'Couldn't you manage another ¥1,000?'" (Labor Center official Takeuchi Masao, interviewed on 10 September 1999). These tactics have helped maintain wage levels, but may also have driven some employers away from the Center. On the street labor market, the macho culture makes it embarrassing for a tehaishi to cut wages—it is much easier to employ fewer men. These factors may help to explain why the recession has hit recruitment levels much harder than wage levels.

8. Fieldnotes, 23 March 1995.

9. For a comparative instance of complex attitudes to casual labor among workers, see Phillips and Whiteside (1985:269–301). They tell how many workers resisted decasualization of the British docks for decades. The more employable workers relished the freedom and high hourly wages available; the less employable workers feared that they would be the first to suffer complete unemployment if the work force were to be decasualized.

10. Ministry of Labor interview, 7 March 1995.

11. Cf. Asahi Shinbun, 3 February 1995, evening edition, p. 3. After the earthquake, single-day contracts rose 65 percent year-on-year, at 5,476 for 31 January. The article quotes a union leaflet as saying "The time has come when we casual construction workers are really needed. . . . "

12. Akiyama et al. (1960 Vol.2:227) describe similar attitudes among Tokyo day laborers.

13. My own simplified term (see pp. 50–51).

Glossary of Yoseba Terms

n noun; v verb; a adjective; abn abbreviation; ad adverb; pn proper noun; np noun phrase; vp verb phrase; ap adjectival phrase; ex exclamation; lit literally; pron pronunciation; Js Japanese.

Abureru v To fail to get work. Slang modification of *afureru*, to overflow; implying "to be excess to requirements."

Abure-teate n Day laborer's dole payment (slang).

Aitai hōshiki np Lit. "face-to-face formula." Recruitment system used in Kamagasaki, where company recruiters bring their minibuses to the Labor Center and negotiate directly with workers.

Amaembo n Lit. "child who indulges." A spoilt brat. Many Kotobuki men describe themselves thus.

Āmen de rāmen np Saying "amen" to get noodles [*rāmen*]. Hence, the practice of attending Christian services purely for the food handouts that follow.

Ana-hori n "Digging holes," slang for construction work.

Ankō n Lit. "angler fish." Kansai slang for a day laborer.

Aokan suru v To sleep rough, lit. "a simple life in the open air."

Arubaito n Part-time job, from German *arbeit*. Hence "arubaitaa," one who does such jobs, also "furii arubaitaa," one who does such jobs without commitment, and its contracted form "furiitaa."

Aru-chū n An alcoholic. From *arukōru* [alcohol] + *chūdoku* [addict].

Asaru v To forage. E.g., "*Gomibako de zanpan o asaru,*" to forage for scraps in rubbish bins.

Baken n A betting slip [for horse racing].

Baren n A bet in which one predicts the first two horses. Cf. *wakuren.*

Bataya n One who makes a living from collecting discarded items, especially cardboard for recycling.

237

Burakumin pn Lit. "hamlet people." Euphemistic term for members of Japan's discriminated outcast minority, formerly known as *Eta* or *Hinin* (qqv). Nowadays "burakumin" itself is a taboo word.

Butakiri n "Getting the chop"—Getting fired midway through a contract, often with wages withheld. "It usually happens about noon, halfway through the day. The boss says 'you're no good, get the hell out of here!' and gives you ¥500 for the bus-fare home." Probably from *butsugiri (ni suru)*, "to cut [hack, chop] a fish into irregular lumps" (Masuda 1974:101) as in *maguro butsugiri*, chopped tuna.

Chinpira n Universal slang term for a junior yakuza.

Chōba-san n Concierge, manager of doya.

Chō-han n Odd and even. Time-honored term for dice gambling.

Chokkō n Lit. "go direct." Worker with semiregular arrangement who goes directly to the work site without needing to negotiate a job.

Chongryun pn The General Association of Korean Residents in Japan. Organization sympathetic to North Korea. Js pron.: *Chōsen Sōren*. Cf. *Mindan*.

Chū-hai n Pre-mixed drink with *shōchū* [qv] and fizzy fruit juice.

Contradistor n A job broker who specializes in setting up contracts for Latin Americans of Japanese descent. Supposed to be Spanish for "contractor."

Dankō n Short for *dantai kōshō*—group negotiations. Union tactic.

Dekasegi n Leaving home to do migrant labor. Hence also *dekasegi rōdōsha*, a migrant laborer.

Dezura n Day wage. One day's pay.

Dokata n A construction worker.

Doya n Slang term for a cheap hotel or flophouse. Derives from *yado* [an inn] with syllables reversed.

Doya-gai n Area with many *doya* [qv].

Doya-ken n Lodging coupon, from local government, usable at cheaper class of *doya* [qv].

Eta n Lit. "filth abundant." Old term for a member of Japan's outcast community. Highly derogatory; now totally taboo and superseded by *Burakumin* [qv].

Ettō n Lit. "passing winter." Annual New Year support campaign for homeless day laborers by city authorities, unions, and volunteers. Here, "Winter Survival Campaign."

Furiitaa [freiter] n See *arubaito*.

Genba n Lit. "present/actual site." Workplace, esp. building site. Also used in maps to indicate "You are here."

Gen'eki n A currently active laborer, capable of getting work.

Getemono n Lit. "odd things." Dogs, snakes, rats, etc. as food.

Gonzō n Kyushu slang for a day laborer, esp. a docker.

Hanba n A work camp, with accommodation, where men work on longer-term contracts. In western Japan, and increasingly elsewhere, also used to mean *rōdō-geshuku* or *ninpu-dashi* [qqv].

Han-keta n A "half-ketaochi." Hence, a *hanba* or *ninpu-dashi* [qqv] that is almost as bad as a *ketaochi* [qv].

Han-tako n Lit. "half-octopus." A labor camp half like a *tako-beya* camp [qv], i.e., almost as bad.

Hinin n Lit. "non-person." Tokugawa period outcast group that overlapped with Eta [qv]. Thought to be one of the origins of the Burakumin [qv].

Hiropon n Old slang term: amphetamines, from brand name.

Hiyatoi rōdōsha/rōmusha np Worker/laborer employed by the day, or for a short period, usually less than a month. Both terms translated as "day laborer" in this work.

Hiyatoi techō np The handbook used by day laborers to record evidence of work done by sticking on *inshi* [qv]; used to claim day laborer dole.

Hiyatoi Zenkyō pn The National Federation of Day Labor Unions.

Hizeni n Money for the day, one day's pay.

Hōgai engo np Extralegal assistance. Temporary help given by authorities to people not eligible for *seikatsu hogo* [qv]. Includes *doya-ken* and *pan-ken* [qqv].

Inshi n Government revenue stamp. Here, one affixed to handbook as evidence of one day's work done. Needed to claim unemployment benefit. Cf. *yami inshi.*

Iryō-han n Lit. "Medical Patrol." Volunteer medical team in Kotobuki.

Jinzai-haken-gyō n Personnel dispatch business. General term for temporary staff agencies. Also most formal and polite way of describing *rōdō geshuku* or *ninpu-dashi* [qqv].

Jitsu-rōdō n Lit. "actual labor." Usually, physical labor.

Jōhatsu suru vp Lit. "to evaporate." To suddenly go missing, to take it on the lam.

Jōyō n A regular worker. Opposite of *rinji* [qv].

Jūminhyō n Certificate of residence. Key bureaucratic document for claiming welfare benefits etc.

Junichirō pn The Kotobuki Day Laborer Union (kanji acronym).

Kai-goroshi n Lit. "working someone till they die." Hence, giving someone a meaningless job instead of dismissing them. Sometimes applied ironically to workers who have lost their freedom, to an employer or *ninpu-dashi* [qv].

Kamagasaki pn The Osaka yoseba. Some older men call it Kasumi-chō. Officially re-named "Airin district"; also called "Nishinari" after the ward in which it lies.

Kan'i shukuhakujo np "Simple lodgings." Formal term for *doya* [qv].

Kao-zuke n [Employment by] knowing someone's face. Implies no work for newcomers.

Kara-ken n Lit. "empty ticket." A *doya-ken* [qv] that is of no value because all the *doya* [qv] that accept them are already full.

Kashira n Lit. "head." Boss, foreman, gang leader, ring leader. Sometimes *kashira-bun*, lit. "head-part." Cf. *Kogashira.*

Katawaku daiku np A carpenter specializing in building wooden frames into which concrete is poured to make foundations.

Katazuke n Tidying up. Simplest, lightest, worst-paid work on building site.

Keiba n Horse racing, the turf.

Keirin n Bicycle racing.

Ketaochi n Origin unclear. A brutally abusive *hanba* or *ninpu-dashi* [qqv].

Kichin-yado n A doss-house. Old-fashioned equivalent of *doya* [qv].

Kinzoku teate np A bonus payable on completion of a laboring contract if no days have been taken off.

Kogashira n A subforeman or recruiter's lieutenant. Cf. *Kashira*.

Kojiki n A vagabond, a tramp. Sometimes, a beggar. Derogatory.

Koseki Tōhon np Family registration certificate. Key bureaucratic document for establishing identity, often kept at one's familial home town.

Kōwan rōdōsha np Lit. "harbor worker." A longshoreman.

Koya n Lit. "small house." A homemade hut or shack.

Kusuri n Medicine. Hence also drugs.

Kyōtei n Motorboat racing.

Maegari n Cash advanced against wages or welfare payment.

Mago'uke n Lit. "grandson-contractor." A sub-subcontractor, one rung down from a *shita-uke* [qv].

Maguro n Lit. "tuna." Mugging of person sleeping in street: victim compared to a tuna lying on a chopping board. Kotobuki slang. Cf. *mogaki, shinogi*.

Make-inu n Lit. "losing dog." A whipping dog, a loser. Not politically correct.

Manmosu n Lit. "mammoth." The giant-size police box in San'ya.

Mig-mig n Filipino term: the Immigration Control Bureau and/or its officials.

Mindan pn The Korean Residents' Union in Japan. Organization sympathetic to South Korea. Js pron same as Korean. Cf. *Chongryun*.

Mogaki n A writhing, violent struggle. Hence a mugging. San'ya equivalent of *maguro, shinogi* [qqv].

Mokuyō Patorōru pn The Thursday Patrol, volunteer group touring parts of Yokohama Thursday nights, handing out blankets, soup etc. to homeless people. A Wednesday Patrol tours Kawasaki.

Moto'uke n The prime contractor on a construction project. Employs day laborers only indirectly, via chains of *shita'uke* and *mago'uke* [qqv].

Muen-botoke n Lit. "unconnected Boddhisatva." One who dies leaving no known relatives.

Nagareru v To drift. Hence *nagaremono* n, a drifter.

Nakama n Friend; comrade.

Nawabari n Lit. "rope stretching." Territory, typically that of a yakuza gang.

Naya n A shed or barn. Also used to describe secure workers' accommodation, as in prewar *naya seido* ["shed system"], controlling workers by confining them to quarters under supervision of *naya-gashira* ("barn boss").

Nikoyon n Lit. "two and four." Old-fashioned slang: day laborer. From the fact that shortly after WWII the daily pay for a registered day laborer was ¥240.

Nikutai-rōdō n Lit. "body labor." Hence manual labor.

Nikkyū n A daily wage. Hence *nikkyū-rōdōsha* n, day laborer.

Ninpu n A laborer, a hand, a navvy.

Ninpu-dashi n Lit. "navvy-sender." Slang term for *rodo-geshuku* [qv].

Ninsoku n Lit. "a person and his feet." A laborer, often a docker.

Ninsoku yoseba n Lit. "place for gathering laborers." A labor camp. First seen in eighteenth century. Likely origin of *yoseba* (qv).

Niyaku n Stevedoring. Hence *niyaku ninpu* np, stevedore.

Nojuku n Lit. "wild-living." Homelessness. Hence *nojukusha* n, a rough sleeper.

Nomi-mawashi n The act of passing round a bottle of alcohol.

Nomiya n A bar or gambling den. In Kotobuki, always the latter.

Nonbē n A drunkard.

Glossary of Yoseba Terms 241

Notarejini, n Death in the gutter. Hence *notarejinu* v, to die destitute.

Ōbeya n Lit. "big room." A room—not necessarily that big—shared by several men.

Ochikobore n Lit. "scatterings." Riff-raff. Not politically correct.

Oyabun n Lit. "father figure." Boss of yakuza gang.

Oyakata n Lit. "father figure." One's patron or boss. Covers senior workers, foremen, owners of small construction firms, etc.

Pachinko n Japanese-style pinball, gambling for prizes [legal] or money [illegal but universal].

Pan-ken n Lit. "bread ticket." Food voucher from local government.

Pin-hane n The percentage of the day wage withheld by the recruiter.

Pū-tarō n Lit. "Jack o' the Wind." Venerable Yokohama/Tokyo area slang term for day laborer.

Rinji a, n Temporary. Abbreviation for *rinji sagyō'in*, temporary operative, formal Japanese for a casual, non-staff employee.

Rōdō-geshuku np A western Japanese institution combining functions of boarding house and casual labor agency.

Rojō seikatsu-sha np "A person living on the street." Official term for homeless person.

Ryūdō-teki na kasō rōdōsha np "Mobile low-class worker." Left-wing jargon for a day laborer.

Sankaku-kōen pn Triangle Park. Famous location in Kamagasaki [qv].

San'ya pn The major yoseba in Tokyo.

Sasashima pn The yoseba in Nagoya. Sometimes pronounced "Sasajima."

Seikatsu hogo np Lit. "livelihood protection." Social security.

Senpaku n Ships, shipping, hence abn for dock work.

Sewanin n An intermediary, an introducer of people. Successful day laborer who introduces friends to employers.

Shaba n The outside [non-yoseba] world. From Sanskrit *saha*. Same term is used by prisoners.

Shabu n Slang term for amphetamines.

Shichibu-zubon n Traditional laborer's baggy pantaloons.

Shinogi n Lit. "tiding over." Pawning one's personal possessions; hence having them stolen by a mugger. Kamagasaki [qv] equivalent of *maguro, mogaki* [qqv].

Shiokuri n Sending money home, aim of many migrant workers.

Shita'uke n Lit. "under-taker." A subcontractor. Cf. *moto'uke, magouke.*

Shittai n Short for *shitsugyō-taisaku* (unemployment countermeasures). Mostly projects cleaning up parks, etc. for low wages paid by local government.

Shittai-rōdōsha np Worker employed on *shittai* [qv] project.

Shoba-dai n Lit. "place money." Payment from street stallholder to yakuza for permission to use a pitch. *Shoba* is the word *basho* (place), reversed.

Shōbu n Lit. "win-lose." Result of a contest. Hence: gambling.

Shōchū n Strong liquor distilled from barley. In Korean: *soju.*

Shokuan Labor exchange. Abbreviation of *Shokugyo Anteijo.*

Suarikomi n Sit-in. Day laborer union campaigning technique used against government or company offices.

Tachinbō n A "standing person." One who waits for work on a street corner. Hence a day laborer; sometimes also a prostitute.

Takadanobaba pn Tokyo district with minor yoseba.

Takibi n An open outdoor fire for keeping warm. A bonfire.

Takidashi n Free food handout by volunteers.

Tako-beya n Lit. "octopus room." A prison-like work camp. Cf. *Han-tako*.

Tamahime-kōen pn Jewel-Princess Park. Famous location in San'ya [qv].

Tedori n Take-home pay. Net income after deductions.

Tehaishi n Lit. "supplier." A street labor recruiter.

Tekkin-kō n A construction worker who specializes in making frameworks of steel rods for reinforced concrete.

Tensen n Lit. "fighting from front to front." Left-wing jargon glamorizing day laborers' practice of moving between yoseba and worksites.

Terasen n Lit. "temple money." The house cut in gambling. From tradition of gambling in Buddhist temple courtyards.

Tobi, also *tobishoku* n Lit. "hawk," "hawk-worker." Construction worker specializing in dangerous, high-altitude work. A steeplejack or spiderman.

Tsukai-sute np, ap Disposable, throw-away. Used to describe companies' treatment of day laborers.

Tsure-shonben np Also *tsure-shon*. The act of several people standing in a line together to urinate. Symbol of camaraderie.

Tsutomeru v To work for someone. Also: to do time in prison.

Wakuren n A bracket quinella bet, where the bracket numbers of the top two finishers are predicted. There may be more than one runner per number. Cf *baren*.

Wan-kappu [One-Cup] pn A sealed glass of saké or shōchū sold for immediate consumption. Brand name, becoming generic.

Yakuza n A gangster. Derives from "ya-ku-za" [8-9-3], a losing combination of cards in a game resembling blackjack.

Yami inshi np Black-market employment stamps. Cf. *inshi*.

Yankara n Slang term for a man who does not work and just sits around the bonfire killing time. From Ainu word meaning *shōchū* [qv].

Yatai n A small wooden stall serving drinks and light meals. Often on wheels.

Yatoware n In yakuza parlance, a hired man who is not a formal member of the gang. Applies to most *nomiya* [qv] staff.

Yobikomi n A barker, a man who encourages customers to enter a massage parlor, brothel, strip club, etc.

Yoi-tomake ex, n (1) "Yo heave-ho," exhortation shouted esp. when pulling an anchor or other heavy weight. (2) A female laborer.

Yojinbō n (1) a metal bar. (2) A bodyguard, bouncer, or bully boy.

Yoriba n Lit. "place where people gather." Alternative to *yoseba* [qv].

Yoseba n Lit. "place where people are gathered." Hence, a day-laboring district. In yakuza slang, a prison.

Zenekon n Abn for *zeneraru kontorakutā*—general contractor. Massive construction companies; often *moto'uke* [qv] on major projects.

Zenka-mono n A man with a criminal record.

Bibliography

Works in Japanese

Akiyama Kenjirō, Mori Hideo, and Yamashita Takeshi, eds. 1960. *Gendai Nippon no Teihen* (The Bottom of Contemporary Japanese Society). Tokyo: San'ichi Shobo. 4 vols.

Aoki Etsu. 1984. *'Ningen' o Sagasu Tabi: Yokohama no 'Furōsha' to Shōnentachi* (A Journey in Search of "Humans": The "Vagrants" and Youths of Yokohama). Tokyo: Minshūsha.

Aoki Hideo. 1988. "Seisha to Shisha no Taiwa—Kamagasaki Ettō Tōsō Kara" (A Dialogue between the Living and the Dead—From the Kamagasaki Winter Struggle), *Kaihō Shakai-gaku Kenkyū* (Liberation Sociology Research) 2:8–24.

———. 1989. *Yoseba Rōdōsha no Sei to Shi* (The Life and Death of the Yoseba Worker). Tokyo: Akashi Shoten.

Arakawa Ikuo. 1970. *Kanri Shakai* (The Control Society). Tokyo: Kodansha.

Arimura Sen. 1987a. *Kamagasaki Doya-gai Manga Nikki* (A Cartoon Diary of the Kamagasaki Slum). Osaka: Nippon Kikanshi Shuppan Sentā (Japan Small Press Publication Center).

———. 1987b. *Kamayan Hyōryūki (Kamagasaki Doya-gai Manga Nikki 2)* (Kamayan's Drifting Diary [A Cartoon Diary of the Kamagasaki Slum, Part 2]). Osaka: Nippon Kikanshi Shuppan Sentā (Japan Small Press Publication Center).

———. 1989. *Kamagasaki Doya-gai Manga Nikki 3* (A Cartoon Diary of the Kamagasaki Slum, Part 3, with English translations by Caroline Uchima). Osaka: Nippon Kikanshi Shuppan Sentā (Japan Small Press Publication Center).

———. 1992. *Hotel New Kamagasaki.* Tokyo: Akita Shoten.

Asahi Shinbun Shakai-bu. 1986. *Tōkyō Chimei-kō* (On Tokyo Place-names). Tokyo: Asahi Shinbunsha. 2 vols.

243

Eguchi Ei'ichi. 1980. *Gendai no 'Teishotoku-sō'* (The Contemporary "Low Income Class"). Tokyo: Miraisha. 3 vols.

Enami Shigeyuki and Mihashi Toshiaki. 1989. *Saimin-kutsu to Hakurankai* (Slums and Expositions). Tokyo: JICC Shuppan-kyoku.

Fukawa Hiroshi. 1994. "Tashūrō Setai Keisei no Igi" ("The Significance of the Formation of Multiple-Occupation Households"), *Yoseba*, 7:88–103.

Fukuoka Yasunori. 1993. *Zai-Nichi Kankoku/Chōsen-jin: Wakai Sedai no Aidentiti* (Japan-resident Koreans: The Identity of the Younger Generation). Tokyo: Chūō Kōronsha.

Funamoto Shūji. 1985. *Damatte Notarejinu-na* (Do Not Be Silent and Die in the Gutter). Tokyo: Renga Shobō Shinsha.

Genki Magazine. 1989. *Kamagasaki Sutorii* (Kamagasaki Story). Osaka: Burēn Sentā [Brain Center].

Gill, Tom. 1999a. "Dai-toshi no Mājinaru-na Otokotachi no Hikakū Kenkyū: Nihon no Yoseba, Amerika no Sukiddo-Rō." ("Comparative Research on Marginal Men: Japan's Yoseba, America's Skid Row"). In *Ningen, Bunka, Kokoro: Kyōto Bunkyō Daigaku Kiyō*, Vol. 2:37–52.

———. 1999b. "Yoseba no Otokotachi: Kekkon, Kaisha Nashi no Seikatsusha" ("The Men of the Yoseba: Lives Without Marriage or the Company"). In Nishikawa Yōko and Ogino Miho, eds., *Kyōdō Kenkyū: Dansei-ron* (Joint Research: Man Theory), 17–43. Kyoto: Jinbun Sho'in.

———. 2000a. "Yamaguchi San no Fumetsu Kikai: Yoseba Rōdōsha no Oi to Shi no Atsukaikata" (Mr. Yamaguchi's Immortality Machine: How Yoseba Workers Deal with Old Age and Death.) In *Ōjōkō: Nihonjin no Sei/Rō/Shi* (On Peaceful Passing: Japanese Views of Life, Old Age and Death). Miyata Noboru and Shintani Takanori, eds. Tokyo: Shōgakukan.

———. forthcoming. "Kanri Shakai Saikentō" ("The Control Society Re-examined"). In *Kokuritsu Rekishi-Minzoku Hakubutsukan Kenkyū Hōkoku: Sei Rō Shi, Nihonjin no Jinseikan* (Research Reports of the Museum of History and Folklore: Life, Old Age, and Death: the Japanese View of Life).

Hasegawa Shirō. 1994. "Sasashima Zenshi—'Suisha' Chimei-kō Kara" ("The Prior History of Sasashima—Starting from Thoughts on the Place-name 'Suisha' "), *Sasashima* magazine, issue 3, pp. 1–8. Nagoya: Sasashima Day Laborer Union.

Hatada Kunio. 1993. *"Kyōdai-gata" Ningen-gaku* (The Study of Humans According to "Sibling Position"). Tokyo: Shufu to Seikatsu-sha.

Hayashi Yukiko. 1988. "Ninsoku Yoseba." In *Sekai Dai Hyakka Jiten*. Tokyo: Heibonsha.

Honma Kei'ichirō. 1993. "Kamagasaki Shōshi Shiron" ("A Preliminary Sketch for a Short History of Kamagasaki"). In Kamagasaki Shiryō Sentā 1993, 24–67.

Imagawa Isao. 1987. *Gendai Kimin-kō* (On Present-Day Outcasts). Tokyo: Tabata Shoten.

Itō Hirokazu. 1987. *Zankoku Kensetsu Gyōkai* (The Cruel Construction Industry). Tokyo: Yell Books.

Kaji Daisuke. 1977. *San'ya Sengo-shi o Ikite* (Living the Postwar History of San'ya). Tokyo: Sekibundō Shuppan. 2 vols.

Kalabaw no Kai, ed. 1993 (1990). *Nakama Janai-ka, Gaikokujin Rōdōsha* (Foreign Workers are Comrades, Right?). Tokyo: Akashi Shoten.

Kamagasaki Shiryō Sentā (Resource Center). 1993. *Kamagasaki, Rekishi to Genzai* (Kamagasaki, Its History and Present Situation). Tokyo: San'ichi Shobō.

Kamata Satoshi. 1994 (1971). *Shinitaeta Fūkei* (The Extinct Landscape). Tokyo: Gendai Kyōyō Bunko (1994); Diamond-sha (1971).

Kama-kyōtō and San'ya Gentō'in. [Kamagasaki United Struggle and San'ya Workplace Struggle Committee] 1974. *Yararetara Yarikaese!* (If They Get You, Get 'Em Back!). Tokyo: Tabata Shoten.

Kan Takayuki. 1986. *Sabetsu Foa Beginaazu* (Discrimination for Beginners). Tokyo: Gendai Shokan.

———, ed. 1988. *Gendai Nippon no Sabetsu* (Discrimination in Contemporary Japan). Tokyo: Akashi Shoten.

Kanzaki Kiyoshi. 1955. *Baishun* (Prostitution). Tokyo: Aoki Shoten.

———. 1974. *San'ya Doya-gai*. Tokyo: Jiji Tsūshinsha.

Katō Yūji. 1991. *Gendai Nippon ni okeru Fuantei Shūgyō Rōdōsha*. (Workers in Unstable Employment in Present-day Japan). Tokyo: Ochanomizu Shobō. Revised edition. First edn. 1980.

Kawahara Emon. 1987. *Kotobuki-chō: Kaze no Konseki*. (Kotobuki-chō: Vestiges of the Wind). Tokyo: Tabata Shoten.

Kawase Seiji-kun Tsuitō Bunshō Henshū I'inkai (Editorial Committee for a Collection of Writings in Memory of Kawase Seiji). 1985. *Kotobuki ni Ikite* (Living in Kotobuki). Yokohama: Kawase Seiji-kun Tsuitō Bunshō Henshū I'inkai.

Kim Joong Myung. 1994. 'Nihon-jin no Shiranai 4.3 Jiken: 1948-nen, 6-man Tōmin wa Naze Korosareta-ka?' ("The April 3 Incident of Which the Japanese Know Nothing: Why Were 60,000 Islanders Killed in 1948?"), *Marco Polo*, April 1994, 61–62.

Kodansha. 1989. *Nihongo Daijiten* (Great Japanese Dictionary). Tokyo: Kodansha.

Kogawa Tetsuo. 1987. *Spēsu o Ikiru Shisō* (A Philosophy of Living Space). Tokyo: Chikuma Shobō.

Koh Son Heui. 1996. *Zainichi Saishūtō Shusshinsha no Seikatsu Katei* (The Life Patterns of Japan-resident Cheju Islanders). Tokyo: Shinkansha.

Kon Wajirō. 1971 (1930). "Honjo Fukagawa Hinmin-kutsu Fukin Fūzoku Shūshū." ("A Collection of Customs from Around the Slum Districts of Honjo and Fukagawa"). First pub. in *Modernologio (Kōgengaku)* (1930). Tokyo: Shun'yōdō. Reprinted in *Kōgengaku*, 1971. Tokyo: Domesu Shuppan, pp. 109–133.

Kondō Yasuo. 1953, 1954, 1955. *Mazushisa Kara no Kaihō* (Liberation from Poverty). Vols. 1, 2, 3. Tokyo: Chūō Kōron-sha.

Kōriyama Yoshie. 1983. *Nikoyon Saijiki* (Diary of a Day Laborer). Tokyo: Sōshoku Shobō.

Kotobuki Labor Center (Kotobuki Rōdō Sentā). 1991–1998. *Kotobuki: Muryō Shokugyō Shōkai Jigyō no Gaikyō* (Kotobuki: The Situation of the Free Work Introduction Enterprise). Vols. 17–24. Yokohama: Kanagawa-ken Rōdō Fukushi Kyōkai (Kanagawa Prefecture Labor and Welfare Association).

———. 1994, 1998. *Kyūshoku-sha ni tai-suru Ankēto Chōsa Kekka* (Results of a Questionaire Survey of Job-seekers). Yokohama: Kotobuki Rōdō Sentā.

Kurihara Akira. 1982. *Kanri Shakai to Minshū Risei* (The Control Society and Popular Rationality). Tokyo: Shin'yōsha.

Kusama Yasoh. 1936. *Donzoku no Hitotachi* (People at Rock Bottom). Tokyo: Genrinsha.

L'Henoret, Andre. 1994. *Deru Kugi wa Utareru* (The Nail That Sticks Out Gets Hammered In). Tokyo: Iwanami Shoten.

Matsubara Iwagorō. 1988 (1888). *Sai-ankoku no Tokyo* (Darkest Tokyo). Tokyo: Iwanami Shoten (Min'yūsha).

Matsunobu Tasuke, ed. 1989. *Yokohama Kindai-shi Sōgō Nen-hyō* (General Year-by-Year Guide to Yokohama's Modern History). Yokohama: Yūrindō.

Matsushige Itsuo. 1988. "Kamagasaki; Nojukusha; Shi ni Oiyaru Sabetsu" ("Kamagasaki; Homeless People; Discrimination to the Death"). In Kan 1988.

Matsuzawa Tessei. 1988a. "Yoseba no Keisei, Kinō, soshite Tatakai" ("The Formation, Functions, and Struggles of the Yoseba"), *Yoseba* 1:169–198.

———. 1990. "Yoseba ni kan-suru Bunken no Kenkyū" ("Research on Writings Related to the Yoseba"), *Yoseba* 3:164–186.

Mizuno Ashira. 1997. *Sono Hi-gurashi wa Paradaisu* (Living by the Day is Paradise). Osaka: Village Press.

Mizushima Hiro'aki. 1993. *Kaasan ga Shinda* (Mother Died). Tokyo: Hitonaru Shobō.

Mori Yasuhiko. 1988. "Mushuku" ("Unregistered Persons"). Encyclopedia entry in *Sekai Dai Hyakka Jiten*. Tokyo: Heibonsha.

Murata Yasuo. 1988. *Nihon no Sabetsu, Sekai no Sabetsu: Sabetsu no Hikaku Shakairon* (Japanese Discrimination, Global Discrimination: A Comparative Social Theory of Discrimination). Tokyo: Akashi Shoten.

Murata Yoshio. 1992. *Yoku Shiyō to Suru no wa Yameta Hō ga Ii* (Better to Give Up Trying to Improve Things). Yokohama: Kotobuki Seinen Renraku Kaigi Seisan Jigyōdan.

Nakada Shirō. 1983. *Hadaka no Derashine* (Naked Vagabonds). Tokyo: Marge Co.

Nakagawa Kiyoshi. 1985. *Nihon no Toshi Kasō* (Japan's Urban Lower Class). Tokyo: Keisō Shobō.

Nobuta-san no Enzai o Harasu Kai (Society to Expose the False Charge against Mr. Nobuta). 1996. "Enzai-shū Nobuta Masao-san no Saishin Seikyū ni Ōji, Tetteiteki-na Jijitsu Shinri o Okonatte Kudasai" ("Please Respond to Demands for a Re-trial of the Falsely Convicted Nobuta Masao and Conduct a Thorough Investigation of the Facts"). Yokohama: Kotobuki Seikatsu-kan.

Nomoto Sankichi. 1974. *Hadashi no Genshijin-tachi* (Barefoot Savages). Tokyo: Tabata Shoten.

Nomura Kichitarō. 1992. "Nobuta-san no Enzai Jiken Keika Hōkoku" ("Report on Progress in the Frame-up Case of Mr. Nobuta"), *Nobuta-san no Enzai o Harasu Kai Nyūsu* (News from the Society to Expose the False Charge against Mr. Nobuta), issue 1, 11 November 1992, 1–8. Yokohama: Kotobuki Seikatsu-kan.

Ōhashi Kaoru. 1972. *Toshi Byōri no Kōzō* (The Structure of Urban Pathology). Tokyo: Kawashima Shoten.

Ōnishi Yutaka. 1994. "Ima, Saizensen Dewa" ("Now, At the Very Front Line"), *Sasashima* magazine, issue 3, pp. 9–12. Nagoya: Sasashima Day Labor Union.

Ōtsuka Yōsuke. 1983. *Rakantachi* (Arhats). Yokohama: Committee to Publish Ōtsuka Yōsuke's Photo Collection *Rakantachi*.

Ōyabu Jū'ichi, ed. 1981. *Kodoku to Zetsubō: Airin Jinsei Tsuiseki Chōsa-shi* (Isolation and Despair: Research Papers in Pursuit of the Airin Lifestyle). Osaka: Gensōsha.

Raz, Jacob. 1996. Yakuza no Bunka Jinruigaku: Ura kara Mita Nippon (Anthropology of Yakuza: Japan as Seen from its "Back Door"). Tokyo: Iwanami Shoten.

Sae Shūichi. 1997 (1983). *Yokohama Sutoriitoraifu* (Yokohama Streetlife). Tokyo: Shakai Sōshisha (Shinchōsha).

Saiki Teruko. 1991 (1982). *Onna Akahige Doya-gai ni Junjōsu: Yokohama Kotobuki-chō Shinsatsu-jo Nikki Kara* (The Female Redbeard Devotes Herself to the Slum: Extracts from the Yokohama Kotobuki-chō Clinic Diary). Tokyo: Ikkōsha.

Saitō Hiroko. 1994. *Kankoku-kei Nihon-jin: Maria Onma no Kiseki o Otte* (A South Korean Japanese: Tracing the Trajectory of Maria Onma). Tokyo: Sairyūsha.

San'ya Rōdōsha Fukushi Kaikan Un'ei I'in-kai (San'ya Workers Welfare Hall Management Committee), ed. 1992. *Yoseba ni Hirakareta Kūkan o* (For an Open Space in the Yoseba). Tokyo: Shakai Hyōron-sha.

Shōji Kōkichi. 1989. *Kanri Shakai to Sekai Shakai* (The Control Society and Global Society). Tokyo: University of Tokyo Press.

Sumida Toshio. 1986. *Geta-naoshi no Ki* (Diary of a Sandal-repairer). Osaka: Kaihō Shuppansha.

Takada Tamakichi. 1974. *Tako-beya Hanseiki* (Half a Lifetime in a Coolie Camp). Tokyo: Taihei Shuppansha.

———. 1977. *Tako-beya Ichi-dai* (A Lifetime in a Coolie Camp). Tokyo: Taihei Shuppansha.

Takamoto Tsutomu. 1993. *Buraku no Genryū: Sen Ni-hyaku Nen no Hishū* (The Origins of the Buraku: 1,200 Years of Sorrow). Tokyo: Sairyūsha.

Takayanagi Kaneyoshi. 1980. *Edo Jidai Hinin no Seikatsu* (The Lives of Hinin in the Edo Period). Tokyo: Osankaku Shuppan.

Takeda Rintarō. 1933. *Kamagasaki*. Tokyo: Chūō Kōron.

Takikawa Masajirō. 1994 (1975). *Hasegawa Heizō, Sono Shōgai to Ninsoku Yoseba* (Hasegawa Heizō, His Life and the Labor Camps). Tokyo: Chūkō Bunko.

Terashima Tamao. 1976. *Rōmusha Tosei* (The Laborer's Profession). Nagoya: Fūbōsha.

248   Bibliography

Tokuji Hisao, ed. 1972. *Nakamura no Machi to Doya: Sono Genjō to Tenbō* (The Town of Nakamura and Its Lodging Houses: Present Circumstances and Prospects). Yokohama: Kanagawa-ken Aisen Hōmu.

Tokyo City Government. 1969. *San'ya Chiku no Rōdō Jijō* (Labor Conditions in the San'ya District).

Tsuchida Hideo. 1966. "Doya-gai no Hikaku Kenkyū" (Comparative Research on Doya-gai), *Osaka Gakugei Daigaku Kiyō*, 15:203–15.

Yamaoka Kyō'ichi. 1984. "Yoseba to wa Nanika" ("What is a Yoseba?"). In *Yoseba no Rekishi kara Mirai o Mitōsu* (Viewing the Future in the Light of the History of the Yoseba), ed. Yamaoka Kyō'ichi, Kazama Ryūji and Munemura Yoshitaka. Tokyo: Mitama/Yama no Kai: 4–18.

Yamamoto Ikio. 1986. *Shōsetsu: Suisha Mushuku* (Suisha Vagabond: A Novel). Nagoya: privately published.

Yokohama-shi Fukushi-kyoku, Kotobuki Seikatsukan (Yokohama City Welfare Bureau, Kotobuki Livelihood Building). 1999. *Heisei Kyū-nendo Kotobuki Seikatsukan Jigyō Hōkoku-shū* (Collected Reports on Activities of the Kotobuki Livelihood Building for FY 1997).

Yokoyama Gennosuke. 1985 (1899). *Nippon no Kasō Shakai* (Japan's Lower Class Society). Tokyo: Iwanami Shoten (Kyōbunkan).

Yoshida Hideo. 1930. *Hikasegi Aiwa* (A Sad Tale of Earning by the Day). Tokyo: Heibonsha.

Yoshida Ryūji. 1995. "Hobohemia to 'Yoseba'—'Yoseba' no Shakai Hendō Kenkyū e Mukete" ("Hobohemia and 'Yoseba'—Toward the Social Change Study of 'Yoseba' "), *Kyōto Shakaigaku Nenpō* (Kyoto Journal of Sociology) 3:77–96.

Periodicals

Kaihō Shakaigaku Kenkyū (Liberation Sociology Research), annual publication of Nippon Kaihō Shakai-gakkai (Japan Association of Liberation Sociology Studies). Vols. 1–10, 1986–1995. Tokyo: Akashi Shoten.

Yoseba, annual publication of Yoseba Gakkai (the Japan Association for the Study of Yoseba; JASY). Vols. 1–13, 1988–2000. Tokyo: Gendai Shokan (Vols. 1–8), Renga Shobō Shinsha (Vols. 9–13).

Works in English

Allen, Matthew. 1994. *Undermining the Japanese Miracle: Work and Conflict in a Coalmining Community*. Cambridge: Cambridge University Press.

Allsop, Kenneth. 1967. *Hard Travellin': The hobo and his history*. London: Hodder and Stoughton.

Anderson, Nels. 1965 (1923). *The Hobo: The Sociology of the Homeless Man*. Chicago and London: Phoenix Books.

Aoki, Hideo. Undated. "Day Workers' Movement in Japan: 'Winter Struggle' at Kamagasaki in Osaka." Unpublished manuscript in the author's possession.

Applebaum, Herbert A. 1981. *Royal Blue: The Culture of Construction Workers*. Fort Worth etc.: Holt, Rinehart and Winston.

Arimura, Sen. 1991. "The comic book diary of Kamayan: the life of a day laborer in Kamagasaki." In *Society and Space* 9:135–149.

Axling, William. 1932. *Kagawa.* London: Student Christian Movement Press.

Bachnik, Jane. 1982. *Deixis and Self/Other Reference in Japanese Discourse.* Working Papers in Sociolinguistics 99. Austin: Southwest Educational Development Laboratory.

Bachnik, Jane, and Charles J. Quinn Jr. 1994. *Situated Meaning: Inside and Outside in Japanese Self, Society and Language.* Princeton and Chichester: Princeton University Press.

Bahr, Howard M. 1967. "The Gradual Disappearance of Skid Row," *Social Problems* 15:41–45.

———. 1971. "Birth Order and Failure: The Evidence from Skid Row," *Quarterly Journal of Studies on Alcohol* 32:669–686.

———. 1973. *Skid Row: An Introduction to Disaffiliation.* New York: Oxford University Press.

Bogue, Donald. 1963. Skid Row in American Cities. Chicago: University of Chicago Press.

Breman, Jan. 1994. *Wage Hunters and Gatherers: Search for Work in the Urban and Rural Economy of South Gujarat.* Delhi: Oxford University Press.

Caldarola, Carlo. 1968. "The *Doya-Gai*: A Japanese Version of Skid Row," *Pacific Affairs* 41:511–525.

Caplow, Theodor, Howard M. Bahr, and David Sternberg. 1968. "Homelessness." In David Sills, ed., *International Encyclopedia of the Social Sciences.* New York: Macmillan: 494–499.

Chalmers, Norma. 1989. *Industrial Relations in Japan: The Peripheral Workforce.* London and New York: Routledge.

Clark, Kenneth. 1965. *Dark Ghetto.* New York: Harper and Row.

Constantine, Peter. 1993. *Japan's Sex Trade: A Journey Through Japan's Erotic Subcultures.* Tokyo: Yenbooks.

Crump, John. 1983. *The Origins of Socialist Thought in Japan.* London: Croom Helm.

Davis, John. 2000. "Blurring the Boundaries of the Buraku(min)." In Eades, Gill and Befu, 110–122.

Davis, Peter. 1995. *If You Came This Way: A Journey through the Lives of the Underclass.* New York: John Wiley.

Day, Sophie. 1999. "Hustling: Individualism Among London Prostitutes." In Day, Stewart, and Papataxiarchis eds., 137–157.

Day, Sophie, Evthymios Papataxiarchis and Michael Stewart eds. 1999. *Lilies of the Field.* Oxford and Boulder: Westview Press.

de Barry, Brett. 1985. "San'ya: Japan's Internal Colony." In Tsurumi 1985: 112–118.

De Vos, George, and Hiroshi Wagatsuma. 1972. *Japan's Invisible Race: Caste in Culture and Personality* (Revised edition). Berkeley, Los Angeles, London: University of California Press.

De Vos, George, and William O. Wetherall. 1983. *Japan's Minorities: Burakumin, Koreans, Ainu and Okinawans* (Minority Rights Group Report No.3). London: Minority Rights Group.

Doi, Takeo. 1973. *The Anatomy of Dependence*, trans. John Bester. Tokyo and New York: Kodansha International.

Dore, Ronald. 1978. *Shinohata: A Portrait of a Japanese Village*. London: Allen Lane.

Douglas, Mary, ed. 1987. *Constructive Drinking: Perspectives on Drink from Anthropology*. Cambridge: Cambridge University Press.

Eades, J. S., Tom Gill and Harumi Befu eds. 2000. *Globalization and Social Change in Contemporary Japan*. Melbourne: Trans Pacific Press.

Fallows, James. 1988. "The Other Japan: A visit to San'ya, a Tokyo slum, reveals the peculiar nature of Japanese poverty," *Atlantic Monthly* (April 1988), 16–20.

Fowler, Edward. 1992. "San'ya: Scenes from Life at the Margins of Japanese Society," *Transactions of the Asiatic Society* (fourth series) 6:141–198.

————. 1996. *San'ya Blues: Laboring Life in Contemporary Tokyo*. Ithaca and London: Cornell University Press.

Fukuoka, Yasunori. 2000. *The Lives of Young Koreans in Japan*, trans. Tom Gill. Melbourne: Trans Pacific Press.

Giamo, Benedict. 1989. *On the Bowery: Confronting Homelessness in American Society*. Iowa City: University of Iowa Press.

Giamo, Benedict, and Jeffrey Grunberg eds. 1992. *Beyond Homelessness: Frames of Reference*. Iowa City: University of Iowa Press.

Giamo, Benedict. 1994. "Order, Disorder and the Homeless in the United States and Japan," *Dōshisha Amerika Kenkyū* (Dōshisha American Research) 31:1–19. Kyoto: Dōshisha University American Studies Research Center.

Gill, Tom. 1992. "The Japanese Morality of Exchange." Unpublished MSc dissertation, London School of Economics.

————. 1994. "Sanya Street Life Under the Heisei Recession," *Japan Quarterly* 41:270–86.

————. 1996. "Kon Wajiro, Modernologist," *Japan Quarterly* 43:198–207.

————. 1999c. "Wage Hunting at the Margins of Urban Japan." In Day, Papataxiarchis, and Stewart, 119–136.

————. 2000b. "Unconventional Moralities, Tolerance and Containment in Urban Japan." In Italo Pardo, ed., *Morals of Legitimacy*. London: Berghahn Books, 229–256.

————. 2000c. "*Yoseba* and *Ninpudashi*: Changing Patterns of Casual Employment in Contemporary Japan." In Eades, Gill and Befu, 123–142.

Gist, Noel, and Sylvia Fleis Fava. 1964. *Urban Society*. New York: Crowell.

Glasser, Irene. 1994. *Homelessness in Global Perspective*. New York: G. K. Hall & Co.

Goetz, Edward G. 1992. "Land use and homeless policy in Los Angeles," *International Journal of Urban and Regional Research* 16:540–554.

Gordon, Andrew. 1985. *The Evolution of Labor Relations in Japan: Heavy Industry, 1853–1955*. Cambridge, Mass., and London: Harvard University Press.

Groth, Paul. 1994. *Living Downtown: The History of Residential Hotels in the United States*. Berkeley, Los Angeles, and London: University of California Press.

Guelcher, Gregory Paul. 1994. "With Gun and Hoe: Japanese Agricultural Emigration to Manchuko, 1932–45." Paper delivered at the Sixth Annual PhD Kenkyūkai Conference, Tokyo.

Harada, S. I. 1975. "Honorifics." In M. Shibutani ed., *Syntax and Semantics 5: Japanese Generative Grammar*. New York: Academic Press.

Hart, Keith. 1973. "Informal Income Opportunities and Urban Employment in Ghana," *Journal of Modern African Studies*, 11:61–89.

Hendry, Joy. 1987. *Understanding Japanese Society*. London, New York, Sydney: Croom Helm.

———. 1995. *Wrapping Culture*. Oxford: Clarendon Press.

Herbert, Wolfgang. 2000. "The *Yakuza* and the Law." In Eades, Gill and Befu, 143–158.

Hester, Jeffrey T. 1991. *Projectile Politics: Ritual Violence and Moral Order in a Day Workers' Community of Urban Japan*. Unpublished paper, University of California at Berkeley.

Hoch, Charles, and Robert A. Slayton. 1989. *New Homeless and Old: Community and the Skid Row Hotel*. Philadelphia: Temple University Press.

Japan Statistical Association. 1987. *Historical Statistics of Japan*. Under editorial supervision of the Statistics Bureau, Management and Coordination Agency. Tokyo: Japan Statistical Association. Bilingual publication.

Jencks, Christopher. 1994. *The Homeless*. Cambridge, Mass. and London: Harvard University Press.

Jones, Gareth Stedman. 1971. *Outcast London*. Oxford: Oxford University Press.

Kalvis, Tim. 1995. " 'A Solitary Island in a Distant Sea': The day labouring district of Kamagasaki, Osaka and the problem of homelessness." Unpublished MA thesis, Institute of Contemporary Japanese Studies, Essex University.

Katayama, Sen. 1918. *The Labor Movement in Japan*. Chicago: Charles H. Kerr.

Kitaguchi, Suehiro. 1999. *An Introduction to the Buraku Issue: Questions and Answers*, trans. Alastair McLaughlin. Richmond, Surrey: Curzon Press.

Koike, Kazuo. 1995. *The Economics of Work in Japan*. Tokyo: LTCB International Library.

Kojima, Hiroshi. 1989. "Coresidence of Young Adults with Their Parents in Japan: Do Sib Size and Birth Order Matter?" Institute of Population Problems Working Paper Series, No.2. Tokyo: Ministry of Health and Welfare.

Komai, Hiroshi. 1995 (1993). *Migrant Workers in Japan*, trans. Jens Wilkinson. London and New York: Kegan Paul International.

Komatsu, Kazuhiko. 1987. "The Dragon Palace Child: An Anthropological and Sociohistorical Approach," *Current Anthropology* 28.4:S31–39.

Kondo, Dorinne. 1990. *Crafting Selves—Power, Gender and Discourses of Identity in a Japanese Workplace*. Chicago and London: University of Chicago Press.

Kusama, Yasoh. 1932. "Coping with Unemployment," *Contemporary Japan* 1:292–300.

Lee, Changsoo, and George De Vos. 1981. *Koreans in Japan: Ethnic Conflict and Accommodation.* Berkeley and Los Angeles: University of California Press.

Leupp, Gary P. 1992. *Servants, Shophands, and Laborers in the Cities of Tokugawa Japan.* Princeton: Princeton University Press.

L'Henoret, A. 1993. *Le Clou qui Depasse: Recit du Japon d'en Bas.* Paris: Editions La Decouverte.

Liebow, Elliot. 1967. *Tally's Corner.* Boston: Little, Brown.

Littler, Craig R. 1982. *The Development of the Labour Process in Capitalist Societies.* London: Heinemann Educational Books.

McCormack, Gavan, and Yoshio Sugimoto. 1988. *The Japanese Trajectory: Modernization and Beyond.* Cambridge: Cambridge University Press.

Management and Coordination Agency. 1960–1999. *Japan Statistical Yearbook.* Tokyo: Management and Coordination Agency. (Bilingual publication; originally published by Prime Minister's Office.)

Marr, Matthew D. 1997. "Maintaining Autonomy: the plight of the American skidrow and Japanese *yoseba*," *Journal of Social Distress and the Homeless* 6(3): 229–250.

Marr, Matthew D., Abel Valenzuela, Janette Kawachi, and Takao Koike. 2000. "Day Laborers in Tokyo, Japan: Preliminary Findings from the San'ya Day Labor Survey." UCLA Center for the Study of Urban Poverty Occasional Working Paper Series. Los Angeles: University of California.

Mars, Gerald. 1987. "Longshore drinking, economic security, and union politics in Newfoundland." In Douglas 1987, 99–101.

Marx, Karl, and Friedrich Engels. 1977 (1888). *The Communist Manifesto,* trans. Samuel Moore. London: Penguin Books.

Masuda, Koh, ed. 1974. *Kenkyusha's New Japanese-English Dictionary,* 4th edition. Tokyo: Kenkyusha.

Matsuzawa, Tessei. 1988b. "Street Labour Markets, Day Labourers, and the Structure of Oppression." In McCormack and Sugimoto 1988, 147–164.

Miller, Ronald J. 1982. *The Demolition of Skid Row.* Lexington and Toronto: D. C. Heath & Co.

Mori, Hideto. 1962. "The Longshoremen of Kobe Harbor," *Orient West* 7: 35–42.

Mouer, Ross, and Yoshio Sugimoto. 1986. *Images of Japanese Society.* London and New York: Kegan Paul International.

Murray, Harry. 1984. "Time in the Streets," *Human Organization* 43:154–61.

Nakane, Chie. 1970. *Japanese Society.* London: Weidenfeld and Nicholson.

Nimura, Kazuo. 1997. *The Ashio Riot of 1907.* Durham (North Carolina) and London: Duke University Press.

Ōnishi, Yutaka. Undated. "Japanese Day Laborers." Unpublished manuscript.

Orwell, George. 1986 (1933). *Down and Out in Paris and London.* London: Penguin Books (Victor Gollancz).

Papataxiarchis, Evthymios. 1999. "A Contest with Money: Gambling and the Politics of Disinterested Sociality in Aegean Greece." In Day, Papataxiarchis, and Stewart, eds., 158–175.

Parker, Carleton H. 1920. *The Casual Laborer and Other Essays*. New York: Harcourt, Brace and Howe.

Parker, L. Craig Jr. 1984. *The Japanese Police System Today: An American Perspective*. Tokyo and New York: Kodansha International.

Peterson, Richard A., and Bruce Wiegand. 1985. "Ordering Disorderly Work Careers on Skid Row," *Research in the Sociology of Work* 3:215–230.

Phillips, Gordon, and Noel Whiteside. 1985. *Casual Labour: The Unemployment Question in the Port Transport Industry, 1880–1970*. Oxford and New York: Oxford University Press.

Price, John. 1972. "A History of the Outcaste: Untouchability in Japan." In De Vos and Wagatsuma 1972, 6–30.

Raz, Jacob. 1992. "Self-presentation and performance in the yakuza way of life: Fieldwork with a Japanese underworld group." In Roger Goodman and Kirsten Refsing, eds., *Ideology and Practice in Modern Japan*. London: Routledge, 210–234.

Roberts, Robert. 1971. *The Classic Slum: Salford life in the first quarter of the century*. Manchester: Manchester University Press.

Rohlen, Thomas. 1974. *For Harmony and Strength: Japanese White-Collar Organization in Anthropological Perspective*. Berkeley and London: University of California Press.

Rooney, James F. 1961. "Group Processes Among Skid Row Winos," *Quarterly Journal of Studies on Alcohol* 22:444–460.

———. 1970. "Societal Forces and the Unattached Male: An Historical Review." In Bahr, ed., 1970.

Rosenberger, Nancy R., ed. 1992. *Japanese Sense of Self*. Cambridge: Cambridge University Press.

Rossi, Peter H. 1989. *Down and Out in America: The Origins of Homelessness*. Chicago and London: University of Chicago Press.

Roth, Cecil. 1969. *A Short History of the Jewish People*. London: East and West Library.

Rubington, Earl. 1968. "The Bottle Gang," *Quarterly Journal of Studies on Alcohol* 29:943–955.

Sassen, Saskia. 1991. *The Global City: New York, London, Tokyo*. Princeton: Princeton University Press.

Shiina, Masae. 1994. "Coping Alone: When Work Separates Families," *Japan Quarterly* 41:26–35.

Smith, Thomas C. 1959. *The Agrarian Origins of Modern Japan*. Stanford: Stanford University Press.

Somerville, Peter. 1992. "Homelessness and the meaning of home: rooflessness or rootlessness?" *International Journal of Urban and Regional Research* 16: 529–539.

Spradley, James P. 1999 (1970). *You Owe Yourself a Drunk: An Ethnography of Urban Nomads.* Prospect Heights, IL.: Waveland Press (Boston: Little, Brown).

Stevens, Carolyn. 1995a. " 'Whose Etto Is It, Anyway?': New Year's Activities in a Yokohama *Yoseba*," *American Asian Review* 13:165–184.

———. 1995b. "Day Laborers, Volunteers, and Welfare in Contemporary Japan," *Urban Anthropology* 24:229–253.

———. 1997. *On the Margins of Japanese Society: Volunteers and the welfare of the urban underclass.* London: Routledge.

Sugimoto, Yoshio. 1997. *An Introduction to Japanese Society.* Cambridge, New York, and Melbourne: Cambridge University Press.

Tobin, Joseph. 1992. "Japanese preschools and the pedagogy of selfhood." In Rosenberger 1992, 21–39.

Tsurumi, E. Patricia, ed. 1985. *The Other Japan: Postwar Realities.* Armonk, N.Y.: M. E. Sharpe.

Ventura, Rey. 1992. *Underground in Japan.* London: Jonathan Cape.

Wallace, Samuel E. 1965. *Skid Row as a Way of Life.* Totowa, N.J.: Bedminister Press.

Walthall, Anne. 1986. *Social Protest and Popular Culture in Eighteenth-Century Japan.* Tucson: University of Arizona Press.

Williams, R. 1912. *The Liverpool Docks Problem.* Liverpool: Northern Publishing Co.

Wiseman, Jaqueline P. 1970. *Stations of the Lost: The Treatment of Skid Row Alcoholics.* Englewood Cliffs: Prentice-Hall. Later editions pub. University of Chicago Press (Chicago and London).

Woodburn, James. 1982. "Egalitarian Societies," *Man* (N.S.) 17:431–451.

———. 1996. " 'Sharing is not a form of exchange': An analysis of property sharing in immediate-return hunter-gatherer societies." Unpublished paper.

Yoshino, I. Roger, and Sueo Murakoshi. 1977. *The Invisible Visible Minority—Japan's Burakumin.* Osaka: Buraku Liberation Institute.

Index

Notes: n = note, thus 234n16 = page 234, note 16.
t = table, thus 215t30 = page 215, table 30.
Multiple notes or tables are indicated by nn, tt.
All place-names in Japan are listed under Japan, locations.